Jean Baudrillard

Jean Baudrillard

A study in cultural metaphysics

CHARLES LEVIN

PRENTICE HALL
HARVESTER WHEATSHEAF

London New York Toronto Sydney Tokyo Singapore
Madrid Mexico City Munich

First published 1996 by
Prentice Hall Europe
Campus 400, Maylands Avenue
Hemel Hempstead
Hertfordshire, HP2 7EZ
A division of
Simon & Schuster International Group

Typeset in 9½/11½pt Melior
by Dorwyn Ltd, Rowlands Castle, Hampshire

Printed and bound in Great Britain by
Biddles Ltd, Guildford and Kings Lynn

Library of Congress Cataloging-in-Publication Data

Levin, Charles.
Jean Baudrillard: a study in cultural metaphysics/Charles Levin.
p. cm. — (Modern cultural theorists)
Includes bibliographical references and index.
ISBN 0–13–433368–3
1. Baudrillard, Jean. 2. Philosophy, French—20th century. I. Title. II. Series.
B2430.B33974L48 1995
194—dc20 95-22659
CIP

British Library Cataloguing in Publication Data

A catalogue record for this book is available from the British Library

ISBN 0–13–433368–3

1 2 3 4 5 00 99 98 97 96

To the students in Comparative Literature and in the Graduate Program in Communications, McGill University 1990–1995

Contents

Acknowledgements

This was not an easy book to write, for various reasons, and so I owe thanks to many more than I can mention for their direct and indirect assistance in assuring its completion.

My intention was to provide an accessible introduction to Baudrillard. To the extent that I have succeeded in saying anything worthwhile, my students at McGill deserve a great deal of credit. They helped me to see that it is no advantage to encrust Baudrillard in academic common sense. If it were, there would have been less reason to read him, or to read about him; and he would have been a different writer. The intelligence and charm of these students was my own best motive for persevering.

Among them, I mention especially Renée Baert, Anne Beaulieu, Jessica Bradley, Malcolm Cecil, Lynn Darroch, Dann Downes, Michelle Gauthier, Linda Hachey, Jesse Hunter, Joseph Jackson, Stacey Johnson, Scott McKenzie, Haidee Wasson, Brennan Wauters, and Peter Van Wyck.

Of my university colleagues, I must first single out Arthur Kroker, of Concordia University, whose extraordinary combination of talents as an imaginative visionary and practical facilitator have made a constructive difference in many careers, including my own. My thanks also to his wife and co-editor, Marilouse. At McGill University, David Crowley, Marike Finlay de Monchy, and George Szantos have in their different ways given me more help over the years than I can measure or repay.

Of all those who have opened promising doors for me, none has been more consistently supportive and nurturing than Ron Burnett, Director of the Graduate Program in Communications at McGill, who also took many hours from his gruelling schedule to read the manuscript. His constructive insight and criticism has been invaluable in the final stages of the work.

I also take great pleasure in expressing my profound appreciation for the sympathetic and inspiring contributions of Catherine

Everett, of the Faculty of Fine Arts, University of Ottawa; and my dear friends, John Fekete and Victoria De Zwaan, of Cultural Studies at Trent University, whose cheerful rationality and hedonistic devotion to enlightenment have long served as a model for my own development.

My most precious words are reserved for Christine Ury, my wife. She has made passion and enchantment the basic dimensions of my existence. And she has taught me the depth and value of life, love and the unconscious.

Chronology: Jean Baudrillard 1929–

1929 Born in the cathedral town of Reims (Marne), 27 July, of peasant ancestors, into a family adapting to the new, urban, bureaucratic France.

1956 Begins ten-year period of teaching as professor of secondary education. Specializes in German social theory and literature. Opposes French colonial policy in Algeria, following the example of Jean-Paul Sartre, and many other left intellectuals.

1962–63 Publishes literary reviews in *Les Temps Moderne*, including an essay on Italo Calvino.

1964–68 Produces a series of standard translations from German, including several works by the playwright Peter Weiss (*Marat/Sade*, Marx and Engels's *The German Ideology*, Muhlmann's *Messianisme revolutionaire du tiers monde*), and Bertold Brecht. Participates in the radical journal *Utopie*, and joins opposition to U.S. policy in Indochina.

1966 In March, defends his 'Thèse de Troisième Cycle' in Sociology at University of Paris X-Nanterre. The title is 'Le système des objets'. In October, begins teaching sociology at Nanterre as assistant, *maître-assistant*, and *maître de conférence*.

1967 Publishes a brief but prescient review of Marshall McLuhan's *Understanding Media* in the Marxist humanist journal *L'homme et la société*.

1968 Plays an active intellectual role in the political ferment approaching and following the general strike in May. Publishes *Le système des objets*.

1970–76 Becomes *maître-assistant* at Nanterre. Publishes a series of major studies, including *La société de consommation*, *Le miroir de la production*, *L'échange symbolique et la mort*. Begins teaching abroad, at the University of California, San Diego, in 1975.

1977–78 Launches a provocative series of antisocialist and anti-poststructuralist essays: high-gloss, pamphlet-style publications which seal his fate as an academic and political outsider: notably, *Oublier Foucault* and *A L'ombre des majorités silencieuses: la fin du social*. His predilection for satirical journalism is becoming more and more evident.

1980– Publishes *De la séduction*. Continues teaching, lecturing, and giving seminars in Canada, the United States, Brazil, West Germany, Australia, Argentina, Spain, Denmark. His works are translated into English, German, Italian, Spanish, Japanese, Danish, Dutch, Portuguese, Greek, Hungarian.

1981 *Simulacres et simulation*.

1983 *Les stratégies fatales*.

1985 *La gauche divine*, a satirical journalistic chronicle of left electoral politics in France, from 1977 to 1984.

1986 *Amérique*. Presents 'habilitation à diriger des recherches' in February at the Sorbonne, under the directorship of the eminent political anthropologist Georges Balandier. This is published the next year as *L'autre par lui-même*, along with the first volume of *Cool Memories*.

1988–95 Begins withdrawal from formal academic life, but remains active as a journalist, essayist, and professional intellectual *bête noir*. There is another stir, this time around *La Guerre du Golfe n'a pas eu lieu* (1991), a collection of Baudrillard's satirical political writings from January–March 1991, previously published in part in the journal *Libération*. *La transparence du mal* (1990), *Cool Memories II* (1990), and *L'illusion de la fin* (1992) appear. Life and travel continue.

Abbreviated titles list

All citations of or references to Baudrillard's works are specified in the text, with the help of the abbreviations listed below. In the case of quotation: when the translation from the French is my own, the abbreviated title of the French original appears in brackets, with the page number, so that the quotation can be checked. For the convenience of the English reader, this will be followed by the abbreviated title and page number of the published English translation, if available. General references to Baudrillard's works will be indicated by the abbreviated title in brackets, the English edition whenever possible.

America	*America*, trans. Chris Turner (London: Verso, 1988).
L'Autre	*L'Autre par lui-même* (Paris: Galilee, 1987).
BE	'*The Beaubourg Effect*: Implosion and Deterrence', in *October* 20 (Spring 1982) 3–13.
Cool	*Cool Memories: I* (English trans.), trans. Chris Turner (Verso: London, 1990).
Death	*Symbolic Exchange and Death*, trans. Iain Hamilton Grant (London: Sage, 1993).
Ecstasy	*The Ecstasy of Communication* (trans. of *L'Autre*), trans. B. & C. Schutze (New York: Semiotext(e), 1988).
ESM	*L'échange symbolique et la mort* (Paris: Gallimard, 1976).
L'espace	'L'Amerique ou la pensée de l'espace', *Citoyenneté et urbanité* (Paris: Esprit, 1991), pp. 155–64.
Evil	*The Evil Demon of Images*, trans. P. Patton & P. Foss (Annandale: Power Institute, 1987).
FA	*Figures de l'Alterité* (Paris: Descartes & Cie, 1994).
FCPES	*For a Critique of the Political Economy of the Sign*, trans. Charles Levin (St. Louis: Telos, 1981).
FF	*Forget Foucault* (trans. of *Oublier*), trans. N. Dufresne (New York: Semiotext(e), 1987).

Follow	*Please Follow Me* (with Sophie Calle, *Suite Vénitienne*), trans. D. Barash & D. Hatfield (Seattle: Bay Press, 1988).
FS	*Fatal Strategies*, trans. Philip Beitchman & W.G.J. Niesluchowski (New York: Semiotext(e), 1990).
GG	*La Guerre du Golfe n'a pas eu lieu* (Paris: Galilée, 1991).
IF	*L'illusion de la fin ou la grève des événement* (Paris: Galilée, 1992).
Live	*Baudrillard Live: Selected Interviews* (ed. Mike Gane) (London: Routledge, 1993).
McLuhan:	'Compte Rendu de Marshall MacLuhan (*sic*): Understanding media: the extensions of man', *L'Homme et la Société*, no. 5 (1967).
MP	*The Mirror of Production*, trans. Mark Poster (St. Louis: Telos, 1975).
Ombre	*A l'ombre des majorités silencieuses ou la fin du social* (Paris: Denoel/Gonthier, 1978).
Oublier	*Oublier Foucault* (Paris: Galilée, 1977).
RLC	'Rituel – Loi – Code', in *Violence et transgression*, eds. Michel Maffesoli & André Bruston (Paris: Editions Anthropos, 1979), pp. 97–107.
SC	*La société de consommation: ses mythes, ses structures* (Paris: Gallimard, 1970).
SD	'Baudrillard: Le sujet et son double' (interview) with François Ewald in *Magazine Littéraire* (Avril, 1989): 19–23.
Seduction	*Seduction*, trans. Brian Singer (Montreal: New World Perspectives, 1990).
Shadow	*In the shadow of the silent majorities/end of the social*, trans. P. Foss, P. Patton, John Johnston (New York: Semiotext(e), 1983).
Simulations	*Simulations*, trans. P. Foss, P. Patton, P. Beitchman (New York: Semiotext(e), 1983).
SO	*Le système des objets* (Paris: Gallimard, 1968).
SS	*Simulation et simulacres* (Paris: Galilée, 1981).
TE	*The Transparency of Evil: Essays on Extreme Phenomena*, trans. James Benedict (London: Verso, 1993).
TM	*La Transparence du Mal: Essai su les phénomènes extrêmes* (Paris: Galilée, 1990).
Vitale:	'Jean Baudrillard: "Une ultime réaction vitale",' interview with François Ewald in *Magazine Littéraire* (Juillet–Aout, 1994): 20–4.

I

Introduction: Historical and cultural context

1

The rules of the game

I just thought everyone knew it was ironic, but apparently they thought I was mad. (Jim Morrison)[1]

THE POLITICS OF CULTURAL METAPHYSICS

This study sets out, especially in Parts II and III, to reconstruct the origins and development of Jean Baudrillard's thought in a more or less conventional way, simplifying his ideas wherever feasible. In order to grasp the full significance of Baudrillard's thought, however, it is important to consider its 'degeneration' as well. Any serious attempt at an exposition of his work must try to address the question why, over the course of his career, Baudrillard has transformed an essentially sociological perspective on culture into the philosophically 'nihilistic' one now so familiar to students of modern and postmodern intellectual history.

Jean Baudrillard is one of the most frequently cited contemporary social theorists. The real depth of his influence is hard to calculate, partly because it often goes unacknowledged; but it is probably as difficult to ignore as that of any major cultural theorist today. Nevertheless, there is something in Baudrillard's approach which does not fit the usual pattern of the sociologist's academic career, even if we compare him only to the radical schools which have formed his principal audience. People seem fascinated by his unusual perceptions. But they dispute his formulations, water them down, or try to squeeze them into a more normal sociopolitical frame of reference. To use one of Baudrillard's favourite tropes: one gets the impression of a body repeatedly fighting off a virus, with diminishing success. Each round of infection twists the normative basis of critical theory a little more. After a while, theory begins to attack itself, and to retreat from itself into schizoid fragments, as if to hide from a growing sense of futility. The scent of opposition remains in the air; but no one can provide a consistent account of its presence or meaning.

It is intriguing to speculate how it is that Baudrillard has achieved so large an audience, in spite of his problematic status within the broad field of cultural studies. The effect of his prose is closer to satire, even to travesty, than to 'critical' or 'emancipatory' discourse. But since no one has been able to dismiss him as a 'mere' artist, his arguments have become something of an embarrassment, at least in the English-speaking academic world, where the social sciences still try to maintain an aura of philosophical and moral respectability. Sometimes Baudrillard expresses so cynical a view of the state of social theory that even his own defiance strikes him as a naive anachronism. Gone is the 'pathos of nihilism', he avers, apparently with more glee than lament: gone is 'that mythic energy which still gave nihilism its radical strength, that sense of cosmic refusal, of dramatic anticipation' (*SS* 233–4). Yet when Baudrillard states that today's 'theories' are just 'floating', like so many currencies, can anyone say that his perception is inaccurate?

With the possible exception of Marshall McLuhan, I cannot think of any academically-based writer who has structured his own message in quite this way: so that the technical failure of his arguments represents their point of maximum efficacy, when they deserve (and very often receive) more attention than they would otherwise have merited. Looking back over the 30 years of published Baudrillard, it is tempting to wonder if the whole semiocritical edifice for which he is so famous was constructed precisely in order to fly apart in our faces. Some of his earlier publications hinted at such perverse intentions. And by 1976 (*ESM*), it was clear that Baudrillard was working against the 'utility' of thought as we conventionally understand it; that his own project was linked directly to moments in intellectual history when the practical formation of ideas was compromised, like the stowaway woodworm in Julian Barnes' recounting of the voyage of Noah's Ark.[2]

What is it that has sustained this note of exceeding dissonance so effectively through the closing decades of our traumatic century? Is it historical indigestion, or the crepitation of the approaching millennium? I cannot offer a satisfying 'explanation' in the scientific sense of that word. But we do know enough about the story of Western intellectual traditions to sense that in Baudrillard, we are dealing with an interesting kind of 'mutation'. The real question is: what do we make of it? Is it one of Nicholas Mosley's 'hopeful monsters'?[3] How can we understand the meaning of a mutation when so many have come to feel, like de Musset more than 150 years ago, that we are already living on remnants, in a time when 'all that was is no more, and all that is to be is not yet'?[4]

In order to get at the potential of this question, I have proposed the concept of 'cultural metaphysics'. Cultural metaphysics is a genre construct whose discursive function is to suggest the possibility of a containing framework within which the tensions and contradictions of radical thought can be explored without having to be resolved or explained away. It is a conceptual holding room for paradox and nonsense, for everything in the contemporary social imaginary that is illegitimate, unpleasant or indeterminate.

Cultural metaphysics is a provisional or 'working' concept, in the sense of a 'working paper', or an ongoing project which is still in the formative stage. It can be understood as a kind of discipline in the sense that discipline is required to write novels and poetry, make films, draw and paint, sculpt, compose, or act. The responsibility of the cultural metaphysician is comparable to the commitment of the artist or thinker who adopts an expressive stance in order to make expression itself the issue, or who represents something in order to explore the problem of representation. Cultural metaphysics hinges on the ideational dimension of this type of activity. But it is not a discipline in the sense that it can be organized as an official body for regulating the accumulation of a specific type of knowledge.

Although what we now treat as metaphysical speculation about culture can be traced to any period of recorded history, cultural metaphysics in the secular sense seems to have risen to prominence in the modern period. I assume that it is the liberalized residue of what we still retroactively think of as culture in the ethnographic sense. The history of the term 'culture' itself affords an excellent illustration of this hypothesis. As Baudrillard has always argued, most pointedly in *For a critique of the political economy of the sign* (*FCPES*) and *Simulations* (*SS*), the term in its current anthropological sense is completely atavistic. The objective, social scientific concept of 'culture' as an expressive totality or collective spirit, distinct from the way other people live, first emerged at the end of the Enlightenment, particularly in the Romantic historical reflections of Herder.[5] It gained professional currency just when such 'ways of life' were beginning to feel the disembedding effects of globalization which are now so integral to contemporary 'life'. The term applies rigorously only to small-scale *symbolic* social organizations, and to some aspects of larger, but still very traditional, pre-industrial civilizations. Beyond that, 'culture' in the collective sense is pure nostalgia. Its predominant form of existence today is 'dis-play' – if not in urban museums, then in protected reservations or isolated colonies (*FCPES* 185–203). In this respect, 'culture' is just like 'nature', which itself exists increasingly in national parks and sanctuaries, like the Gombe Reserve on Lake Tanganyika in Tanzania.[6]

The very concept of culture as an exclusive, bounded, societal structure only arose when the historical phenomenon to which it now refers had already crested. This is one of Baudrillard's most important metaphysical insights: that the manic power of the dominant term in academic and social scientific discourse is probably a defensive symptom of pathological mourning (what he calls 'melancholia') – or worse, of lethargy and aphanisis: 'the brutal disaffection of saturated systems' (*SS* 234). In other words, the contemporary scientization of 'culture' reflects the passing of culture from the field of ordinary experience. We notice it, name it, and study it, just as it begins to fade from memory: only then does social awareness of the symbolic existence we take for granted emerge from the dedifferentiated field of unconscious bodily perception and pass momentarily into the academic figure/ground gestalt of conscious or linguistic articulation.

All our lively debates about culture, according to this perspective, are really about something else, something which probably never occurred in the form we have conceived it, and which is now 'disappearing'. In fact, the speculations and pronouncements about culture which constitute the discursive substance of cultural metaphysics as a genre, including those in the present study, are probably best understood as secondary substitutes for 'cultural life' as we imagine it once to have existed, perhaps in our own family history.

There is an important sense in which all, or most, social science, is really cultural metaphysics. The genealogical link between the contemporary academic discourse on culture and the 'disappearance' of traditional culture as an experiential field is most striking in those instances where cultural metaphysics attempts to function as a normative or predictive body of knowledge, as in the claim to understand the 'laws' of 'development' (psychological, moral, economic); or in the 'research' correlating violence in the 'media' with violence in society (leading to the banning of children's cartoons); or 'clinical data' establishing a causal link between child abuse and 'multiple personality', pornography and rape, or the 'decline of family values' and crime, decadence, and anomie. It is impossible today to predict the eventual scientific value of any statement plucked from the great welter of official and professional words about culture in modern societies; but we can be reasonably sure that our willingness to believe the fantastic things we hear increases with waning confidence in the traditional cultural mechanisms for moulding and controlling behaviour.

Though cultural metaphysics would never thrive as a genre without protected speech and liberalization of norms and values, it still bears traces of the restrictive authoritarianism characteristic of traditional cultural systems. The paradox is evident in the fact that every radical cultural interest group – from transsexuals to Christian fundamentalists – has its own cultural engineering programme already worked out and ready to implement. Stand-up urinals will be eliminated from all bathrooms and the Bible will be taught as 'creation science'. Most traditional cultural forms of social control were organized around conventionalized images of the body in the world, usually dimorphic in conception. These convenient binary constructions were drawn from the intermediate range of perception typical of the unassisted organs of bodily sensation and cognition. We now characterize them as 'symbolic', as if they had arisen from some other world of spiritual intentionality which we no longer understand. The ritual and emotional core of such cosmic systems usually related to questions arising from experiences of birth, death, sex and gender, which in turn influenced the structure of kinship systems, relationships of social authority, and radial patterns of meaning. In the balance of emotional maturity and wisdom, the current politics offers few notable advances over these older ways of seeing. The crucial difference is that traditional cultures evolved through complex multivariant processes, whereas the cultural engineers of today actively plan to impose their premeditated systems, from the top down if necessary. The stable, homeostatic type of semiotic regulation described retroactively by cultural anthropologists is difficult to conceive on the scale of contemporary societal systems. What seemed to our ancestors like a binary universe made of yin and yang now strikes us as an impossibly complex interacting continuum of chemical, genetic, social and emotional histories. Yet digital abstraction has achieved a power of penetration into phenomena which already invalidates the bodily order of perception. It may soon loop back to the roots of cognition itself, transforming the way we experience the intermediate zone of ordinary perception, where the psychosomatic body still manages to squeeze past the pincering pressure of the imperceptibly large and small. From the standpoint of cultural metaphysics, then, we would be wise to consider the possibility of something like social simulation, as Baudrillard has described it.

Cultural metaphysics in this larger, political sense can be understood as a symptom of generalized panic in the industrialized world over the loss of community. The atavistic strain of cultural authoritarianism, such as one finds in Heidegger, is essentially a reaction to modernization and secularization. It answers people's need to belong to a group that is good and right and pure – or, in other words, a group purged of all that is thought to be bad, wrong, dirty. This 'retrospective consciousness of the lost community', as Jean-Luc Nancy calls it, is by no means exclusive to modernity (or even to the West). 'Our history begins with the departure of Ulysses . . . [and with] Penelope, who reweaves the fabric of intimacy without ever managing to complete it.'[7] What is specific to modernity, particularly the contemporary scene, is the academization and scientization of these timeless anxieties about identity, sexuality and 'evil'. In a world where the only culture is cultural metaphysics, superstition becomes social theory: 'What society looks toward is no longer a return to the promised land, but a general disaster that is already upon us, woven into the fabric of day to day life'.[8]

The other side of cultural metaphysics, however, is dispassionate contemplation. It offers not only a valve for the evacuation of floating social anxieties, but potentially also a vehicle, or holding environment, where the residues of discharged panic can accumulate for observation. How else might the anguished and distorted leavings of the psychosocial process become available as materials for reflection? In this secondary, metabolic role, cultural metaphysics suggests a model for working through the disturbing anomalies of social experience. It is a way of elaborating the psychodynamics of the uncanny and the aesthetics of the grotesque, which address the paradoxes of the exteriorized and mechanized image as catalysts of cultural experience and thought.

Although Baudrillard can be and has been interpreted as a panic theorist, my reading emphasizes the contemplative element of his work, which I believe affords genuine insight into the vicissitudes of the social process. To that extent, my views have an affinity with

Gianni Vattimo's postmodern reading of Nietzsche and Heidegger. (Incidentally, the latter seems to be an unacknowledged elaboration of Baudrillard's critique of the political economy of the sign.[9]) Through a kind of philosophical piggybacking on what Vattimo calls the nihilistic 'reduction of Being to exchange value', cultural metaphysics is able to heighten (or to debase?) the rational, cumulative, proto-scientific efforts of history and social science to the level of pure speculation, denuded of all pretence at referentiality and practicality. Thus, cultural metaphysics transforms the intellectual content of the human sciences into a self-contained aesthetic sphere, where one is more free (but never completely so, unfortunately) to elaborate, divide and connect, rhizomatically, without any necessary prior reference to an organizing principle or practical structure, such as left and right, serious and frivolous, true and false. The ideal is of a social thought experiment occurring in a discursive space void of moral parameters.

Baudrillard's cultural metaphysics is a kind of 'Critique of Pure Critique'. It is radical mainly because it questions the self-image of the intellectual as a privileged agent, and thus undermines the whole moral basis for cultural studies as a respectable discipline with a function and a purpose and a *raison d'être*. As should be clear by now, the basic speculative value in this kind of discourse is aesthetic. Like a good Nietzschean, Baudrillard is not interested in goodness, because it claims to be general and objective (something in accordance with which intellectuals think they should be trying to shape the world). He is more attuned to the problem of diversity. The difficulty of diversity from the point of view of academic respectability is that it cannot be 'conceived' or 'planned' (or meaningfully judged). It is an inherently unpredictable interrelation of particulars and singularities, not the holistic field of integrated causes and effects the social sciences seek. Diversity cannot be justified on grounds other than a mere preference for diversity – that is, a belief that in the absence and unlikeliness of Truth and Goodness, we must settle for variety, which exists naturally, and thrives when conditions are open.

ONTOLOGICAL OPTIONS

A profound thinker never really convinces us of anything; he or she can only awaken us to the choices we have made, and make us wonder about their meaning and their consequences. Baudrillard is that kind of thinker. When plumbed to the murky bottom, his thought confronts us with a difficult choice which lies at the root of our intuitions about the relationship between politics and knowledge. I will discuss this theme at some length in the last part of the book; but it may help the reader to provide a rough sketch of the problem at the beginning.

The alternatives that Baudrillard illuminates, with remarkable insight, in my view, are the following: either one stakes everything on a particular *vision*, thus committing oneself to the pretence (or paranoid psychopathology) of certainty; or else one refuses to take the outcome of the knowledge-seeking process quite so seriously, and one places all of one's faith in the 'rules of the game'. The choice may sound simpler than it really is.

The first option (the decision to be zealous on behalf of a comprehensive vision) is what tends to make knowledge of any kind such a menace. Nevertheless, certainty is very appealing because it offers security and peace of mind. The promise of protection is the standard exchange value for faith, loyalty and obedience.

In contrast, the rules of the game offer little compensation for the loss of protection which occurs when one is cast out into the desert of professional scepticism (and that is precisely where Baudrillard tries to take his readers). To choose the rules of the game is to minimize the value, in the larger scheme of things, of any single point of view or piece of knowledge. The visionary can discern what is important and what is not because he or she knows what the larger scheme of things is. The gamesplayer makes a different kind of determination: he or she argues that because we don't know the scheme of things, every hierarchy must be treated formally as ascriptive and provisional. It is one of the preconditions of the game that the means of dismantling any determination, any vision, must be ready at hand, and universally available. This seems foolish to many people, either because it threatens the social order, or because it makes criticism of the social order more difficult. But it is the only non-visionary way.

Yet it takes a certain vision to resist the lure of vision. The frustrating dilemma for the postmodern intellectual is that in the end the impersonal rules of the game require as much emotional investment, zealotry and faith as any fundamentalist campaign, because the game still has to be defended against the constant human effort to put the fix in. So we are never free of the problem of conviction: we are always forced to put down a wager on something. The difference between choosing a vision and choosing the empty rules of the game is that in the vision, we back one definite content against another; whereas in the game, we bet on an otherwise debatable public form over any possible content.

In reality most of us never finally make this kind of choice. We tend towards one extreme or the other, hovering between absolute faith and total scepticism. The balance of our lives is lived largely in the gaps, where existence refuses to conform either to the coherence of vision or to the formal rationality of the rules of the game. Baudrillard somehow manages to be at both extremes simultaneously: he is a radical visionary who nevertheless treats the problem of existence itself as a kind of game whose rules are magical and ritual rather than rational (for example, *Seduction*, *FS*). He is perhaps the first trained social analyst to confront us with this paradox at the level of theory itself. It is easy at first to classify him as an absolutist, because he does present a total vision of the world in a relentlessly reductionistic style. But if one stays with his reasoning long enough, this intellectual totalitarianism becomes ridiculous. The more one investigates the arguments, or puzzles over their appeal, the more one is struck by the moments of irony, the flashes of self-exposure and calculated cynicism, which seem designed to undermine our trust in any intellectual vision, not least Baudrillard's own. In the end, it is impossible to decide whether Baudrillard really wants to be the Emperor, His tailor, the boy who sees Him naked, or the court jester.

Given the difficulties of interpretation raised by Baudrillard's elusive posture, it may ease the burden on the reader to know where the present author stands as one of his expositors. Because I am supported mainly by my psychoanalytic income, I am used to being in the 'gap', where explicate knowledge is sparse, and 'rules' don't compute. Faced with Baudrillard's ontological choice between vision and play, however, I much prefer to play by the rules of the game, rather than to know by means of second sight. Intellectually, of course, I am attracted by cosmic apparitions like a moth to the flame; and I have indulged that predilection in my account of Baudrillard. But in practice, I trust only democratic forms: the rule of law; the formalities of habeas corpus and due process; the prejudice in favour of the political primacy of the individual, and the fiction of his or her moral independence; the convention that the burden of proof should be heavy, and be carried by the accuser; and the absolute political and moral guarantee of communicative freedom and free association. My reasons are very simple. No philosophical deconstruction of these individual rights and freedoms ever made their absence less detrimental. No political promise offered in exchange for their suspension is ever kept. And finally, nineteenth-century predictions that individuality sublated by the collectivity would re-emerge in a higher, finer form have not panned out historically.

THE PUBLIC SPHERE AND THE DEVIL'S SHARE

In Part VII of this study, I shall argue that Baudrillard's analysis of the crisis of modernity suggests a more favourable assessment of the liberal democratic option than is currently entertained on behalf of enlightened social action. This hardly sounds like a Baudrillardian proposal, of course. Baudrillard emphasizes the irrationality of the human soul. He confronts us with the psychosomatic violence of symbolic exchange as the existential ground of social being. From this perspective, the rational individuality upon which a liberal order depends appears as a devitalized abstraction feeding parasitically off the turbulent social body; liberalism will never work because the identity and transparency of the liberal individual is an historically and culturally determined fiction – a refusal to acknowledge the 'devil's share'.

For me, the answer to this argument is already implicit in Baudrillard's critique. Who ever said that individuals are supposed to be identical with themselves? And since when has it been a philosophical or political requirement of rationality that it be the sole and exclusive personality trait? An understanding of Baudrillard's fundamental objections to the liberal illusion of rationality is likely to bring the thoughtful reader back to an awareness of the profound historical reasons for the rise of that illusion in the first place, and its indispensability in the conduct of post-traditional social life. It is precisely because, in the last analysis, we are bound by symbolic exchange, slaves to seduction, exiled by some inner fatality, that we need to cultivate a liberal order, if only to contain our passions and to foster our diversity in the age of technology.

The critics of liberalism are probably right when they say that a democracy based on the juridico-political concept of the individual is incapable of producing a collective culture rich and vital enough to inspire loyalty and conviction. Yet for the radical dissident, surely this is its most attractive feature. The shallowness of democratic culture encourages a welcome loss of faith in public symbols. The result is a gradual deliteralization of societally-constituted identities. With luck, the myth of a connecting social substance will gradually fade, along with the theology of incorporation, the fantasy that we can escape from ourselves, that we are 'not alone', because society is 'there for us', waiting.

The liberal principle of unrestricted discussion is the historical twin of modern market technology – starting with the printing press. The public sphere thus created is a dangerous place, where anti-societal diseases spawn and spread. It creates an opening in the social body, an entry into individual and social consciousness, for everything foreign and unpredictable – whatever cannot be mastered easily through the traditional homeostatic mechanisms of cultural control. It fosters a desire for radical freedom which refuses to be protected from itself, or to respect the prickly sensibilities of others. This much more dangerous liberal demand for freedom of social forms goes directly against the grain of conventional collectivist thought, left wing or right wing, and the moral imperatives of goodness, justice and equality.

That this anarchic current of radical liberalism is implicit in Baudrillard's otherwise apparently anti-liberal writing goes a long way towards explaining why his reception by academic cultural theorists has been so ambivalent. With the important exception of Foucault, Baudrillard is almost unique among major contemporary critical theorists for his frank recognition of human aggressivity. He does not mistake violence and competition for epiphenomena, transient effects which will disappear with re-education in some communitarian utopia. He is prepared to deal with the possibility that violence is in the human soul, and it is here that he connects most deeply with the emotional essence of radical liberalism.

The further one searches, the more human aggression seems related to the desire for certainty. The traditional liberal response to it is essentially the same as in psychoanalysis: put it into words, images – process it in semiotic or symbolic form; but don't do it or believe it (unless you do it to yourself, or have a consenting partner). Those are the rules of the game. There is nothing more for liberals to concern themselves with, except possibly cultural metaphysics. In other words, liberalism has no substance, and no specific content. It is impossible to be *just* a liberal in the way that a socialist can be a socialist, or a fascist a fascist. One can only *defend* the rational forms of liberal convention, one cannot *live* them. From an existentialist point of view, then, liberalism is really just an excuse, a rationalization, a cover. A form of polite bad faith. I espouse it in the hope of persuading people to leave me alone and let me be what I am – which might be anything at all, but very rarely an embodiment of liberalism. In making that concession, I concede that others can and should be different, even when, behind such rational calculations, there breathes within me a monster that would dominate the universe. Whatever I am, whatever I have become, whatever I dream, I have somehow learned that I am better off not expecting my vision to turn into the state religion. The centre of gravity of my irrational, heterogeneous, decentred self will naturally lie somewhere within my history and social circle, my own little sado-masochistic coterie, my coven of witches, my hermaphrodites, my fellow Kabuki actors, my multiple personalities, my clairvoyants and conycatchers – if and when I find them. I am playing a game. Yet, infantile as my game may be, I am mature enough to realize that it isn't everybody's. Other bodies have other emergent properties with different psycho-social consequences. I learn to tolerate the fact that my creed is not universally recommended, adopted, enforced by the police, taught in the schools.

So the liberal answer lies in some intuition about a metagame, a game of games – in effect, to use Baudrillard's vocabulary, a *simulation*. The fantasy of the open society is exactly that: a proposal to mime a coherent social life based on formal adherence to a set of metarules which in fact do nothing more than let everyone go their own way.

It is tempting to believe that this is the formula for a multicultural utopia. But there are good reasons to be doubtful. We have never had a genuinely open society; and the liberal democratic approximations of that ideal do not have an encouraging record. Even if one looks on the bright side of what Marcuse called 'repressive tolerance', the impression is that the abstractness of the metarules has a withering effect on ritual and symbolic forms of life. No doubt the idea of individual freedom is partly responsible for the desiccation of traditional cultures. Proof of pluralism still lies too much in the pudding of market process. Moreover, the indifferent extension of formal freedoms presupposes an underlying provision for social equality which requires some degree of enforcement in order to be credible. Unfortunately, no culture based on ritual symbolic forms, with their cosmic hierarchical playacting, can possibly survive strict application of the equality rule. Something irrational always survives, of course. Societal life will always be governed by ceremony, anxiety, fantastic projections. But many believe that in the modern democracies, these residual cultural modalities no longer articulate a deeply felt internal connection between people. There may be nominal membership in a group, class, institution, juridically-derived collectivity, or technologically-fostered community; but there is no *Gemeinschaft* as the German sociologists would say – no sense of belonging in one's soul. Lots and lots of society, getting more aggressive all the time, and increasingly global in circumference; but not much that is genuinely social in the profoundest sense of that word.

It is with this apperception that Baudrillard simply drops out of the contemporary political universe. In compensation, through the medium of cultural metaphysics, he tries to reconstitute a thoroughly primitive and pre-scientific conception of the rules of the game: ambivalent reciprocity as the fundamental social modality, symbolic exchange as its ritual or ceremonial form, seduction as the game of games, and the fatal strategy as the ultimate principle of closure. Psychologically these may very well be the deepest rules of play. And perhaps they would seem more appropriate still if we really believed that modernity had reached the point of no return.

2

Cultural metaphysics

Fantastic literature . . . does not introduce novelty, so much as uncover all that needs to remain hidden if the world is to be comfortably 'known'.[1]

If the roster of the International Psychoanalytic Association is only the edge of a much vaster network, then there are a lot of people in the world who know a secret: that the relationship between dreaming and living is uncanny, and if permitted, may drastically reorder the conventional perception of one's own existence, the intentional structures which inform the process of living a life.

Are as many aware that the social world has a secret dimension as uncanny as dreams? Freud's technical appropriation of the dream as a piece of equipment designed for individual living is only a special part of a more general modern phenomenon, which might be described as the rise of deritualized forms of mythic self-reflection. Cinema provides a simple way to think about this. Just as Freud was formalizing the critical and transgressive functions of psychic fantasy, the film medium was beginning to objectify collective fantasy: in the 1890s, the private dream screen was doubled by the technology of cinematic reverie, and was perhaps even facilitated by the latter. Pasolini called it the 'hypnotic *monstrum*'.[2]

If psychoanalysis and cinema have resituated fantasy in the explicate order – in effect, as domains of active and controversial reflexivity – then what might be the philosophical or social scientific response running parallel to this historical development? Various terms come to mind. 'Theory' is one of them. Jonathan Culler has pointed out how we have come to use that word as a nickname. He links it with the rise of an intensive cross-disciplinary jargon of indeterminate epistemological status.[3] Allan Megill describes a coherent tradition of 'crisis thought'.[4] Foucault sometimes called this genealogy, after Nietzsche. For many the preferred term is 'deconstruction' (Derrida) or schizoanalysis (Deleuze and Guattari). Like the dream, and like the voyeuristic pleasures of cinematic art, these forms of intellectual engagement tend to privilege the experience of regression and the structure of repetition, as if they had been drawn into the Ovidian world of uncanny transformations and *unintended* consequences. Jonathan Dollimore captures this perfectly in his concept of transgressive reinscription: 'a *turning* back upon something and a perverting of it typically if not exclusively through inversion and displacement'. Dollimore is quite definite about the role of regression and the importance of systematic repetition. 'The idea seems strange: is not transgression a liberation from, a moving beyond: a break out, perhaps even a progression?'[5] Not necessarily. There are many variations on this theme, some conventional, some radical, but taken together, they seem to constitute what Richard Rorty has described as a 'new genre' – 'neither the evaluation of the relative merits of literary productions, nor intellectual history, nor moral philosophy, nor epistemology, nor social prophecy, but all of these things mingled together'.[6] It is an oddly libertarian sort of mandarin art which might be called 'cultural metaphysics'.

But why the grandiose 'cultural *metaphysics*'? Why not cultural theory, cultural criticism, cultural studies, critique, communications, aesthetics? There is no doubt that with a little effort Baudrillard's writing can be fitted under these headings; but words like 'theory', 'critique' and 'study' resonate with inappropriate overtones of academic or social responsibility. One advantage of the term 'metaphysics' is that it no longer has any connotations of legitimacy. Nor does it imply any discursive distance from the 'object'. Curiously, it is now metaphysics alone – once considered the science of grounds and reasons – which confidently declares itself without foundation or justification (which is exactly where we are likely to find Baudrillard).

Another advantage of 'metaphysics' is that it has become (at least for those who can make sense of Baudrillard) frankly mythical in its preoccupations. Cultural metaphysics offers one of the few remaining public theatres – along with the cinema – for rehearsing the forms of infantile pre-operational thinking, the language of the pre-societal body, of everything and nothing, life and death, presence and absence, me and not me, beauty and the beast, projection, incorporation, awe, angst and passion.

Of course, Baudrillard is certainly not the first, nor the only cultural metaphysician. The list of his European forebears would take us all the way back to classical Athenian comedy and Menippean satire; they are likely to be found wherever an educated, metropolitan culture has flourished. Among them may be counted a number of independent 'thinkers' who are now taken quite seriously, including in modern times Kierkegaard, Nietzsche,

Bataille, Marshall McLuhan, Dorothy Dinnerstein, Gilles Deleuze, Teresa Brennan, Camille Paglia. But his closest contemporaries are perhaps in other fields: among film directors, Pasolini, Tarkovsky, Cronenberg; and among writers, Swift, Borges, Calvino, William Burroughs, Philip Dick, Thomas Pynchon.

THE UNCANNY

> Theory does not derive its legitimacy from established facts, but from future events. Its value is not in the past events it can illuminate, but in the shockwave of events it prefigures. It does not act upon consciousness, but directly on the course of things from which it draws its energy. It therefore has to be distinguished from the academic practice of philosophy and from all that is written with an eye to the history of ideas.[7]

This brief passage from *Cool Memories* captures the circular nature of Baudrillard's relationship to the ambient culture – not only to the avant-garde, but to the social scientific community at large. Like a hybrid Plato-Warhol, Baudrillard has always worked between the adjoining faces of representation (or imitation) and its objects, charting the collapse of the imagination into the world and the world into the image, the fusion of the mimer and the mimed. 'Theory' (as he calls it above) achieves this not only descriptively, but as a participant in the processes described, pretending to act 'directly on the course of things from which it draws its energy'. Few who enter his texts can now think of 'simulation' apart from things as they seem to be. This curious self-propagating quality – the 'Baudrillard effect', as it might be called – can be detected in a whole range of cultural phenomena, from experimental art practices to the sociology of Anthony Giddens. To read Baudrillard is to sense how social reality and social theory emulate each other, perhaps even become each other. The following chapters will investigate this transaction, tracing the development of his 'theory-fiction' to the point where it has even begun to document its own absorption and *dépassement* in a world which is partially of its own creation.

Cultural metaphysics is often marked by a specific type of prophetic impulse: not to speak the Truth in the name of God, like a promising or threatening biblical figure; but to report a bewildering identification with the 'not-me', whose alien forces seemed, at the moment of encounter, to have coursed through the world and left nothing over but the traces of something odd, sometimes a foreboding. The cultural metaphysician would like to speak of this experience, but there is little for him or her to point to. The regular features of everyday life have not changed, yet they have somehow become strange and peculiar-seeming, perhaps through an elusive glimpse of a vague possibility concealed in the familiar textures of the most ordinary phenomena: what Freud called *Unheimlich* – the uncanny.

If Baudrillard's metaphysical theme is mimesis, the uncanny destiny of representation, his sociological theme is the sacred and the profane, not in the formal, Durkheimian sense, but as an odyssey through modernity: 'the phenomenology of a sort of personal discovery, which repeats, in other dimensions, what might have been the primitive experience of emigration' (L'éspace 158). His writings have become, in part, a work of mourning – ecstatic or paradoxical mourning, we might call it. Starting with the problem of culture in everyday life, they have concentrated increasingly on the task of reviewing the failed idealizations of self-reflexive political philosophy, from Romanticism to Foucault. To follow Baudrillard in this pilgrim's regress is to become implicated in a public act of renunciation: Baudrillard's letting go of the ancient dream of social ecstasy, of symbolic exchange and festive collectivity. It is as if he wanted 'to prevent the realization of the social for fear of damaging the concept and forever destroying the hopes that surround it' (*Cool* 170).

This last statement contains an important clue to an overlooked aspect of Baudrillard's unusual style of commentary: his wish to preserve in the imagination what cannot be realized, or even recognized, in the pragmatic historical world. In this respect, Baudrillard's writings are uncharacteristic of radical critique. They stand in awe of the inevitable impasse in communication between psychic reality and social reality. Instead of trying to abolish this distinction, as do the conventional utopians, Baudrillard resists almost anything that would threaten it, a fact which some have mistaken for political conservatism or cynicism. Perhaps this is his thought for our age: that the will to close the gap between fantasy and society is equivocal – not simply an expression of the emancipatory spirit, a natural impulse of the 'id', or a 'revolutionary strategy of desire', but also, and more deeply, a clever ruse of the superego. It is not difficult to discern this in contemporary political culture: the terroristic intention to repress and control is only perfunctorily concealed in the contemporary uses of once revolutionary slogans like 'the personal is the political'. In the style of exorcism, Baudrillard's secret strategy – what he has come to call his 'fatal strategy' – has been to ward off piety by dishing out ironic nonsense, just as Freud, when forced to sign a document attesting to his good treatment by the Nazis after the *Anschluss*, added with a flourish of the pen: 'I heartily recommend the Gestapo to everyone!' Thus, in *The Evil Demon of Images*, Baudrillard explains his denunciation of the 'immorality' of the image:

> [it] correspond[s] to the unrestrained film buff that I am and have always wished to remain – that is, in a sense, uncultured and fascinated. There is a kind of primal pleasure, of anthropological joy in images, a kind of brute fascination unencumbered by aesthetic, moral, social or political judgements. It is because of this that I suggest that they are immoral, and that their fundamental power lies in this immorality. (*Evil* 27)

Baudrillard's mock complaint about the proliferation of the image carries nostalgic Romantic undertones which may be compared to Wim Wenders's search for *Heimat* (or spiritual home) in films like *Tokyo-Ga* and *Until the End of the World*. Wenders explicitly characterizes the unrestrained reproducibility of the image as a troubling division within modern experience. *Heimat* is the object of longing in that condition of 'transcendental homelessness' which Georg Lukács attributed to modern culture.[8] Its resonance extends from Proust's 'lost time' to the 'white hotel' of D.M. Thomas's fictionalized Freud.[9] In *Tokyo-Ga*, Werner Herzog evokes it when he tells Wenders, while looking out over Tokyo from the 'Eiffel Tower', that he can no longer find any images on earth which correspond to what is inside himself – he may have to travel to the moon to get them: 'The simple truth is that there aren't any images around now'.[10] It is precisely this sentiment which Baudrillard attempts to evoke with his immoderate declaration: 'Today . . . reality has already incorporated the hyperrealist dimension of simulation so that we are now living entirely within the "aesthetic" hallucination of reality' (*Death* 74). Herzog was looking for an image that had not already been reproduced, so that *he* could *represent* it. But as Baudrillard points out, 'the very definition of the real is *that of which it is possible to provide an equivalent reproduction* . . . [but this has become] *that which is always already reproduced*' (*Death* 73). There is no longer a sufficient difference between image and reality to permit an act of representation in the traditional sense (*Evil* 26). It is as if the sheer ubiquity of the reproduced image has sapped us of our capacity to see the world with imagination.

Of course, this is nonsense. But from the point of view of cultural metaphysics, it is a compelling thought, a manifestation of the

Unheimlich, as Wim Wenders shows near the conclusion of *Until the End of the World*. The penultimate scenes of that film are set in an enclave of exiles in the Australian outback. It is the eve of the millennium, the year 2000. A nuclear crisis may have destroyed the world, but no one can be certain, for all the communication lines have been cut. At any rate, something has wiped out all the memory banks. The refugee community is safe because it is geographically so isolated. Sam (William Hurt) has returned on a mission to restore sight to his blind mother (Jeanne Moreau). He has been round the world, tracking his relatives in the postmodern diaspora, and interviewing them while wearing a new image device his father Henry (Max von Sydow) has invented. It is hoped that with the aid of this technology, Sam will be able to transfer the encoded brain image of his memories of these interviews so that they can be reproduced in his mother's brain, thus enabling her to 'see' her family again. Unfortunately, Sam's sight has been suffering as a result of the encoding procedures. But the experiment is a success: his mother manages to have some painful visual experiences, then dies. The friendly aboriginals sense that her death, and Sam's sensory disorientation, have something to do with the Western 'disease of images'; they leave the camp. Meanwhile, Sam and his girlfriend Claire (Solveig Dommartin) become hopelessly addicted to video recordings of their own dreams, which they play over and over, in a somnambulistic stupor. Eventually, it turns out that the world has survived the nuclear crisis, and the exiles are saved. But in the last scene, Claire is shown orbiting around the earth in a satellite station, monitoring the global environment. It is as if the earth is no longer really a place where she can live; it is an enormous artefact, and she has been absorbed into its self-regulating feedback loop. The gap between psychic reality and social reality has closed to the point where there is no longer any possibility of living out the fantasy that one contains an interiority secret within that world. There is no home, or place that you can go inside. Everything is just as it was before, and yet, in another sense, as Baudrillard would say, it is as if everything had 'disappeared'.

It is with this last enigma that the point of Baudrillard's theory of simulation eludes many readers. They feel quite rightly that if reality is disappearing, as Baudrillard proposes, then it must once have been 'present' in some definitive, 'objective' sense which seems epistemologically questionable. Or else they feel that with the theory of 'third-order' simulacra, Baudrillard's line of argument has slipped hopelessly into self-cancelling relativism. As I shall argue in this study, the only answer to these epistemological criticisms is to suggest that we resist the temptation to read Baudrillard's metaphors literally; but this means decompressing our overdeveloped 'Western' sense of moral and political urgency. If that can be done, then a valid Baudrillard will be discovered, a worthwhile man of letters who is neither a naive realist nor a naive relativist, but an astute cultural metaphysician allegorizing the shifting relationships between psyche and society.

A NOTE ON FRENCH POLITICS

The French were understandably uncomfortable after the military defeat of Nazi Germany. People wanted to distance themselves from the awful trauma of occupation and collaboration. The rapid onset of the Cold War provided France with an opportunity to save face by pursuing a 'third way' between the frontier ideologies of capitalism and communism. This alternative was not liberal social democracy, but patriotic republican authoritarianism, whose roots can be traced from Napoleon through De Gaulle to Chirac. The elite French political class needed to provide the state with an outward aura of geopolitical independence. In reality, as Dien-Bien-Phu and the Algerian war make clear, this pretension was an international farce comparable with the adventures of Mussolini. Nevertheless, it had some political advantages, especially in French intellectual culture. What had led to withering stultification in McCarthyite America sustained a more enlightened, open-minded tendency in France.

It is also important to remember that the French Communist Party (PCF) was skilful in appropriating the glories of the *résistance*, and so the decline of Soviet prestige was slower in France than it was in the English-speaking world. This meant that one could still dare to express old-fashioned revolutionary thoughts from within the academic establishment. Even after the revolt against the old left in 1968, a basically libertarian thinker like Foucault could publicly advocate a bloody proletarian dictatorship without losing credibility as a scholar. When he had been a student at the elite Ecole Normale Supérieure in the immediate postwar years, the cream of the French crop were steeped in the politics of revolutionary collectivism.

The Algerian war of liberation was an important variable in the French political equation. The global neutrality of France did not prevent internal polarization over colonial policy, which could be identified with American imperialism. In consequence, the moderates like Albert Camus and Raymond Aron were marginalized and ridiculed by the intelligentsia. France had never really had a stable democratic culture to begin with, and De Gaulle's attempts to repress political opposition to the colonialist policies of the French state radicalized many intellectuals, including Baudrillard.

The internal political splitting quickly led to fragmentation, especially on the left. From the end of the German occupation, Stalinism had come under criticism from the left in *Les temps modernes* (where Baudrillard would later publish some literary review articles), and from disaffected Fourth International Trotskyists, particularly Cornelius Castoriadis, Claude Lefort, and Jean-François Lyotard, who grouped pseudonymously under the banner of *Socialisme ou Barbarie*. In 1955, Merleau Ponty published *Les aventures de la dialectique*; and the following year, immediately after the Twentieth Party Congress in the Soviet Union, where Khrushchev seemed to announce a new era, Russian tanks put down the Hungarian worker's council revolt.[11] In the early 1960s, Roger Garaudy, a sort of French Communist Party philosopher-general who espoused a conciliatory form of Marxist humanism, was mercilessly hounded from the faculty of Clermont-Ferrand.[12] At the same time, student political organizations were growing allergic to the official organized left, and turning to anarchist and situationist theory.[13]

By March of 1968, the chemistry of contestation had boiled over at the University of Paris at Nanterre, where Baudrillard was an assistant in sociology. Student frustration with Gaullist educational reform had sparked a massive, left-countercultural revolt against the state. This heady period is still universally described as 'May '68' or the 'events of May'. It is said that at its height, 10 million individuals participated in the rebellion directly. Even the ORTF (Office de la Radio-Télévision Française) was shut down, and De Gaulle had to broadcast his appeals to the nation from an empty television studio. Yet it was the credibility of traditional left organizations which suffered most during this period. Within the party apparatus, Garaudy and Louis Aragon, the ageing surrealist poet, apparently supported the students, but were overruled. Nervous about public disorder, the PCF attempted to stall the general strike through its powerful union arm, the Confédération générale du travail (CGT). Meanwhile, the Soviets once again deployed their tank divisions, this time to suppress the Prague Spring of Alexander Dubček's 'socialism with a human face'.

But the steady decline in the academic influence of the Communist Party seemed to have almost no bearing on the intellectual stature of Marx. Unlike the Americans, the French well understood the difference between the communist movement and Marx's cosmopolitan social, historical and philosophical writings. Apart from Raymond Aron, no academically respectable French social philosopher directly questioned the essential wisdom of Marxian social theory – certainly no member of the *Tel Quel* group, or any of the prominent structuralist and poststructuralist thinkers. The atmosphere of infallibility was such that, in 1972, when Baudrillard published *Pour une critique de l'économie politique du signe*, Marx's 'scientific' credentials were arguably at their highest stage of development. Even then, Baudrillard's devastating cross-examination, which culminated the following year in *The Mirror of Production*, did not reject Marxian concepts, so much as turn them against themselves. Some commentators have argued that Baudrillard's critique of Marx in fact offers a useful reinterpretation of his thought relevant for the present age. There is no doubt that Baudrillard's writings from 1968 to 1976 constitute an important attempt to update the great economist's contribution to social thought. But no modern thinker has offered a more cogent account – from within Marx's own categories of thought – of the complicity of Marx's ideas in the prevailing order of civilization, nor a more compelling interrogation of their desirability.

In the intervening years, Marx's headlock on the French intelligentsia has loosened, and there have been many theoretical realignments, though Baudrillard has remained politically unattached. After the publication in French of Solzhenitsyn's *Gulag Archipelago* in 1974, it actually became fashionable to be anti-Marxist in Paris; the *nouveaux philosophes* appeared on the scene, and Bernard-Henri Levy's *Barbarism with a Human Face* created a media sensation. Baudrillard remained aloof from these developments. He was apparently wooed from various quarters, right and left, during this period, but seems to have succeeded in alienating all prospective allies. Certainly the publication of *Oublier Foucault* in 1977 did not endear him to the academic poststructuralist establishment; and socialists have with good reason spurned him since the appearance of *Les majorités silencieuses ou la fin du social* and *La gauche divine*. He has also maintained an ambiguous relationship, sometimes unpopular, but often insightful, to feminist theory and discourse.

Baudrillard's political strategy, if it may fairly be called that, is to remain equidistant (like a classical psychoanalyst) from all parties, to align himself with nothing that exists officially in the present. Of course, it is true that for a period in the 1970s and 1980s, his ideas became associated with significant developments linking post-structuralism and postmodernism (particularly as these terms were used in the art world), and this led to an important series of English translations and discussions in and around journals like *semio-texte* and *sub-stance* in New York, and the Power Institute of Fine Arts and the 'Working Papers' Collection in Australia. These developments in some ways echo the earlier neo-surrealist and Dadaist influences surrounding the student movement in France, and the more sophisticated post-68 aesthetics emerging in part through Baudrillard's collaboration with the art/theory journal *Traverses.* Baudrillard also founded the independent radical journal *Utopie*, a testing ground for much of the radical media theory which emerged in the 1970s. Given the enormous influence of Baudrillard's work, however, it is important to underline its non-prescriptive relationship to the whole variety of political and art practices which have drawn on his insights. One of his great strengths as a thinker lies in the ability to stay an idiosyncratic course through the world of academic thought; it is precisely this quality, so difficult to generalize or formalize, which has inspired the intellectual ferment around his work. In an interview just prior to the publication of *Da la séduction*, Baudrillard yielded to his critics' charge that he may be guilty of a certain nostalgic Romanticism, of 'resurrecting the myth of the noble savage'. In reply, he said that he was thinking about the need for 'a new type of relationship between humanity and reality in the here and now: a way of life that would permit the rediscovery of intensity, play, and challenge. . . . But it is much too soon to deduce any new political attitudes from these reflections'.[14]

II

Becoming an object

3

Baudrillard as an emergent property

It is sometimes argued in systems theory that an organization of some kind – let us say, an ecological system – will give rise on occasion to oscillating rhythms or uncharacteristic patterns which transgress the homeostatic norms of the system itself, though they develop and are sustained within the parameters of the system as it normally functions. The screeching of electric guitar 'feedback' is an example of such an effect. When the 'pick up' on the guitar which registers the vibration of the strings is aimed directly into the speakers of the amplifier, the amplified transmission is fed back through the pick-ups and retransmitted through the system in such a way as to set off a cyclic escalation producing an oscillating wail. Jimi Hendrix's well-known Woodstock rendition of 'The Star-Spangled Banner' is a case in point. What is remarkable about this kind of effect is that it becomes self-sustaining, or independent of the initial, causal 'pluck' of the guitar string. The wail is sustained indefinitely and eccentrically, with a unique pitch and timbre, long after the original vibration of the string has ceased. We might say that in such a case, there has somehow been summoned up within the established sound system a *new* system, or an *emergent property*, which functions quasi-autonomously, according to a logic of its own which is not entirely reducible to the functioning order from which it arose and upon which it continues to depend indirectly for its existence.

The concept of the 'runaway' system is an important theme in Baudrillard, and his own writings can themselves be understood as an example of the same. If we think of his intellectual and historical background as a kind of 'conceptual ecology', we can say that Baudrillard's discourse follows the course of an 'emergent property'; it is the achievement of a new conceptual or rhetorical state whose principles are irreducible to the functional norms of the order from which it initially arose. In terms of the guitar feedback cycle, Baudrillard's thought moves deliberately from musical tone to controlled noise. His first two books, *Le système des objets* (1968) and *La société de consommation* (1970), can be compared to ordinary picking or plucking, in the sense that these books strum the strings of the conventional order of European social scientific thought (culling and harvesting the fruits of his observations of commercial culture). The next two books, *For a Critique of the Political Economy of the Sign* (1972) and *The Mirror of Production* (1973), offer a theoretical elaboration of the earlier studies, in which the agitation of the strings is registered and expanded by the pick-ups and the amplifier, to be expressed through the speakers. The result is an accumulating tension which seems about to burst in *L'échange symbolique et la mort* (1976), as Baudrillard 'turns', swinging in the direction of the amplifier, to position his guitar in front of the speakers, so that the effect can be rechannelled as cause, the sign becoming referent, theory becoming action, discourse turning into world. *Seduction* (1980) completes this first cycle, launching the emergent property of a new discursive practice, oscillating frantically between nostalgia and hope, fear and desire.

The image of Jean Baudrillard as a sort of academic Jimi Hendrix is, as the French would say, 'drôle' – he is now 65 years old – but the comparison is not entirely facetious. A connoisseur of Baudrillard might want to emphasize how the subtlety and originality of his contributions, like those of Jimi Hendrix, have been overshadowed by his notoriety as a performer (this is in fact a theme of the present study). But one can easily imagine how a critic with a different agenda might prefer to tease out the elements of phallic narcissism in Baudrillard's work, and in competitive French culture theory generally.

The discussion so far illustrates, incidentally, how easily an argument (or an 'image') can spin out of control, as soon as we try to amplify and elaborate its terms. In fact, this very thought has arisen in part as an unintended consequence of the extended metaphor about the emergent properties of systems and thus itself serves as an example of an emergent property: in this case the well-known 'sliding' effect which occurs when sometimes only very slight tensions in a textual 'economy' are fed back into the text systematically, forming a closed circuit which produces wildly variant readings, the internal coherence and cogency of which are often quite remarkable.[1]

If there is a kind of turning point in Baudrillard's work, as I have suggested, this seems to reiterate a familiar pattern in the biography of modern ideas. For example, there is said to have been a 'turning' (*Kehre*) in Heidegger's thought after *Being and Time*, and also a 'turn' in Wittgenstein's thinking after the *Tractatus*. Many consider the whole course of modern philosophy to have been set by a 'linguistic turn'.[2] Moreover, all these turns have a common feature: they involve a movement inwards, especially in the sense of a withdrawal into the interior of language (if there is such a place), a retreat from the claims of traditional philosophy to organize and to use language in ways reaching 'beyond words' to link up with the world in a more original and fundamental sense. Baudrillard's turn is certainly related to the general linguistic contraction of contemporary thought, and cannot be understood apart from it. Yet it would be a mistake to identify Baudrillard too closely with this trend, for the cross-currents of his thought are ambivalent. His way of thinking is often refractory to the contemporary language paradigm in very important respects which we will be in a better position to explore later.

There is indeed a point when one realizes that Baudrillard's thought has somehow broken away from familiar ways of approaching social phenomena. His ideas seem to spin off in a tightening spiral, 'imploding' even their own internal logic in what he would later call the 'fatal strategy'. For the moment, we can sum up the concept of 'fatal strategy' by saying that it is a deliberate attempt to identify with the object, or even to become one. This is a conscious and systematic perversion of the Hegelian subject–object dialectic, in which the outcome of the history of Spirit is no longer conceived as the triumph of the concrete universal, but as a kind of squalid failure of transcendence and collapse into the abstract particular. There are moments when the effect is like the ravings of the cynical philosopher tramp 'Johnny' in Mike Leigh's film *Naked* (1993). After *Seduction*, what Baudrillard produces is intended to be received as a fragmented figment of a deranged process, seemingly the result of a refusal to integrate different mental activities: a direct 'attack on linking', as the late Wilfrid Bion would say.[3]

Turning himself into this 'bizarre object' has been, to say the least, a precarious strategy for Baudrillard, one easily misunderstood even by indulgent readers; his thought does sometimes seem in danger of disappearing into the very process of cultural commodification whose alternatives he has so long sought to articulate. Like the ceremonial destruction of goods in the traditional west coast tribal potlatches, the Baudrillardian symbolic 'happening', in which social scientific ideas are ritually torched and cast adrift on a metaphysical sea, has generated its own kind of underground currency in the academic world. One can discern in his tendency to caricature himself, especially in his more personal writings, such as *America* and *Cool Memories*, that at times he may even have verged on self-disgust. As in Arthur Danto's definition of art – the 'self-consuming artifact' – the 'object' that Baudrillard would become is too useless to be 'recuperated' as a proper commodity. In his own words, '[It] is a kind of "theory–fiction" where things in the end simply fall apart by themselves. There is a kind of auto-destruction . . . not, in any case, a centralization of the arguments' (*Live* 202).

Thus, Baudrillard's position within the contemporary intellectual universe is studiously anomic, even compared with the most radical linguistic solipsisms and social constructionisms. And yet, as I have stated above, 'it is intended to be received'. This fact raises the question of how it is possible successfully to issue the sort of negative invitation that Baudrillard does; and on what terms such an invitation can be taken up without negating its subversive intent. Some answers will emerge as we go along, especially when we review the concepts of symbolic exchange, simulation and seduction, and explore his characteristic use of theoretical language as a medium for paradoxical performative speech acts.

For the moment, we can only pretend that the pieces of Baudrillard's self-destructive thought manage somehow to hold together in spite of him. In this respect, he is rather like one of his own metaphors drawn from 'Chaos Theory', a 'strange attractor' around which a turbulent infinity loops in a finite space, producing a stable but unpredictable disorder, so that 'against its will, energy is doing something productive, like the devil in medieval history . . . [it] does something against its own will and, by self-entanglement, produces beauty'.[4]

It will be easier to understand how Baudrillard's repudiation of intellectual tradition has already become a part of that tradition (and why this must be so), if first we examine carefully his use of the 'language paradigm' to throw light on the emergence of commodity culture and the structures of political economy, as traditionally understood in the social sciences. Only then can we begin to evaluate his contribution as a whole. Let us begin with a rough outline of his thought; the rest of our study will proceed from there, by means of progressive elaboration and review.

4

The imitation of the self

It is not the purpose of critical thought to place the object on the orphaned royal throne once occupied by the subject. On that throne the object would be nothing but an idol. The purpose of critical thought is to abolish the hierarchy.[1]

Arguably the most lucid exposition of Baudrillard's development as a thinker has been provided by Baudrillard himself, in a book which has been issued in English with the title *The Ecstasy of Communication*. This was originally Baudrillard's doctoral *Habilitation* at the Sorbonne, and its French title, *L'autre par lui-même* – The Other, By Himself – nicely expresses his sense of having merged already with the bizarre object of his own fatal strategy. In a kind of retrospective gloom, he pictures himself as Orpheus glancing back on the shade of Eurydice – and thus symbolically consigns his own work to an eternity in Hell. To offer his *oeuvre* as a completed task to the Sorbonne examiners, like a life that has fulfilled its destiny and now seeks judgement, would be to pretend that it has 'developed in a coherent manner', fulfilling in its final shape an original plan which in fact never existed. Caught in this reflexive epistemological snare, Baudrillard states that he will have to present his work as an 'exercise in simulation', thus furnishing through the work itself another illustration of one of its own principal themes: the problematic of simulation. He concludes:

I can hardly examine the question of sociological verisimilitude, to which, moreover, I could only answer with the greatest of difficulty; rather I must put myself in the place of an imaginary traveler who stumbles upon these writings as upon a lost manuscript and who, for lack of supporting evidence, would attempt to reconstitute the society they describe. (p. 10)

The implied reference to a misplaced civilization is significant, because Baudrillard's fantastic evocations of the cultural present are always cast against the shimmering backdrop of a lost world. There are many remnants to be explored in this landscape, but the capital city (Baudrillard's sinking Atlantis, if you will) is classical European thought, as conceived in ancient Greece, and operationalized since the Renaissance. This is the Promethean cosmos which the 'antihumanism' of the French structuralists and post-structuralists was intended to overthrow: the anthropocentric universe of a 'subject' (individual or collective) appropriating nature as an inert 'object' in the linear time of progressive history.

For Baudrillard, unlike those who have continued the attack on 'Western' thought, Promethean man is already disappearing from view, as we ourselves disappear into the increasingly hived-off cultural space of simulation. This ever more autonomized and reified space of civilization (the 'third order' simulacrum we shall examine later) has the character of a neutralized field or network, designed for a kind of functional play, in which all the participants interact in the imaginary dimension constituted and governed by the 'rules of the game'. The game's *raison d'être* is obscure; but its rationale seems to approximate Kantian aesthetics: the free play of the senses, the imagination, and the understanding, with a purposiveness without a purpose; in other words, the point of the game is none other than its own technological elaboration.

According to this view, human culture is no longer the 'second nature' which social critics like to 'demystify' as an historical construction, and to denounce as an error in collective moral judgement. For Baudrillard, the civilizing process is not a 'secondary process', situated somewhere on the receiving end of a Newtonian cause–effect relationship with nature. It now absorbs its original or causal preconditions into its own functioning, which has become a 'primary process' in its own right, virtually self-sustaining and thus progressively more insulated from any kind of Otherness. In Baudrillard's theory of cultural evolution, modernity represents that moment when we are no longer content to compromise with Otherness, or to 'exorcise' it magically through ritual (what Baudrillard first theorized as the ambivalence of 'symbolic exchange'). We now claim to penetrate Otherness, to get inside it (conquest) in order to discover exactly how it works (science), so that we can colonize it (engineering), or build an example of it (as in the Turing test, successful simulation is our proof of understanding). For Baudrillard, modernity is a form of domestication. In the modernist Imaginary, Otherness (or alterity) is simply dissolved into ourselves. The question whether this transformation is a matter of philosophical perspective, or whether it represents an objective historical process, or some combination of the two, is probably one of the central questions of cultural metaphysics. If we follow Baudrillard's reasoning, then this humanist interpretation of global historical development turns in upon itself in what he considers an 'objective irony', an irony which confronts us in the objects themselves. In other words, through its own militant constructionism, in the climactic triumph of human history, the human itself will 'disappear' into the object of its own creation, will be dissolved in the construction of the human project itself: it is the object, not the human 'subject', which will set the tone of play, and emerge as the most interesting (though perhaps not 'dominant') participant in the game of civilization.[2]

Something like this scenario is described in the last chapter of Anthony Burgess's novel, *The End of the World News*. The explosion of planet earth is now generations behind, and the enclosed technological space on the escaping starship *America* eliminates all sensory links with the biospherical world of 'natural' objects. Since everything within the range of bodily experience is humanly constructed, it is not surprising that the students on the ship refuse to accept literally the story about the world their ancestors once inhabited, because it sounds too much like an unsubstantiated myth of origins: 'mother earth' is just another human construction.

Burgess's portrait of the final collapse of modernity captures an important aspect of Baudrillard's preoccupation with semiosis and simulation. But as he makes clear, we should not identify the social function of simulation too narrowly with modern technology, which represents only the latest phase in the evolution of simulacra. The idea that the cosmos is a semiotic construction by and for humans belongs originally to religious fundamentalism. It is much older than the classical conception of 'nature'. The discovery of the precedence of inanimate objects over man and over his signs had no wide currency until Darwin. The implications are still tacitly denied, largely through the illusion, clung to by the otherwise atheistic Westernized intelligentsia, that language and culture confer an ontological privilege on humans, insulating them from the consequences of physical, animal existence.

Thus we may take Baudrillard's opening comment in *L'autre par lui-même*, that 'Everything began with objects', in at least two ways. It is a statement about the first issue he took up in his writing – the study of the social object in late capitalist society – but also an ontological metaphor, like St John's 'In the beginning was the word' or Faust's 'In the beginning was the deed'. Before there was social being there was the thing: in the beginning was the object. The philosopher and pornographer Georges Bataille, who had a great influence on Baudrillard, summed up this view as follows:

> We do not know ourselves distinctly and clearly until the day we see ourselves from the outside as another. Moreover, this will depend on our first having distinguished the other on the plane where manufactured things have appeared to us distinctly.[3]

The subject only comes into being as the effect of positing a discrete object; he or she is thus grounded in the 'plane of objects'[4] where the world appears as a vast collection of separate things, of which the human subject is perhaps the most beautiful and the most exotic. Those who are familiar with Heidegger will recognize here, in Bataille and in Baudrillard, the theme of the 'forgetting of Being', in which the subject takes on the discrete character of 'ontic' phenomena, in a controlling relationship to them (the object). For Heidegger, both the subject and object are Platonic abstractions whose splitting and opposition 'conceals Being' and thus constitutes the 'Ge-Stell', or enframing, of technology as the ominous 'destiny' of 'Western metaphysics'.[5]

For Baudrillard, therefore, at the time of writing *Le système des objets*, the central psychological metaphor of the object was the Lacanian figure of the *mirror*, the projective surface in whose reflection the subject appears to himself as a discrete and coherent being, solid and cohesive like a thing, uniform and symmetrical like an artefact, functional and purposive like an instrument. In the 1960s, when Baudrillard began to write, the world of objects (as always, arranged as an expressive organization of culture) could still be interpreted as a reflection of the Promethean cosmos of modern European history, the 'humanist' stage upon which a subject acts out a dramatic 'scene' (the unconscious, history) of imaginary and symbolic relations. This was the long-established principle of modernism, so well expressed by Marx in 1844:

> In creating a *world of objects*, by his practical activity, in *his work upon* inorganic nature, man proves himself a conscious species being, i.e. as a being that treats the species as its own essential being. . . . [Man] produces universally [and] reproduces the whole of nature. . . . The object of labor is, therefore, the *objectification of man's species life*; for he duplicates himself not only, as in consciousness, intellectually, but also actively, in reality, and therefore he contemplates himself in a world that he has created.[6]

5

Things traditional and modern

[N]owhere do things flourish which are not a combination of inert elements . . .. (Saussure)[1]

According to the report *Charting the Biosphere*, put out by an organization called Systematics Agenda 2000, there are anywhere from 10 to 100 million living species on earth, of which only 1.4 million have been documented and another ten thousand or more become extinct every year. The biologists add that these totals include about 3.5 million viruses and bacteria, of which 9000 have so far been identified.

How many objects are there in the world? If in the age of Linnaeus and the encyclopedists, a taxonomy of unnatural flora and fauna (including 'found' objects) had begun, it might have succeeded in cataloguing everything, if time had stopped at the end of the eighteenth century. But that was just the point in history when inanimate things took off, when the volume of artefacts began to expand geometrically, at a pace far greater even than the human population explosion.

Enormous as is the labour we expend to produce all these objects, it is probably exceeded many times by the sheer drudgery of organizing them, maintaining them, cleaning them, storing them, disposing of them: in short, of consuming what we produce. Objects require constant gardening: from the front lawn to the Tuileries, civilization is a vast obsessional enterprise, in which an enormous amount of effort is expended in order to bring about certain orderly effects, and to create the impression that the wild and weedy world of 'nature' has been held at bay. Since the neolithic revolution, civilization has been synonymous with deforestation. Perhaps culture is merely the process of putting trees back in the streets and fields.

Ethnographic history teaches that every society privileges certain objects, from furniture to foodstuffs, which are produced and maintained in prescribed ways. Materials are worked into recognizable patterns, shapes, colours, which become the bearers of characteristic meanings. Usually, these calculated arrangements are executed according to a strict code which is transmitted through fixed social infrastructures, such as inherited status, artisanal tradition and behavioural custom. The symbolism of the traditional social object is usually an integrated expression of a public or shared culture.

If we can ascribe a definite organization to the traditional object, it should be no surprise that social objects in late capitalist society also exist in some kind of order. But the principles which govern the organization of the modern object are very different from the traditional ones, according to Baudrillard.

The modern object exists in a different way because the physical and social links connecting its production, its value, its significance, its function and its possession (to name only a few aspects of an object's life) tend to be invisible. In the advanced capitalist societies, there is not the same kind of integrated core of tradition, lived overtly in customary roles and relations, transmitted explicitly as a code governing both the making and interpreting of objects. Instead, there is what Baudrillard calls an abstract 'system' of objects.

Both the traditional order and the modern system have a way of transcribing the inert, material quality of things into forms of social communication, rather as if they had some alchemical power to divert the object of use into a lexicon for the articulation of a culture or a way of life. Like the order of traditional things, the system of objects is a system of communication. But instead of transforming the object into a symbol by integrating it into the nexus of social relationships within which it takes on a unique meaning for the conversants, as in traditional societies, the system of objects *abstracts* the object from its social context and turns it into a sign. As sign, the object becomes an interchangeable unit, no longer an expression emerging from a relationship of symbolic exchange, but a discrete element in a chain of signification, infinitely transmissible and recombinable, like the digital, diacritical elements which make up the 'combinatory' of the phonetic alphabet.

The power of the object system can be seen in the way that its 'logic' or 'code' appropriates the symbolic object and reproduces the symbol as a sign of itself: the same object extrapolated and recirculated as commodity. This capacity of the object system to absorb any and every remnant of alterity, of difference from the system, as in the recuperation of the symbolic object, generates a kind of secondary set of connotations, in which the differences between the traditional and modern, the hand-crafted and the machine-produced, symbolic exchange and sign function, are reinscribed at the level of the object system itself as differential sign relationships, encoding oppositions in socioeconomic status, class membership and 'style'. Still more impressively, the object system has the power to divert whole sectors of traditional artisanship to the commodity market, thus converting religious, peasant or tribal cultures into production sites for industrial capitalism. The form and even the exquisite craftsmanship of the traditional object are often very well preserved, even in the contemporary production process, but the symbolic relationships inscribed on the object in its traditional context are abstracted, decomposed and reinserted, as discrete, diacritical elements, into new chains of signification, circulating and recombining through the interplay of signs. The oriental carpet is a classic case in point.[2]

Baudrillard's thesis is that an entire cultural transformation can be read in the mundane texts of the everyday life around us. But how does one decode this historical development? How does one 'read' the process through which traditional, artisanal, symbolic objects are turned into floating signs? What is the 'language' of objects, and how do we learn to interpret it?

A good example can be found in the evolution of domestic living space, from precapitalist times to the present. Even before we try to compare the arrangement of objects, the term 'living space' itself provides an important clue. The concept of living space is abstract and functional; it defines a neutral field of variables, rather than an emotionally charged, semantically dense, 'essentialist' idea, like 'home'. A space is a generalized medium which one occupies, and fills with the signs of one's presence. It is not a *place* one is born into, whose shapes and textures are already heavy with the meanings of a personal destiny, anticipated in the historical memory of the generations of the family, whose very being is inseparable from its dwelling place. A living space is not connected in any definite way to the concept of place. In the modern high rise, the 'apartment' even transcends specific ties to the material character of the building, and approaches the pure concept of boundary. At the extreme, there is no 'voice' with a local 'accent', but something more like an abstract writing space, a sort of screen, devoid of local features, in which the signs of one's presence can be rearranged and substituted in endless combinations, according to various 'life style strategies'. At this point, the 'logic of consumption' has penetrated the interiority of the 'home' through the 'exteriority of the sign': the 'organic family space', whose 'symbolic scheme is largely that of the body' (*FCPES* 67), has been evacuated and remodelled as a specialized medium for the circulation of commodities.

In semiological terms, the 'rhetorical' transformation of living spaces, from the precapitalist, 'feudal' household – through the bourgeois home – to the modern 'home environment', can be traced on a continuum from the condensed meaning of the symbol to the displaced articulation of the sign. For example, the traditional patriarchal, peasant household was organized as a communal, quasi-public place, centred on the 'hearth', whose deep cultural significance can be traced to classical times, and remains virtually inseparable from the concept of home in some European languages (in German, *Heim und Herd* [hearth and home]; or the poetic Italian, *focolare*). The rich and multi-layered referential structure of the fireplace barely survives in contemporary accommodations. The hearth has become a syntactical element in the articulation of the 'living room' area, functionally displaced by central heating, which reduces it to a kind of consumer option with pleasant associations (perhaps fitted with a gas burner and simulated logs), outshone by the television, whose lurid blue light clashes slightly with the atmospherics of burning embers.

At an intermediate stage on this scale, ranging from the post-nomadic agrarian to the postmodern, we find the traditional bourgeois model of domestic organization, circa 1850 (not much later), which remains the enduring reference model for the mobile classes in Europe (*FCPES* 41), and certain sectors of North American society, against which the contemporary modular style of domesticity as a 'syntagmatic calculus' must compete. In the modular style, the symbolic condensations of communal family life have been systematically broken down into fungible units, recombined, and redistributed throughout the living space according to a 'technical' (but not necessarily practical) logic of interlocking functionality (*SO* 24). In the bourgeois home, redolent with aristocratic connotations carried over from the *anciens régimes*, the hearth remains sacrosanct, although its deep symbolic resonance is already starting to be specialized – disembedded from the cyclical rhythms of feudal life. In the premodern household, the still unsegregated generations converged in the arena of the 'home fires', which combined the forms and functions of cooking, heating, gathering, working and sleeping all into one more or less integrated or overlapping, convivial, dramatic scene. In the classical bourgeois home, the process of functional differentiation just manages to preserve the cosmic metaphor of the hearth, but only by redistributing it into more distinct groupings of objects whose meanings have been withdrawn from the communal sphere of symbolic exchange to be privatized, individualized and intensified in their specialized meaning. Early bourgeois residential arrangements were still linked to the body scheme, more fragmented than the precapitalist household, but psychically still more immediate – not as coolly schizoid – as the diacritical codes which govern modular systems of ambient signification in contemporary 'model homes'.

In the marginal and 'bygone' objects belonging to what Baudrillard calls the 'non-functional' system, the 'anthropomorphic' dimension of symbolic relations has not been fully abstracted into the commodity culture.[3] For example, the bourgeois mirror is metaphoric in relation to the contiguous logic of modern interior design (*SO* 27–8). The almost overbearing symbolism of the mirror, its function as spatial witness to the interiority and identity of the family (always reflecting the reassuring redundancy of the opulent surroundings), can be measured against the opaque signification of the living room television set, 'isolated in a corner on a pedestal' which 'constitutes an eccentric pole opposing the traditional centre of the room', henceforth 'redistributed as a field of vision' (*SO* 56). As for the mirror itself, it has been taken out of its frame and shattered into a series of smaller, 'functional' reflecting surfaces, each designed for the specific types of living space, and sometimes incorporated into the household 'combinatory' as a design feature employed in order to create 'ambient' illusions of space, abundance and movement. This pure 'immanence' (as opposed to the implied transcendence of the bourgeois mirror) is also the fate of the centralized, symbolically charged clock, particularly the grandfather clock and the mantlepiece clock (*SO* 29), which have since been diffused throughout the household as a subordinate component of innumerable other objects: the radio, television set, VCR, stove, wristwatch, various timers, alarm devices and ornaments.

6

Oppositional semiotics: the nonsubject of meaning

Baudrillard's comparative analysis of domestic interiors offers an early glimpse of his characteristic fascination with the meaning of cultural surfaces. In the late 1960s and early 1970s, his approach was still coloured by a somewhat moralistic interpretation of history. He had not yet postulated the radical cultural logics of simulation and seduction. Yet behind his sober dissection of the 'class logic' whereby 'through objects a stratified society speaks' (*FCPES* 38), the concerns of cultural metaphysics are foreshadowed in a preoccupation – one might even call it a fetishistic delight – with the perverse, obsessional, mundane structures of domestic appearances.

Baudrillard's fascination with absurd details transports us into a fantastic petit bourgeois theatre where 'everything is protected and surrounded'.

> The table is covered with a table cloth [and] a plastic table cloth cover. Drapes and double drapes . . . carpets, slipcovers, coasters, wainscotting, lampshades. Each trinket sits on a doily, each flower in its pot, each pot in its saucer . . . . Even in the garden each cluster is encircled with wirenetting, each path is outlined by bricks, mosaics or flagstones. . . . The obsession . . . is not merely to possess, but to underline [each possession] two or three times . . . to show how well one possesses. (*FCPES* 42)

And this in turn is underlined

> by an all-powerful puritan morality of ritual hygiene: the triumph of varnish, polish, veneer, plating, wax, encaustic, lacqueur, glaze, glass, plastic . . . a whole ethic of protection, care and cleanliness which converges with the disciplinary ritual of framing . . . concentric circles and property: shutters, drapes, double drapes, wainscotting, plinths, wallpaper, table covers, doilies, bedspreads, blotters . . . of the same order as the symmetrical arrangements, where things are duplicated in order to be reflected: yet another redundancy. (*FCPES* 44)

Evidently, the surface (spatial or 'syntagmatic') organization of the object world yields information about deeper structures of being in the social world. There is a transcoding process at work – a vertical homology between the mode of production and the expressive arrangement of objects in social space – which is susceptible to the sort of binary analysis proposed by Lévi-Strauss. Even in these early studies, however, Baudrillard's semiotic was eccentric to the normal uses of structuralist method. *Le système des objets* prefigures the strategy of pushing concepts to literal extremes. He does not confine himself to abstracting a set of differential oppositions, to remain on a sort of narrative level of things; he seems to penetrate into the very being of the objects, to 'think' the objects as forms of signification, by converting the structuralist metalanguage itself into a first order description language, so that the objects themselves appear to embody the terms of the structural semiotic, and to intersect on an historical plane of reference.

The argument in these texts depends upon an opposition between symbol and sign which derives much of its power from the well-known metaphor–metonymy distinction developed by Jacobson, into which Lacan translated Freud's theory of the dream work: the mechanisms of condensation (metaphor) and displacement (metonymy). For example, the artisanal object could easily be identified as more metaphoric than metonymic in its social construction: its metacommunicational style is semantic rather than syntactic, motivated rather than arbitrary, it is treated more as an entity in its own right than as a relation to be articulated; it links to other objects semantically by means of similarity rather than syntactically by means of contiguity. It refers to an interiority which is transcendent, as a signified, rather than to an exteriority which is immanent, a signifier. And so on. Pushed to its limit, this comparative historical approach can generate some bizarre effects, with radical consequences for structuralist and poststructuralist theory. A close reading of *Le système des objets* already reveals the complicity of the sophisticated language models with modernist and postmodernist value hierarchies. In the latter, metonymy is privileged over metaphor, writing over speech, the sign over the symbol, the signifier over the signified, immanence over transcendence, exteriority over interiority, syntax over semantics . . . . In Baudrillard's phenomenology of the object, the whole bias of formalist language theory is uncovered through the temporal frame of reference: all the categories and values of the linguistic turn are revealed with astonishing consistency as derivatives of the contingent textures of the lived world of social objects in historical transition. It is almost as if the objects themselves function metalinguistically in Baudrillard's analysis, whilst the formal concepts of Saussure and Jacobson (and by implication, Derrida and Kristeva) are accorded merely phenomenal status, as observed symptoms of the present age.

In *For a Critique of the Political Economy of the Sign*, Baudrillard proposed a revision of the theory of commodity fetishism which follows straight from this refraction of the language paradigm back onto the world. According to this new view, the fetish is not an alienated agency, robbed from a subject, and projected onto an object, as Marx claimed (see Chapter 9 below); it is more like a defensive construction, initiated by the subject, and achieved through the reductive objectification of structural oppositions (see Chapter 15). The term *reification* would then refer to the general cultural form serving as a mould for these subjective constructions (fetishes). The reified cultural form does not involve the misapprehension of a subjective quality as a thing (false consciousness, misplaced concreteness, etc.), but the restructuring of subjectivity itself through the instantiation of a system of equivalence based on the hierarchical opposition of the fetishized value terms: in the case of the commodity, the system of exchange value, or money; in the case of the body, the phallic order of gender signification. The classical Hegelian explanation offered by the critical theorists (e.g. the Frankfurt School) would then appear to have been misleading: the mechanisms of fetishization and reification would not lie in a 'veiling of consciousness' (a sort of ideological deception), but rather in the rhetorical effects of systematic closure, a sort of 'totalization via signs' (*FCPES* 101).

In order to explore the concept of fetishism as a form of anxiety about losing control over the play of meanings, Baudrillard displaces critical theory's traditional moral and epistemological concern with the problem of truth (and lies). Perhaps most important in this regard is Baudrillard's challenge to Marx's paradigm of production. Like Book One of the Old Testament, Marx tended to assume that production contains the transcendental moment of human truth, whilst consumption represents a debased moment of heteronomy and downfall. In contrast, Baudrillard takes production, rather than consumption, as the paradigm case of reified systematicity, and the constitutive moment of fetishistic relationships. For Baudrillard, the element of 'mystification' which Marx attributed to the commodity lies in making, rather than exchanging or consuming. If Marx devalued consumption as a passive relation to the object, Baudrillard characterizes productivity as a kind of passive aggressive or controlling relation to the object. Production is a means of bringing the feared difference of the object into line with the subject's projections. On this account, production is fetishistic because it is a form of reduction, in which the object is stripped of unwanted meanings, whereas consumption might (if it could be freed from the productivist 'code') involve a moment of openness to what is new and unknown in the object.

Unlike the classical and moralistic critical theorists, such as Georg Lukács, Theodor Adorno, and countless contemporary cultural critics, Baudrillard never pretends that it is possible for humans not to use each other as objects, or not to project themselves onto objects. He is never so naive as to blame ordinary human transference relationships on capitalism and its particular forms of deception (such as Gramsci's 'hegemony', Althusser's 'ideological state apparatus', or Habermas's 'systematically distorted communication', etc.). Baudrillard starts from the recognition that social relations are necessarily mediated by objects, and distinguishes the specific problem of commodity fetishism from this general condition of social being. According to Baudrillard, there is a fundamental tension between Marx's definition of the commodity as a social *form* (comprising the opposition use value/exchange value), and his essentialist theory of fetishism as the 'alienation' of a consciousness. The latter implies an animist projection onto an object, which Baudrillard equates with ethnocentric European and Christian perceptions of pagan religion. This tendency to confuse fetishism with psychological investment in the object (the 'worship of graven images') suggests that it is a characteristic of Western moral philosophy to confuse semantic activity and imagination with social pathology (corruption and deception). For Baudrillard, the act of meaning always involves 'projection', if only because meaning can never arise solely from a subject's relation to itself. There must always be another, and this *other* never has the status of a transparent consciousness. *The problem of fetishism*, in Baudrillard's view, *is not the consumer's emotional involvement in the object as such, but the place of the object in an independent system of signification.* Here, the difference between meaning and signification is that meaning involves a subjective projection which accepts the object's ultimate power over the subject, whereas signification tries to deny the object's power by reducing its alterity to a manipulable form – a kind of subjection of the nonsubject. In this productivistic form of consumption, as Baudrillard defines it, the aim is not the appropriation and enjoyment of the object, but the metonymic ingestion of a reified systematicity through the valorization of a sign. Fetishism is a 'passion for the code' (*FCPES* 92).

Here, it is useful to consider Baudrillard's argument that the sign owes its discrete character to the structuralist's reification of the signifying process (*FCPES* 199). The sign object itself implies a reification. In a sense, then, structuralism, and its systems of opposition, describe not just a methodological reduction of the continuous to the discrete, but a *real* one, at the level of lived social relations. But (as we have just seen) even basic structuralist categories like the arbitrary (versus the motivated), the discrete (versus the continuous) must be relativized in their use, for they are produced by the problematic of the sign itself (*FCPES* 149–52). This is true, for example, of the metaphor/metonymy pair. Structural oppositions function generically only in rather impoverished codes (*SO* 223) such as the system of objects. The system of objects cannot be a language in the true sense because it lacks an adequate syntax and functions with a 'repertoire' rather than a diction (*SO* 222). It is more like an 'order of classification' – in other words, a taxonomy (*SO* 224). On this basis, consumption can be interpreted as the performance of metaphoric and metonymic operations on a synchronic structural grid. At the level of contrasting social configurations, the metaphor/metonymy pair plays a diachronic role in articulating the historical transition from the *symbolic* object's grounding in a subject or social relation to the *sign* object's formal autonomy as an element in a system of signification which is socially context-free.

7

The object of life

'The more you consume, the less you live.' – Graffiti, Paris, May 1968.

'Le futur C'est Mieux que la Couture!' – Franco Moschino T-shirt.

According to a recent North American study of objects, 'most traditional peoples have emphasized the integrated or social self at the expense of personal uniqueness, whereas modern Western culture has tended to stress the differential, uniquely individual self [to the degree that] runaway fragmentation is more of an actual possibility in our own culture'.[1]

It is doubtful whether there was ever such a thing as an 'integrated self', even in the most solidary and homogeneous of traditional societies. Baudrillard does, however, emphasize the pursuit of individual difference or singularity through the object system peculiar to modern consumer societies. By singularity, he is not referring to the depth dimension of character, or the inaccessible reaches of unconscious interiority, but rather to a kind of false self cobbled together by the consumer through the manipulation of the marginal differences which constitute the sign object. For Baudrillard, consumption (*consommation*) is, strictly speaking, not the satisfaction of a need through the appropriation of a use value, but the manipulation of signs as an active (but closed) relationship to the object system, where the latter is invested as a potential mirror of the unique self. Just as Marx conceived capitalist production as the isolation of the labourer from the social relationships in which his or her product is valued, exchanged and consumed, so consumption in Baudrillard's sense draws the consumer out of the symbolic dimension of social interaction, and isolates him from others in a private psychological relationship with the object system, through which he mediates his relationship with himself. The sign object transforms the collective, communal, religious or family occasions of the object into the generalized *idea* of a social relationship (e.g. status, power, prestige, love, fulfilment, meaning), which is consumed privately as a 'sign-value'. This power of the object system to elicit or interpellate a privatized unit of consumption is not restricted to individuals; the act of consumption tends to empty out every social relationship, as if to reduce the group to a crowd, the community to a queue, the family to a socio-economic unit, and the couple to partners in consumption, as in the pair Jerome-and-Sylvie in George Perec's novel *Les choses* (*SO* 236).

From the sociologist's and marketer's perspective, the subjective lure of social isolation, abstraction and serialization appears in the form of what Baudrillard calls 'personalization'. Personalization is what every consumer object in its systematic form promises. It is that feature of the commodity generated from the interplay of the 'model' (e.g. the Rolls-Royce Silver Wraith, the Dior 'creation') in its simulation of absolute singularity (the schematic embodiment of the ideal object of its type), and the 'series', with its endless range of available or affordable variants (an abstract field of 'indefinite substitution') (*SO* 172, 163–84). The ad hoc synthesis of model and series, constantly modifying each other in the discourse and behaviour of consumption, produces the paradoxical effect of social integration through individual choice (personalization): the 'miracle of the system' (*SO* 172). 'In the act of personalized consumption, it is clear that the subject in his very demand to be a *subject*, merely produces himself as the *object* of economic demand' (*SO* 181; emphasis in original).

Baudrillard's psychological descriptions of the 'logic of consumption', particularly his analysis of the dynamic of personalization through the semiotic appropriation of model and series, suggest that each private act within the terms of the object system is a modern version of that 'deep play' which Clifford Geertz analyzed in the 'text' of the Balinese cockfight: a collective expression of the cultural values which constitute the basic personality structure of a society. Here the issue is not whether the individual acts alone or within a group. Baudrillard's concern is a general one, transcending the obvious fact that human psychology is richer and more specific than the semiotics of 'personalization' and the calculus of sumptuary competition. His point is that the ideology of individualism encouraged by capitalist market relations does not generate in and of itself a literal autonomy or independence of personality. On the contrary, personalization implies for Baudrillard a mechanism of social integration whose most developed form in our society is not the interaction of personalities (something already brought to exquisite heights in the elitist cultures of Europe and the Orient), but a kind of compacting, in which solidarity and conformity 'implode' into the Brownian motion of statistical masses of people, the flows and breaks studied not by sociologists and ethnographers, but by experts in crowd control (and wild philosophers like Elias Canetti[2] or Gilles Deleuze and Felix Guattari[3]). Baudrillard's analyses of the Centre Pompidou (*BE*) or the Gulf War (*GG*) are essentially ethnographic reports on the 'deep play' of Anglo-European 'consumption'. They are not meant to be read as social science, or even as descriptions of actual people in the light of practical politics, but as attempts at participant observation of the cultural unconscious.

As we shall explore in more detail later, the absorptive power of the object system is, according to Baudrillard, perhaps most impressive in the domain of its own meliorist ideology – Individualism, Freedom, Transcendence, Revolution – those idealizations of capitalism's ultimate historical meaning and purpose which have functioned so effectively as dynamic and liberating agents of social progress. Because the paradigm of consumption privileges the moment of abstraction so thoroughly, it expands naturally into what Baudrillard calls a 'total idealist practice', which extends systematically beyond the sphere of the object and interpersonal relations to embrace the general order of communication, culture, history and politics (*SO* 236). Revolution is consumed in the idea of revolution, not just in the 'revolutionary new product', or in designer T-shirt slogans, but more fundamentally in the traditional political arena, which is gradually resolving itself into a permanent 'mass-mediatized' crisis (the 'Red Brigades' in Italy, the constitutional wars in Canada) wherein Revolution becomes eternal and thus eternally consumable on the same plane as any commodity afloat on the waves of fashion. The effect of universal social semiosis is to reproduce through signs 'the fleeting materiality of the project of living itself' (*SO* 237), so that in a sense, there are no longer any 'projects' even in the political sense, but only objects as signs of the destruction of projects through consumption.

Here one begins to see how Baudrillard defines the special field of consumption as if it were a text, along with the consequences of such a move. But there is a nuance in this approach that is habitually overlooked. Baudrillard may in a sense be applying (or misapplying) concepts appropriate for textual analysis, as if they were analytical tools, or part of a repertoire of interpretation, or objective classification, but he is much more vigorously working towards the reverse effect: namely, the suggestion that actual material practices 'out there' in the 'real' world of political economy are objective correlatives of semiolinguistic reading practices. These variants of the structuralist 'revolution in thought' (the great 'epistemological break' of which Althusser wrote) are not neutral methods devised for analyzing cultural phenomena, but unconscious reflections of consummative experience, which spill over into the thinking of social and literary theorists and emerge as apparently independent theory or philosophy. Structuralism, applied Lacanian psychoanalysis, and also their critical negation in 'post-structuralism', are thus interpretable, in a Baudrillardian frame of reference, as deeply implicated derivatives of the consumer society, intellectual analogues of a 'totally idealist practice'.

Thus it emerges (though not nearly so explicitly in Baudrillard's earlier texts) that there are no limits to the Baudrillardian model of consumption (*SO* 238), in the same way that there are no limits to the deconstruction of a text, and the destruction or absorption of all its interpretations. As we shall see in much more detail later (Chapter 19), the paradigm of consumption, like that of poststructuralist reading, is not desire, but the death-instinct. There is always a 'lack' at the centre, a disappointed demand for totality, a Nirvana principle[4] which drives the indefinite substitutions of consumption, deconstruction, analysis and interpretation: the 'idea' is consumed, realized and destroyed, through the very fact that it can be autonomized and thus appropriated as a sign in which the personal relationship is abolished. In this ironic vulgarization of the Idea, *The Object System* becomes in effect a parodic inversion of Platonism – the social simulacrum – just as Deleuze had proposed in the same year (1968) for philosophy.[5] Consumption does not substitute the relationship mechanically or metonymically; it does not fill the void, it *describes* and celebrates the encounter with absence, highlighting its edges like the marking of a fetish, touching the object only as a point of articulation (Lacan's *point de capiton*) in a signifying chain. Deconstruction mimics this, and perhaps it is the 'lack' itself, as traced by the manipulation of signs, which is finally consumed and destroyed in contemporary critical theory.

8

The Baudrillard effect

The organization of objects in the average modern nation state is abstract in at least three distinct ways: 1) the object is lifted out of a 'local' economic context and placed in a 'global' (or much larger) economic context – in other words, it is transposed into the 'system' of 'exchange value' which fosters wholly different modalities of production, distribution and consumption; 2) the conversion to exchange value in turn has the effect of disambiguating the object by making it interchangeable with all other objects against a 'universal' standard – the generalized form of equivalence – which seems to strip the object of its particular symbolic meaning; 3) the object takes on what Baudrillard calls 'sign value', by which he means that when the object becomes a commodity in Marx's sense, it *also* becomes a term (or conjunction of terms) in an abstract discourse of consumption, governed by 'codes', 'models', and various idealizations and rationalizations. The sign value of an object is achieved through semiotic strategies of signification in order to simulate particularity and meaning for objects – especially the standardized and mass-produced ones – which have been stripped down to fungibility as terms of exchange in the market culture. Sign exchange value assigns the object a position within a social hierarchy (real or imagined) and a potential meaning which seems to suggest a social context, or at least the possibility of constructing one where there actually is none.

When Baudrillard uses the term 'system', he does not intend the system itself to be understood as a rational abstraction or a universal structure existing independently of material social reality. Of course, rationalizations, abstractions and structures must be counted among the relational beings which masquerade as objective qualities and entities in the cultural environment of consumption: ideas of functionality, naturalness, elegance, ambience, control, satisfaction and so on. The discourse of sign exchange value articulates a powerful rhetoric of unity in variety: the unique, the universal and the uniform all at the same time. But the 'system' of which it is a part, and which it helps to instantiate, does not exist separately from the universe of particular and tangible things in which we actually live. There is no Realm of Pure Forms from which the real and chaotic experience of imperfect beings somehow derives. Baudrillard's metaphor of the 'code' governing the political economy of the sign is nothing more than the common preconscious hypothesis we form on the basis of our necessarily limited experience of the sign form embodied in particular commodities. One may never have seen an advertisement or a picture of a particular commodity, but one senses implicitly the connection of every consumer object with the discourse of objects: the food on your plate and the picture in the menu or behind the counter of the 'item' you have ordered are inseparable at the moment of consumption – the object and the sign are fused together in a cultural 'system' which is independent of immediate social conditions at any of its entry points.

So the cultural system does not exist apart from its material instantiation in the actual, disorganized world of real objects. When Baudrillard speaks of a 'system' in that special sense of sign exchange value and the political economy of the sign – the object system – he is presupposing the emergence of a whole new class of increasingly technical objects whose very purpose is to link together other objects in social space. In other words, the systemic element derives from the fact that since the rise of industrialization, a number of institutional arrangements and technologies (organizations of objects) have emerged which have the power suddenly to connect objects up in ever more extensive and generalized ways. Mechanized and then automatic production generates a great variety of standardized objects which can be recognized wherever one goes, thus gradually, and then massively, transforming the character of physical space. Markets set up lines of distribution between points of exchange which vastly accelerate the rate of proliferation and expand the range of any one commodity's existence. They homogenize and generalize the forms of the social object, not because they represent a universal idea, but because they are stitched together from endless tracks in the real world.

The introduction of the telegraph in nineteenth-century America offers an excellent example of the 'material' character of this process of 'abstraction'. The possibility of more or less instant relay of information in Morse code effectively destroyed what might once have seemed a fixed identity between transportation and transmission. With the telegraph, communication outstripped the pace of travel, and had the effect of bunching locations in space together at any chosen point of simultaneous control. The monitoring of the railroad track could thus be centralized, but the 'centre' might be anywhere in the network.

The relationship of the telegraph and the railroad illustrates the basic notion of systems theory and the catch phrase that the 'system is the solution,' in that the integrated switched system is more important than any of its components.[1]

The collapse of geographical space also permitted the standardization of time and the synchronization of local commodities markets into a single integrated market system. This had a critical impact on the price system and the pattern of trade. In effect, some of the conditions for self-regulating supply–demand coordination of the economy (as imagined in classical economics) were now being realized on a national and international scale. We have grown used to the idea of round-the-clock global banking and trade in which every transaction involves a critical response to the total 'system' conditions, rather than the local circumstances of any of the participants (though our bodies seem to be rebelling, in the form of illness and depression, against the disruption of biorhythms enabled by the mechanical clock plus electricity plus chemicals). The high degree of abstraction and generalization presupposed by this degree of international integration depends upon a physical and technical reorganization of social space which has taken more than a century to put in place.

Inspired by formalist analyses such as Harold Innis's *Empire and Communication*, Anthony Giddens has tried to shift the description of social systems away from the Parsonian problems of order, boundaries and integration, towards an analysis of the time- and space-binding characteristics of social systems. The following account of the preconditions of modernity nicely condenses the sociological assumptions underlying Baudrillard's theory of consumption.

The dynamism of modernity derives from the *separation of time and space* and their recombination in forms which permit the precise time-space 'zoning' of social life; the *disembedding* of social systems . . . and the *reflexive ordering and reordering* of social relations in the light of continual inputs of knowledge affecting the actions of individuals and groups.

The 'emptying of time' is in large part the precondition for the 'emptying of space' . . . [C]oordination across time is the basis of the control of space. The development of 'empty space' may be understood in terms of the separation of *space* from *place*. . . . 'Place' is best conceptualized by means of the idea of locale, which refers to the physical settings of social activity as situated geographically. In pre-modern societies, space and place largely coincide. . . . The advent of modernity increasingly tears space away from place by fostering relations between 'absent' others. In conditions of modernity place becomes increasingly *phantasmagoric*: that is to say, locales are thoroughly penetrated by and shaped in terms of social influences quite distant from them. What structures the locale is not simply that which is present on the scene; the 'visible form' conceals the distanciated relations which determine its nature.[2]

The 'phantasmagoric' ambience here presented as social science is really just a sober restatement of that sense of the uncanny which McLuhan and Baudrillard have managed to project into the Imaginary of contemporary technological experience. This 'Baudrillard effect' is wonderfully captured by Wim Wenders in *Tokyo-Ga* (1983), particularly at one moment in the film when he is gliding home in a taxi through the late night Tokyo traffic, watching the television above the rear view mirror. It is the end of the broadcast day. John Wayne rides off into the sunset, and the Japanese national anthem is played.

Perhaps the proliferation of images has already destroyed too much. Perhaps images at one with the world are already lost forever. When John Wayne left, it wasn't the stars and stripes that appeared, but rather the red ball of the Japanese flag. And while I was falling asleep, I had the craziest thought: here I am now in the centre of the world. Every shitty TV set no matter where is the centre of the world. The centre has become a ludicrous idea – the world as well – an image of the world, a ludicrous idea, the more TV sets there are on the globe. And here I am, in the country that builds them all for the whole world so that the whole world can watch the American images.

The 'system of objects' arises only within the context of advanced capitalism, and is instantiated in the material networks and institutional arrangements which capitalism lays down (railroad tracks, telegraph lines, warehouses, pavement, hoardings, billboards, outlets, towers, power lines, telephone lines, radio transmitters, magazines, television sets, satellites and dishes). But it does acquire a certain functional independence from the always local instantiation of the infrastructure of modernity. The *cultural* aspects, or in other words, the 'models' for the kinds of signification which constitute consumer activity and contribute to the moment of consumption itself, are easily transmitted into other cultures where material and political conditions do not yet exist for the emergence of a full-blown object system. The penetration of rock'n'roll, Jazz and denim jeans into the Soviet Union, prior to Perestroika, is just one well-publicized example: somehow, the 'system' gets picked up like a language; its 'grammar' and its semantic 'structure' can be roughed out on the basis of minimal inputs. Much of the contextual information required for interpreting the system gets transmitted along with the jeans and the records, whose appearance on the black market entrains an invisible string of implied connections. This occurs even though the supporting cultural infrastructure exists in faraway places like New York, Paris, London, Montreal, places about which the young Russian consumers at that time had only the most 'abstract' knowledge. Of course, the American, French, British and Canadian consumers who buy so many of these articles rarely know much about places like Hong Kong, Jakarta, Singapore and Manila, where an increasing proportion of the commodities they consume are actually made.

The materiality of the abstraction process which Baudrillard described is especially evident in the fact that a growing proportion of the commodities 'produced' are not in fact 'objects' in the ordinary sense of the term. They cannot actually be handled; their purchase and exchange occurs only in coded or symbolic form, and their existence is 'virtual'. Of course, 'information' is just such a commodity. Although information may only be an 'object' in some obscure philosophical sense, from a socioeconomic perspective, it certainly deserves a place in the system of objects as a common item of sign exchange value.

It was Marx who saw that the first great period of capital accumulation depended upon the socialization and commodification of living labour as 'abstract labour power', that is, the systematic reorganization of productive energy through its organic disembodiment and cultural disembedding (to use Giddens's term). In the early stages of industrialization, labourers are isolated from the social body (the traditional community), so that the ability to work can in turn be extracted from the biological body (each individual man, woman and child), to be converted into exchange value and reinvestible surplus. The brutal extraction of human energy in the nineteenth century was of course nothing new. Greeks, Romans, Chinese, Arabs and Africans had long conducted a thriving trade in labouring bodies before the Europeans came on the scene. The genius of Capital was to organize the extraction process into a smoothly running form of supply and demand, fully integrated with the expanded commodity market in a generalized system of exchange, so that labour would freely present itself on the market, and would not have to be housed, fed and constrained to work by the master, like the unwieldy and inconvenient slave.

to Baudrillard, the advent of digitalized 'information' he most recent refinement of the commodity form, mately heralds the supercession of the object system drillard's reasoning is that the political economy of the sig retains cumbersome ties to the traditional referential constraints of the world of appearances, signification and representation: the traditional identity of space and place, the traditional nonidentity of presence and absence. Digitalization achieves a new functional level of analytic abstraction, a microscopic decomposition of the object, which permits in turn a more fine-grained recomposition or synthesis, which is no longer tied to the original at any point except the coded interface of the transformative process.

There is no doubt that we have moved into a new phase of history analogous to the grand systematization of labour power in the consolidation of capital. If the latter period, culminating in the political economy of the sign, corresponds to what Baudrillard has termed a 'second-order simulacrum' (the first being the traditional societies of representation), then the new system underway involves a third-order level of simulation, characterized by digitalization, which permits a much more generalized and accelerated process of converting life materials into abstract values for circulation and exchange. Foucault has called this bio-power, but the issue is not bio-power itself, which has always existed, but its social and technological *form*, as Baudrillard points out.

It is worth making a brief aside here, to discuss the issue of 'form'. As we shall see later, especially with regard to structuralism, one of Baudrillard's most important early insights was that formalist methodologies which seem to lack critical distance from their objects of study tend to be the best predictors of structural transformation in the social process. Marshall McLuhan's brilliant slogan, 'the medium is the message', much scorned by academic conservatives and radicals alike, was probably Baudrillard's first example. In his review of *Understanding Media*, he argued prophetically that McLuhan's catchphrase should be interpreted as 'the very formula of alienation in a technical society' (*McLuhan* 230). Baudrillard has always remained consistent with the view (*FCPES* 175) that McLuhan's hypotheses about social communication are 'worth reexamining' because of the way they seem to reflect and confirm the 'abstraction' of social life through the 'imposition of models'.

Just as the critical discovery by Marx was not exploitation, which has always existed (usually in much more brutal fashion), but the *form* of the commodity, so the critical discovery today is not bio-power, as if that were something new, but the deepening significance of digital form in the reproduction of the social body (*Death* 57ff.). The cultural imaginary has long recognized the implications of the synthetically reconstituted body, but usually this has been conceived in the representational modality of the Zulu robot myths, or Mary Shelley's *Frankenstein*. Since *The Fly* (1958), and then *Star Trek*, the idea of an invisible structural decomposition and transfer of bodies has taken hold of the popular imagination. We do not yet have teleportation, but we do have cloning, and the prospects of bio-engineering have risen sharply since 'the cracking of the DNA code', which has led to the rapid development of new lab technologies for genetic research. For Baudrillard, all this confirms that we are moving through a series of cultural commutations leading thematically in the direction of simulation through greater and greater powers of analytic abstraction. It is as if the opening moves of classical philosophy are being played out in a kind of epistemological endgame. Plato saw imitation as a destabilizing corruption of the norm, and Aristotle saw it as the central motif of learning. They have both been vindicated in the modern problematic of simulation.

According to Baudrillard, the first order of social simulation involved the steady dilution of primitive symbolic exchange in the medium of representation and perspectival *trompe-l'œil*. This stage corresponded roughly with the development of writing and the repressive effects of farming on economies of natural abundance.[3] It culminates in the great classical era of the Renaissance, as described by Foucault in *The Order of Things*. Second-order simulation covers a brief period of *productive* 'liberations', often codified in legal constitutional form: the release from feudal bondage of the labourer, the release of property from symbolic obligations, the release from representational bondage of the sign, the release of politics from the bonds of social hierarchy, the release from mythology of sexuality, the release of discourse from theology and of knowledge from traditional taboo (for example, laws against dissection of corpses and desecration of graves). These productive liberations unleashed a tremendous industrial process, whose effect on the order of representation was well described by Marx in *The Communist Manifesto*: 'all that is solid melts into air'. It was industrial simulation (serial production) which generated the object system and the political economy of the sign. The current third-order phase of simulation is defined by the digital attenuation of the difference which remains between appearance and reality, copy and original, map and territory. And if we are to believe Baudrillard, then we are already well into the fourth order of simulation, the viral or carcinogenic phase, whose narrative Baudrillard began with 'Clone story' in the mid-1970s (*SS* 145–56).

III

Baudrillard in the politics of theory: Marxism, structuralism and the critique of everyday life

INTRODUCTION

The whole structure of Baudrillard's thought revolves around the problem of the aesthetic status and the ideological role of objects in society. The dominant theme throughout his career might well be summed up in the phrase 'the object comes alive', or 'the object has a life of its own'. Nevertheless, as he reminds us in *L'autre par lui-même*, his articulation of this theme has undergone 'considerable inflection' since his early work. He describes how it follows a kind of 'double spiral' from 'the dialectic of alienation to the giddiness of transparency' (*Ecstasy* 79). This rather dramatic self-description may at first seem obscure, but it is not at all an exaggeration of the intensity with which his thought has evolved. It is easy to become disoriented in the vertigo of Baudrillard's arguments, and to lose sight of their basis in the more traditional Hegelian problematic of subject–object relations. In order fully to appreciate the 'destiny of the object' in his thought, therefore, we must comprehend the problematic of intention, interpretation and structure from which it arose.

In *Le système des objets* (1968), the reference in the title to the possibility of analyzing a 'system' of objects draws clearly from two traditions of social theory which had yet to be brought together on this theme: the Marxist theory of the commodity in capitalist society and the structuralist analysis of systems of social signification. The first level of this relationship can be stated as follows: at a time when structuralist and Hegelian paradigms were considered historically antithetical and epistemologically incompatible, Baudrillard chose nevertheless to draw deeply on the analytic technique of semiological criticism in order to elucidate dialectical categories of critical theory such as 'exchange value', 'commodity fetishism', 'reification' and 'culture industry'. Anyone who cares to read what Baudrillard wrote between 1968 and 1972 will see his purpose clearly enough. The critical concepts are mostly derived from the Hegelian tradition, particularly from Marx and 'Western Marxists' such as Walter Benjamin and Herbert Marcuse. But these categories are shown to be inconclusive, even somewhat vacuous. In consequence, the language of structural analysis is deployed – not in order to replace the critical vocabulary, but in order to give it some much needed descriptive content. (Baudrillard's capacity to squeeze descriptive juice from stony jargon is one of the most notable features of his writing.)

At the time Baudrillard was working through these issues, however, the communication between critical theory and structuralism was indirect at best, and there was by no means an exact fit between concepts coinciding in terms like 'system', 'subject', 'object' and 'ideology'. Indeed their respective readings of Marx are quite different at several crucial points. In view of these difficulties, it is preferable to treat the prehistory of these themes in separate parts, including an outline of related currents on the French postwar intellectual scene.

9

Commodity fetishism and the theory of reification

Karl Marx defined commodities as 'something two-fold, both objects of utility, and . . . depositories of value': in other words, as both use values and exchange values.[1] The use value of a commodity is its aspect as 'an object outside us, a thing that by its properties satisfies human wants of some sort or another'.[2] According to Marx, there can be no commodity which does not comprise some use value. But there can be use values which are not commodities, because the commodity is also an exchange value, and the exchange value of an object is never intrinsic to the object itself. 'Turn and examine a single commodity . . . as we will . . . it seems impossible to grasp it [i.e. exchange value].'[3]

> Value . . . does not stalk about with a label describing what it is. It is value, rather, that converts every product into a social hieroglyphic. . . . We try to decipher the hieroglyphic, to get behind the secret of our own social products; for to stamp an object of utility as a value, is just as much a social product as language.[4]

For Marx, the aforementioned 'secret', in abbreviated form, is *labour*. 'Human labour-power in motion . . . creates value, but is not itself value. It becomes value only in its congealed state, when embodied in the form of some object.'[5] Consequently, exchange value, unlike use value, is an abstraction, and 'the exchange of commodities is evidently an act characterized by a total abstraction from use-value'.[6] Exchange value has no relation to the particularity of the object; it is the common property of all objects produced in capitalist society, i.e. an 'expression' of 'the labour-time socially necessary for its production',[7] or 'abstract human labour'. The result of this fact, Marx argued, is that '[exchange] value can only manifest itself in the social relation of commodity to commodity'.[8] In fact, if use values are, in a sense, the substance of objects, exchange value is the *form* which makes them *interchangeable*, delivers them over to a system of exchange which is indifferent to the concrete qualities of objects as such. But what makes the system complete – what closes it into the fully developed capital it forms – is the commodification of labour itself. When the system of exchange value achieves this level of autonomy, the commodity, as an element in that system, appears to forsake all reference to its origins in human labour, and becomes 'a very queer thing, abounding in metaphysical subtleties and theological niceties'.[9] Marx described this subterfuge of the object as 'commodity fetishism'.

Critical theory may be said to have begun, if not with Marx himself, then with Georg Lukács's adoption of Marx's theory of commodity fetishism as the basis for a theory of capitalist sociocultural development as a process of 'reification'. In his classic work on Marxist philosophy, *History and Class Consciousness*,[10] Lukács was attempting to move away from the positivistic and economistic tendencies of institutionalized Marxism which had developed since the Second International and the Bolshevik Revolution. The theory of reification, set forth in the long essay, 'Reification and the proletariat', was a brilliant elaboration on Marx's classic chapter on 'The fetishism of commodities and the secret thereof' in *Capital*.

In the metaphor of fetishism, Marx was of course restating the theme of the producer's alienation from his own product in the capitalist system of production. The worker's labour reappeared as an alien and hostile force, in the form of capital, or accumulated exchange value. In short, the fruits of his own labour were turned against him. But the term 'fetishism' also seemed to allude to the cognitive problems posed by the capitalist system. Clearly, the consequences of the rise of the exchange value system were not only social, but epistemological. In a sense, therefore, Marx was not only explaining how the capitalist system worked, but accounting for previous failures to understand it. Such, at any rate, was Georg Lukács's reading of *Capital*.

It is still debated to what extent Marx wished to carry the fetish metaphor beyond the production model of a subject *making* an object: to apply it to the 'communication' model of subjects *interacting* with subjects in society generally. Marx made frequent use in *Capital* of a number of highly suggestive phrases: 'the *language* of commodities'; 'The enigmatical character of the equivalent form which escapes the notice of the bourgeois political economist'; 'the mystical character of commodities'; 'the magic and necromancy which surrounds the products of labour [in capitalist society]'; the 'riddle' of the commodity, the commodity as a 'social hieroglyph' and so on.[11] Along with this, he conjured up a picture of the capitalist world as, in part, 'an immense accumulation of commodities';[12] and he described the realm of commodities as a kind of society within society, with a life of its own, interacting with itself, all to the amazement of the human onlooker.

> The relation of the producers to the sum total of their own labour is presented to them as a social relation, existing not between themselves, but between the products of their labour.[13]

> Their own social action takes the form of the action of objects, which rule the producers instead of being ruled by them.[14]

It seems clear that Marx wanted his critique to embrace not only the commodification of labour and the direct mechanisms of exploitation, but also, at least, the alienated character of exchange relationships as such. The statement of the metaphor, the sense of the displacement of meaning from one realm to another, appears over and over in the text: 'The mutual relations of the producers . . .' Marx says again, 'take the form of a social relation between the products.'[15]

Now there are, very broadly, two schools of interpretation with regard to the theme of fetishism in this 'mature' work of political economy. The first, which Lukács and later critical theorists wished to refute, treats commodity fetishism as a kind of 'veil' which is torn aside as soon as Marx's explanation is grasped. This is supported by Marx's own forcefully reductive terminology, in which 'the characters who appear on the economic stage are but the personifications of the economic relations that exist between them'.[16] But Marx also stated that his own discovery (of abstract human labour, and its general form of equivalence) 'by no means dissipates the mist through which the social character of labour *appears to us to be an objective character of the products themselves*'.[17] And Marx seemed to grant the illusion of this 'objective character' a measure of historical substance when he stated, for example:

> The life process of society, which is based on the process of material production, does not strip off its mystical veil until it is treated as production by freely associated men, and is consciously regulated by them in accordance with a settled plan.[18]

Marx's 'mystical veil' was nevertheless an *embodied* mystical veil, embodied in real social relations which, *ipso facto*, would not 'dissipate' until the social system itself was fundamentally altered.[19]

Lukács seized on the implication that the commodity ruled more than just the economic life of capitalist society, and transformed it into the key to a sociophilosophical interpretation of Marx's work. Casting the whole issue in Weberian terms as a crisis of understanding, Lukács attempted to show that the commodity in fully developed capitalist society was becoming 'the universal structuring principle' and that the 'commodity structure' could 'penetrate society in all its aspects and . . . remould it in its own image'.[20]

> The problem of commodities must not be considered in isolation or even regarded as the central problem in economics, but as the central, structural problem of capitalism in all its aspects. Only in this case can the structure of commodity-relations be made to yield a model of all the object forms of bourgeois society together with all the subject forms corresponding to them.[21]

To the extent that the emergence of the commodity form signalled a gradual but 'thorough-going capitalist rationalization of society as a whole',[22] Lukács described the process generically as 'reification', and uncovered its influence even in the forms of cognition themselves, as they were expressed in the classic antinomies of 'bourgeois' thought. What appeared to economists, sociologists and philosophers as an opaque 'second nature', with its own intrinsic laws of movement, Lukács would conceive as a dynamic, historical totality, the product of a human agency which had not yet come to grips with its own constitutive powers, had not yet achieved true, historical self-consciousness.

Lukács's attempt to reclaim the Hegelian dialectic for historical materialism, and thereby to restore the constitutive role of the subject in Marxist philosophy, was greeted at the time with mixed feelings in the communist establishment, but it had a profound influence on members of what came to be known as the Frankfurt School of philosophy who were interested in problems of culture in capitalist society. In particular, this perspective was adopted by Max Horkheimer, the director of the Institute for Social Research, in his programmatic essay 'Traditional and critical theory';[23] but it exercised an enduring influence on other writers associated with the Institute, such as Theodor Adorno, Herbert Marcuse,[24] and also Walter Benjamin.

In France, after the Second World War, Maurice Merleau-Ponty devoted an important chapter of *Adventures of the Dialectic* to Lukács's work, and described the tradition which Lukács had inaugurated as 'Western Marxism'.[25] It should also be noted that Lukács's *History and Class Consciousness*, in which he elaborated the theory of reification, became available in French translation more than a decade before it appeared in English.[26] His work was given much consideration by prominent Marxist and neo-Marxist thinkers associated with the *Arguments* group, such as Kostas Axelos, Pierre Fougeyrollas, Edgar Morin and Henri Lefebvre, who also translated and discussed the work of critical theorists such as Herbert Marcuse. However, Lukács's boldly anthropocentric schema was not received well among French structuralists, who were beginning to dominate the intellectual scene at this time. Louis Althusser, for example, denounced Lukács's theory of the historical mission of the proletariat as an anachronistic avatar of Hegelian subject–object identity, and linked his 'humanism' with Marx's 'immature' *Paris Manuscripts*, although these had still not been published in 1923, the year Lukács worked out his interpretation of Marx.[27] Furthermore, Althusser viewed Marx's chapter on commodity fetishism in *Capital* as a regression from his 'mature', production-centred 'science', characterizing it as 'regrettable' because 'all the theoreticians of alienation and reification have founded their idealist interpretations on it'.[28] Althusser correctly argued that the theory of reification – at least as Lukács had presented it – would ground the critique of political economy in the experience of the subject. Baudrillard's way around this stricture was through quasi-ethnographic exploration of the sphere of consumption in 'everyday life' – what one commentator describes as a 'passive empirical analysis'.[29] Baudrillard has always been able to retain some link to the 'subject' by recontextualizing structuralist and poststructuralist thought from a dialectical point of view (albeit through a 'negative dialectic' closer to Nietzsche and Adorno than to Hegel). Althusser, for his part, bitterly opposed any such perspective, and declared the analysis of reification – this 'last trace of Hegelian influence' – a deviation from the 'correct' analysis of the capitalist system. Nevertheless, it should be pointed out that Lucien Goldmann, an important Marxist sociologist and literary critic who played a significant role in the structuralist movement, was perhaps Lukács's most consistent advocate in France during the 1960s.[30] It should also be remembered that the stigma placed on Hegelian thought by poststructuralists like Michel Foucault and Gilles Deleuze was never as strong in Europe as it became in the English-speaking world, especially Britain, where Althusserian ideas gained a strong hold on oppositional cultural theory.

WALTER BENJAMIN

As we have just seen, the notion of an historic shift in the social being of objects is implicit in Marx's account of the rise of the exchange value system. But Marx grasped the object primarily as a means, whose end was the maintenance, ultimately the improvement, of life. The transhistorical perspective from which he viewed and criticized the commodity system was the production of use values and the problem of their allocation according to needs – their rational distribution. In *Le système des objets* and *La société de consommation*, Baudrillard was looking for a way to conceptualize the commodity as a change in the *form* of the social object – as a cultural transformation – and for this purpose, the notion of use value proved inconclusive.

Baudrillard was interested in the way objects are 'practised' socially. This presented a number of problems, not least of which had to do with how these object-practices could be articulated critically without reducing their meaning to ready-made categories. At this level, at least, the frame of reference could not be structured around allegedly 'authentic' values – such as utility – without destroying the moment of specificity on which interpretation depended. It was also, Baudrillard argued, pointless to speak of the 'alienation' of such values, even with respect to the sometimes intense personal psychological investment in the marginal differences between products. How does one question the satisfaction of someone who buys a waste bin with flower designs or an 'anti-magnetic' razor?

> No theory of needs permits us to give priority to one experience of satisfaction over any other. If the demand for personal value is so profound that in the absence of anything else it gets embodied in 'personalized' objects, how can this movement be condemned, and in the name of what 'authentic' essence of value? (*SO* 182)

Another problem lay in the technical status of objects. Baudrillard grasped the emergence of the object from its symbolic nexus in traditional societies primarily against the backdrop of the industrial revolution and the rise of competitive capitalism, as Marx had described it in *Capital*. Hence, the obvious heuristic schema for situating the issue of technicity was the gradual, but, as Marx had shown, socially and historically decisive, replacement of artisanal labour by serial production (*SO* 58–60). Not only could one begin to generalize about technical organization with reference to these contrasting modes of production, but (as we saw in Chapters 5 and 6) one could even speak of the very different social concepts which would tend to cluster around the products of mechanized industry, as opposed to the things produced by craftsmen. This was, in fact, one of the great themes developed by Walter Benjamin in his well-known essay, 'The work of art in the age of mechanical reproduction'.[31]

While Benjamin was concerned with the 'loss of aura' implicit in the serialized object (the reproduction of works of art was his paradigm case), and the way in which serial production eliminated the unique presence of the object, its reference beyond the sphere of objects, or, in other words, its symbolic, 'vertical' tie with a human origin and purpose, he was also sensitive to the new constellations of meaning and activity surrounding the object, and how technical developments interrelated with, or even produced, qualitatively different forms of experience. In this sense, it is possible to imagine that Benjamin would intuitively have understood McLuhan's phrase, 'the medium is the message', and like Baudrillard, that he would have related it to the form of reification and to the development of a new social logic of signification.[32] However, precisely where Benjamin identified the forms of reified sociation with the greatest specificity, as with the film industry, his judgement seemed to be overwhelmed by the immediacy of technologically fostered collective experience and mass political organization. The latter seemed to herald an egalitarian culture which would sweep aside the domination implicit in the 'aura' of symbolic objects, with their economic links to an archaic system of privilege.

It is not difficult to see how Marx's great metaphor of the 'socialization of production' under capitalism determined some of Benjamin's conclusions.[33] But he was nevertheless not entirely sanguine about the collapse of traditional authority signalized in this new social ontology of things designed by and for reproducibility. In a later essay, 'Some motifs in Baudelaire', Benjamin stressed the loss, in the new technical habitus, of what Weber had called 'enchantment'. Here, he no longer defines aura as the haughty distance of ritual authority, mirroring the aesthetic and political passivity of the masses. In contrast to the modern 'rationalization' of life which Weber described, Benjamin's aura became instead the 'reciprocity' of the crafted object whose human and social origins are still legible: 'To perceive the aura of an object we look at means to invest it with the ability to look at us in return.'[34] In the disenchanted world, however, 'the eye of the city dweller is overburdened with protective functions' in which 'there is no daydreaming surrender to faraway things'. Benjamin quotes Georg Simmel to the effect that 'before buses, railroads and trams . . . people were never put in a position of having to stare at one another for minutes or even hours on end without exchanging a word'.[35] Here, Benjamin is concerned with the muteness not only of serial experience and social organization, but also of the standardized object which mirrors them. And Benjamin's allusions to the 'personality' of the traditional or ceremonial object, and to a kind of social dialogue once implicit in the aura of things, anticipate one of Baudrillard's major themes: the marginalization of symbolic exchange by the sign form, which suppresses the ambivalence and the reciprocity of the social relationship. Benjamin had grasped the manner in which the emerging hegemony of the commodity form would recompose an expressive, relatively anthropomorphic social environment into a field neutralized for the circulation of unbound elements in an impersonal system of 'communication'.

As Baudrillard would point out, however, serial production has by no means eliminated the artisanal or symbolic object, whose relics connote unique, natural and authentic qualities – references to a kind of 'origin' – which 'seem to escape the system of objects' and to 'contradict the demands of a functional calculus in order to respond to the vows of another order' (*SO* 89). Evidently, in the ambiguous status of the 'bygone object [*ancien objet*]', a diachronic or historical thread of references still survives within the commodity system. As Jack Goody and Ian Watt point out, modernity is

> inevitably committed to an ever-increasing series of culture lags. The content of the cultural tradition grows continually, and in so far as it affects any particular individual he becomes a palimpsest composed of layers of belief and attitudes belonging to different stages in historical time.[36]

But although quite divergent social ontologies and values are able to coexist in the sign culture, the temporal dimension of the object – its very bygone status – has itself become a privileged commodity, whose traces are constantly being redistributed as new differential features of other objects. As we have already seen, the complexity of this transitional coding complex is especially clear in the evolution of private living accommodations:

> Whatever one's social level in France today [1969], one's domicile is not necessarily perceived as a 'consumption' good. The question of residence is still very loosely associated with patrimonial goods in general, and its symbolic scheme remains largely that of the body . . . . For the logic of consumption to penetrate here, the exteriority of the sign is required . . . . One must avoid the appearance of filiation and identification . . . . Only a certain discretionary income permits one to play with objects as status signs – a stage of fashion and the 'game' where the symbolic and the utilitarian are both exhausted. . . . In France, at least – the margin of free play for the mobile combinatory of prestige or for the game of substitution is limited. (*FCPES* 69)

10

The object in postwar French culture

Apart from German critical theory, there were more general and secular sources for Baudrillard's orientation towards the social object. Probably the most important of these was the widespread belief, in postwar France, that American capitalist culture bore within itself universalizing and levelling tendencies which were quickly spreading to the Continent. Indeed, Baudrillard seems to have relished the embarrassment of the French cultural elite over the superior appeal of American consumerism. Together with the appearance of television (which was still very gradual in France in the early 1960s, in contrast with Britain),[1] the rapidly expanding market for mass-produced commodities was the most potent symbol of this cultural transition.

France has for some time been notorious for the power of its technocrats and the rapid pace of its modernization programmes in industry, energy and architecture. The imposing Georges Pompidou National Centre of Art and Culture remains a prominent sign, in the heart of Paris, of this 'modernizing' trend. It is the subject of one of Baudrillard's seminal essays, *L'effet Beaubourg*, which appeared in 1977, the same year as the centre opened. The location of the centre on the Plateau Beaubourg was part of a massive redevelopment plan, conceived in 1968, for the site of the old market halls, Les Halles. The plan for a cultural complex in the quarter was introduced the following year. There was political opposition to the project, especially from the left intelligentsia, who saw it as a cynical potlatch glorifying the state in the name of an otherwise impoverished arts community. The Beaubourg, as it came to be called, was an 'Ideological State Apparatus', reinforcing the 'integration of pro-American power politics through an Atlantic conception of artistic production'.[2] Ironically, it was also the home of *Traverses*, a radical aesthetics journal which Baudrillard served as an editor and a principal contributor for many years.

Baudrillard's analysis of the 'Beaubourg effect' could not have been more scathing; yet it hardly represents 'political opposition' to the new centre in the usual sense (cf. *Live* 64). Attempting to distance himself as much as possible from the traditional moralism of the French cultural left, he ignored the obvious opportunity to question the political pattern behind the Centre Pompidou: centralization of power into a closed system, transparent from the outside but impervious to the surrounding environment; the displacement of local culture by official culture through administrative fiat; the physical dislocation of a disadvantaged community; and the hidden socioeconomic costs of gentrification. Instead, Baudrillard concentrated exclusively on the design of the new building, approaching it as a symptom of profound transformations on a global scale: transformations beyond the purview of the national political class, with its internal struggles to harness or to resist the explosive force of an expanding capitalist system. Even Beaubourg's appearance heralds the dissolution of classical politics, with their Newtonian dynamics of power and conflict. In contrast, the tangled lattice of the exposed superstructure evokes the image of an absorptive cybernetic network, saturated with the frantic success of its public function as a cultural 'attraction' for the 'people'. Baudrillard interprets Beaubourg as the microcosm of an accumulating social density, in which one can see, as the crowds are processed through its sheathing, that public space has already reached a 'critical mass'. This is a point of 'implosion' or 'reversion', where the field of classical political action – the social – begins slowly to collapse in upon itself like a dying star. Indeed, the 'death of the social' figures everywhere in the structure of Beaubourg. With its outer shell of tubes and piping, reminiscent of the ubiquitous, totalitarian 'ductwork' in Terry Gilliam's *Brazil* (1985), the traditional architectural body scheme is turned inside out. The crowds descending upon the building are given the same spatial status as all the other utility systems. Every available square metre is reserved for the housing of the cultural services and the curated objects, whilst the functional processes of the building itself are evacuated into the colour-coded conduit system of exterior funnelling suspended on a skeleton of steelwork: white for the ventilation system, blue for the air conditioning, green for fire prevention systems, yellow for electricity, red for people (escalators, corridors, stairwells).

Baudrillard's apocalyptic reading of the fate of French culture and urban life represents the culmination of a general movement within French social theory, during the decades after the war, to draw critical attention to the impoverishment of 'everyday life in the modern world'. At the centre of this tendency was the eminent philosopher, sociologist and former member of the French

Communist Party, Henri Lefebvre, one of Baudrillard's mentors, whom he would eventually join as professor of sociology at the University of Paris (Nanterre). Lefebvre published a series of books on the theme of everyday life after the war,[3] drawing not only on the insights of critical theory, but, to a certain extent, on the language paradigm favoured by the structuralists – although he persistently criticized their objectivist orientation and authored a series of rebuttals to Althusser.[4] In Marxist circles in general (outside the CP) there was an outcry in defence of the 'particular' (as against the rational or Hegelian 'universal') which paralleled similar, though earlier developments in critical theory. This was reflected especially in certain tendencies of structuralism typified by the work of Roland Barthes, but also in the attempts to synthesize Marxism and phenomenology or existentialism. In his *Critique of Dialectical Reason*, Jean-Paul Sartre wanted to combine the specificity of micrological analysis with the totalizing sweep of Marxian dialectic, and cited Lefebvre's 'progressive-regressive method' as a means of accomplishing this.[5]

In recent interviews, Baudrillard has indicated the importance of Sartre for his intellectual development (*Live* 20). His early association with *Les Temps Modernes* probably reflects this. Of course, like many in his generation of intellectuals in France, Baudrillard was repelled by the universalism and moralism of Sartre's postwar 'humanist' synthesis. But he was never openly hostile to existentialism, whose concern with an absurdly precarious subjectivity persists in all Baudrillard's work. It serves as an implicit reference point for measuring the power of social objectifications. There is a strong echo of Sartre in Baudrillard's view that the object is 'nothing' but the reified social relations which have converged behind it (*FCPES* 63, 212).

Not far removed from Sartre's ambivalent subservience to Stalinism was the work of two other groups which achieved some notoriety in the 1960s. One was the *Socialisme ou Barbarie* collective, which included Cornelius Castoriadis, Jean-François Lyotard and Claude Lefort, a student of Merleau-Ponty.[6] In connection with Baudrillard, their work – particularly that of Castoriadis – is most significant for its analysis of the repressive dimensions of Marx's work. The other was the *Situationiste Internationale*, a neo-Surrealist anti-organization which included activist students such as Raoul Vaneigem, and Guy Debord, who published a scathing attack in 1967 on the commodification of culture entitled *La société du spectacle*.[7] Although Baudrillard early rejected the overly simplistic assumptions of the spectacle theory, many years later he would say that he had 'always been a Situationist' in his instinctive approach to the political analysis of culture (*Live* 181).

Many of these writers, including Baudrillard and Lefebvre, became involved in one way or another in the extraordinary 'eruption' – '*les événements de mai*' – during the spring of 1968, when university students evolved a sustained and demonstrative protest directed at De Gaulle's regime – which was nearly toppled – and against what was perceived to be the mindless conformism of the consumer society. Although the focus of the general strike which ensued became increasingly conventional as the large trade unions became involved, the overriding issue, as far as the students were concerned, was the semantic crisis of capitalism. Students compared the irrelevance of much of their university training to the meaningless routine of most productive labour; and many workers agreed with this analysis, scaling their demands towards a wholesale reorganization of work relationships and working environments.

Many of the issues of the strike came in a direct line of descent from the surrealists, whose politicized aesthetic, enunciated in such manifestos as André Breton's 'Surrealist situation of the object', combined easily with the argument of Marcuse and others that the commodity culture was creating 'false needs', distorting human desires, and stifling the creative impulse to transform the *status quo* and humanize the political process.[8] It was from the perspective of a Marxism fused with existentialist and surrealist values that many involved in the uprising would interpret the structuralist movement as an ideological expression of technocratic consciousness and authoritarian order. The connection was perceived especially in the structuralists' tendency to set aside or abolish the issue of linguistic and symbolic reference, and to reduce human and social activities to closed signifying systems, thus 'autonomizing' their own discourse in a self-justifying and self-referential circle reminiscent of the strategies of bureaucratic power.[9]

No one had anticipated this response to structuralism more than Henri Lefebvre, who located the 'decline of referentials'[10] as a major feature of the 'bureaucratic society of controlled consumption', and of a 'discarded, decayed, functionalized, structuralized and "specialized" everyday life . . .' from which 'a cry of loneliness rises . . . the intolerable loneliness of unceasing communication and information'.[11] It was in fact Lefebvre who had coined the phrase 'critique of everyday life' and who had been one of the first to call for more nuanced Marxist analyses of modern culture in France. Although Lefebvre was well known for his hostility to structuralism, like Paul Ricoeur he demonstrated that it was possible to appropriate many of its insights without succumbing to its neo-positivist epistemology. Lefebvre did not deny that a certain cooperation between linguistic, aesthetic and anthropological views was proving fruitful in the study of 'neo-capitalist' culture, and he integrated these into his own critical sociology.

Lefebvre's somewhat Lukácsian motif was the fragmentation of society into progressively more specialized partial and disconnected systems; everyday life itself had already become the stagnant backwater in this constellating process. Even language was succumbing to the tendency to break up into separate spheres of interest of increasingly unrelated content: communication in everyday life, according to Lefebvre, was marked by the growing prevalence of signals.[12] This observation drew not only from Lefebvre's own special concern with the dehumanization of the urban environment, with its automated inefficiency, but from the prolific growth of an anonymous commodity culture. 'We are surrounded by emptiness, but it is an emptiness filled with signs', he declared.[13]

The connection with what Roland Barthes had said in *Mythologies*, an illuminating collection of *feuilletons* devoted to the *faits divers* and bric-à-brac of modern popular culture, seems obvious now. But whereas Barthes, from a resolutely structuralist point of view, saw the 'referential illusion' as the essence of ideological thinking in Western cultures (of which realism in literature was but one example), Lefebvre saw the 'decline of referentials' as an historical phenomenon intimately bound up with the ongoing dissolution of traditional society, the ominous 'progress' towards a cybernetic civilization and the realization of the structuralist obsession with reified systems, self-regulating order. Baudrillard's early writings were clearly an attempt to marry these opposing perspectives on the semantic crisis.

The theme of declining (or illusory) linguistic and symbolic powers of reference has always been near the heart of the various rhetorics of social and conceptual 'crisis'. It was Husserl's preoccupation when he proposed a science of the *lebenswelt* which would restore the prescientific experience of the world as the ground of natural and mathematical knowledge.[14] Existentialism had already begun to thematize the issue as a crisis of collective faith; the sense of the 'arbitrary' as a decisive new dimension of social life was summed up in the concept of the absurd, and situated historically through Nietzsche's claim about the death of God. And even the positivists joined the discussion by pointing out the meaninglessness of traditional referents and proposing alternative languages to suit the age. From this point of view, it is possible to see structuralism as, in part, one of the heirs of the positivist programme.

Writers like Walter Benjamin, Theodor Adorno, and later, in France, Henri Lefebvre, attempted to situate these debates on the more mundane level of experience in ordinary life. Viewing the whole problem of reference in the structured historical perspective of Marx's critique of political economy, they interpreted the crisis not as the death of meaning, but as a series of *shifts* in meaning which had a concrete basis in changes in social life, mutations in social structure and developments of 'material production'. These shifts could be formulated in terms of *things* as well as language, which meant, of course, that the emerging 'critique of everyday life' could with justification frequently adopt the point of view of a bygone, artisanal and perhaps more genuinely communal era in order to gain historical perspective on the rise of the 'commodity'.

This emphasis on the [communal] 'other' of capitalism was particularly evident in the writings of Georges Bataille, whose career, like Henri Lefebvre's, spanned the period before and after the war, and included an early association with the surrealist movement. But what is especially important about Bataille's work, with respect to any interpretation of Baudrillard, is his critical perspective on classical political economy, from which he did not ultimately exclude Marx. Bataille was convinced that the essence of societal structures prior to capitalism could not be deemed 'economic' in the sense that the significant social object was always the means of expressing a symbolic and ritual transcendence – or 'transgression' – not, as Marx believed, as the means of the *material* reproduction of life.[15] He disagreed with the standard theory that primitive economies were based on barter and, not unlike Lévi-Strauss, drew on the authority of Marcel Mauss's study of *The Gift*[16] to formulate a counter-theory of exchange whose basis was 'not the need to acquire which [exchange] satisfies today, but the contrary need of destruction and loss'. 'The archaic form of exchange has been identified by Mauss under the name of *potlatch*', he pointed out.[17] In Bataille's view, the primitive relation to the object was not consumption, but *consummation*, a nonrationalizable social process related to his theory that important meanings could only arise out of nonmeaning, or from uncodified or decodified social material.[18] For Bataille, meaning always arose in and through *excess*, and excess – or transgression – was by definition beyond the rational ends of production. It was very much in the context of Bataille's *part maudite* that Baudrillard received Lévi-Strauss's theories of primitive exchange as a clue to an alternative to exchange based on equivalence in capitalist society. But Bataille did not only foreshadow the theory of symbolic exchange. His rejection of Western, productivist economies implied that Marx's critique of political economy had not gone as far as it should in getting to the root of the capitalist malaise.[19]

The surrealists were notorious for their fascination with the aesthetic possibilities of randomly juxtaposing ordinary, everyday objects, and stripping them of their utilitarian dimension. The theme of random juxtaposition resurfaced in France after the war in the structuralist tendency to privilege relations of contiguity in general. The watchwords were discontinuity and the death of the subject. The relations of meaning were arbitrary, not necessary or intentional, and so there was no point in trying to ground them in human agency. Taken to an extreme, this emphasis on aleatory parataxis could be interpreted as reflecting or conjuring up a world entirely devoid of human intentionality – a mere collection or 'heap' of things. This was exactly how the world appeared in the novels of Robbe-Grillet. According to one critic, Robbe-Grillet's '*Nouveau Roman*' seemed to propose 'the idea of a universe in which people are merely objects and objects are endowed with an almost human hostility'.[20] Lucien Goldmann attempted to demonstrate that there was a 'rigorous homology'[21] between the structure of social reification and the structure of the *Nouveau Roman*. For Goldmann, the analogy between Robbe-Grillet's work and the ordinary experience of capitalist society was 'marked by the appearance of an autonomous world of objects, with its own structures and its own laws and through which alone human reality can still to a certain extent express itself'.[22] Roland Barthes, on the other hand, was less disturbed by the social implications of Robbe-Grillet's aesthetic than by the fact that it seemed to be an attempt to vindicate novelistic realism; but he did point out that there would be an 'inevitable inference from the [hypothetical] non-signifying nature of things to the nonsignifying nature of situations and men',[23] and added, with a note of irony, that 'if nature signifies, it can be a certain acme of culture to make it designify'.[24]

The relation between what Goldmann saw as an increasingly alienated social experience and the concerns of modern fiction was made even more explicit in a short but compelling novel by Georges Perec entitled *Les choses*, which appeared in 1965 and won the Prix Renaudot.[25] *Les choses* depicted a young married couple, Sylvie and Jerome, living in a state of almost total absorption in a kind of netherworld of commodities, things, objets d'art. But the novel's central concern was this *demi-monde* of consumption itself; Sylvie-and-Jerome only wafted from object to object, almost unnoticed, merging with the system of objects. Their relationships were quite literally 'reified'. Nothing in the novel escaped the metonymic terror of things, their differences, their substitutions, their relationships with each other.[26]

11

The structuralist articulation of the object

'Toute passage a l'acte est une solution imaginaire.' (*TM* 154)

In contrast to the critical theorist's attention to problems of reification and alienation in society, the structuralists tended to emphasize the *active* function of the object in any cognitive relationship, and the passivity of the social subject. No doubt, this is one way of grasping the mutual hostility of Hegelian and structuralist thought. But it is also the basis for an interesting counterpoint in Baudrillard's early work, up to and including *The Mirror of Production*. During this period, structuralism does not serve merely as a foil for critical theory; as we have seen, it also provides a method for *interpreting* the commodity culture posited by critical theory, and thus for exploring the 'physiognomy' of reification. Baudrillard's initial theoretical impulse seems to have been quite well summed up by Theodor Adorno:

> Life transforms itself into the ideology of reification . . . . Hence, the task of criticism must be not so much to search for the particular interest-group to which cultural phenomena are to be assigned, but rather to decipher the general social tendencies which are expressed in these phenomena . . . . Cultural criticism must become social physiognomy.[1]

For Baudrillard, the key to this task lies in the characteristically structuralist inflection of the language paradigm.

The structuralist perspective on the social object can be traced back to the work of Durkheim and Mauss in *Primitive Classification*:

> It was because men were grouped, and thought of themselves in the form of groups, that in their ideas they grouped other things, and in the beginning the two modes of grouping were merged to the point of being indistinguishable. Moieties were the first genera, clans the first species. Things were thought to be integral parts of society, and it was their place in society which determined their place in nature.[2]

This hypothesis of an intimate bond between social organization and the social meaning of objects reappeared in Lévi-Strauss's

Totemism and in *The Savage Mind*.[3] The significance of Lévi-Strauss's approach, however, lay in another direction from Durkheimian functionalism: the object would no longer appear as a homogeneous, unified 'thing', but as a type of meaningful relation – in other words, as a *sign*. This was crucial to Lévi-Strauss's approach not only because it suggested a link between systems of exchange and systems of meaning (such as myth), but because for Lévi-Strauss 'the promotion of the object to the rank of sign'[4] encapsulated the immemorial transition from nature to culture which inaugurated all societies, and language itself.

Taking inspiration from Marcel Mauss's 'precept that all social phenomena can be assimilated to language',[5] Lévi-Strauss declared: 'Whatever the moment and circumstances of its appearance in the chain of animal life, language could only have been born in one fell swoop. Things could not have begun to signify progressively.'[6] In effect, it was as if a sudden convergence of signifier and signified had carved up the mute world into discrete entries in a limitless and circulating lexicon. Objects were immediately social, immediately endowed with significance.

In answer to the question 'whether all phenomena in which social anthropology is interested really do manifest themselves as signs, such as a stock of tools, various techniques, and modes of production and consumption',[7] Lévi-Strauss replied that 'A stone axe can be a sign . . . [in so far as] it takes the place of the different implement which another society employs for the same purpose.'[8]

> One cannot study the gods without knowing their icons; rites without analyzing the objects and the substances which the officiant makes or manipulates; social rules independently of the things which correspond to them. . . . If men communicate by means of symbols and signs, then, for anthropology . . . everything is symbol and sign, when it acts as intermediary between two subjects.[9]

This was effectively a proposal to develop the '*science that studies the life of signs within society*', whose province had been 'staked out in advance' by Saussure.[10] But if the territory was conceded without struggle, there were nevertheless several pockets of resistance to semiological reduction, which Baudrillard would make into reference points for the themes of critical theory.

SYSTEMATIC APORIAS

Umberto Eco has described the essence of the semiological approach in the following words: 'A cultural unit is defined inasmuch as it is *placed* in a *system* of other cultural units which are opposed to it and circumscribe it. *We are concerned with values which issue from a system.*'[11] This statement contains a very complex problematic. To work as Lévi-Strauss suggests, the sign must be conceived as an *arbitrary* unit of meaning. If the cultural unit or sign has no intrinsic relation to any referent, the meaning must be posited as a function of the *systematicity* of the signifying elements themselves. The meaning of anything functioning as a sign must derive from the *differences* between the elements of a *conventional* system of signification. Meaning then appears to be an endowment of the system: it comes from the sign, but not from what the sign 'refers' to, in so far as that is thought to be located outside the system.[12] But if it is the 'system' which 'motivates' the sign relationship (signifier–signified), in the absence of a functioning referent, there still remains some question as to the motivation of the system itself. Either there must be some agency (motivation) outside the system, constituting the system, or else the system itself, as a whole – as an effective structure – is *not* arbitrary, but natural, given, an 'unmoved mover'. It must come into being 'all at once', as Lévi-Strauss said.

It is in the latter sense that structuralism tends to assume the *immediacy* and primacy of systems and the derived character of intentionality and human agency. Language is adopted as the paradigm of systems and structures – and the structures of language are endowed with a functional autonomy and determining power which dispenses with acts of meaning and reference as aspects of the semantic process.

The logical problems with this approach still tend to be suppressed, perhaps because Western thought has acquired such a stake in the epistemological privileging of language. Nevertheless, if we accept the system definition of signification then we are stuck with a variant of Bertrand Russell's paradox: the problem of the ontological status of the putative system of signs itself. Does the meaning of the term 'system' function like that of a sign, i.e. as a relationship between a signifier and a signified in a system of signs? Is 'system' (as sign) part of the "system" (as system)? If it is, then in what sense can its apparent reference to a "system" be a literal and objective one? If 'system' is part of "system", then it can have no privileged reference outside the system of signs, and is itself caught up in the differential play of signs; so there can be no *real* "system" within which the meaning of 'system' (as a sign) can be determined.

On the other hand, if there *is* a real system, and the system of signs is not itself a sign, then the term 'system' must have an objective reference (to the actual system of signs), which means that the sign refers independently of the system to something beyond the system, namely the system itself, and therefore cannot be a part of it. Like a Moebius band, the sign is always outside the system of which it is a part, and the system is always inside the play of the sign which it is supposed to contain.

Not all structuralists assume that the systems they analyze are wholly self-governing or objective entities (which means, of course, that they are only "systems" in the weakest possible sense). For example, one way around the problem of realism is to argue that "systems" are always the products of the structuralist's activity as a model-builder or "bricoleur". This position, which was Baudrillard's in *Le système des objets*, allows that structures and systems are historically determined and open-ended: that "language" is part of a larger environment of phenomena which in many ways supercedes the internal relations between signs.

So long as the concept of structure retains its epistemological priority, however, subjectivity appears either as a God-like constitutional creativity – a variant of Rationalism – or as a mere meaning effect, an extension of systematic or structural properties. The first accounts of structuralist "activity" are markedly rationalistic in character. The model constructed by the observer is conceived as abstracting the essential and eliminating continuous features so that the model is formal and its elements are all discrete, allowing for substitutions and variations within the system.[13] Even Roland Barthes, during his early structuralist phase, adopted this view:

> Structure is . . . actually a *simulacrum* of the object. . . . The imitated object makes something appear which remained invisible or, if one prefers, unintelligible in the natural object. Structural man takes the real, decomposes it, then recomposes it. . . . The simulacrum is intellect added to object . . .[14]

From this point of view, structure implies a constituting activity. But the issue is never settled whether the intentional character of the "simulacrum" applies also to systems which the structuralist cannot claim to have constructed, such as a "linguistic system", or the "system of exchange value". If it does, then every subject reinvents language and political economy from scratch, with Fichtean prowess. If it does not, then every subject is him or herself merely a structural effect, a by-product of the relations between the signs in the system. Of course, these aporias presuppose that the structuralist's models of 'objective' systems are themselves objective. On the other hand, a Marxist in the Hegelian tradition might suggest as an alternative that the objective character of these systems – especially of the signifying systems with which semiology is so fascinated – is an extrapolation from the formal, systemic and discrete qualities of the structuralist's *model*: in sum, that the objective systems are actually reifications of subjective activity.

In the general field of sociological theory, Anthony Giddens has attempted to resolve the aporia of agency and structure through the development of a sociological theory of "structuration" which views all social phenomena simultaneously as confluent processes of structure-structuring and structuring-structured. For Giddens, every social agent is engaged actively in making structures and matching them, in structuring and being structured at the same time. The same duality necessarily conditions the activities of the professional social observer, who must negotiate the "double hermeneutic" of modelling and being modelled, which is always in principle a remodelling of the already modelled object of his or her investigations. Of course, to be consistent, Giddens would have to acknowledge that structuration theory is itself implicated in the "hermeneutic circle". In fact, he concedes the paradox in a way which strengthens, rather than undermines, his thesis: he argues that the double hermeneutic expresses a peculiar condition of modernity which has deeper implications for social theory than the mere truism that social life is reflexive. According to Giddens, it is not just the *agency* of culture, community or subjectivity, which intervenes in the 'system', and is adapted by it, like a variable in relation to the homeostatic whole. Under the conditions of modernity, reflexivity has been generalized well beyond this, so that it functions on an entirely new level. The entire social system functions massively in this self-reflexive manner, absorbing professional discourse and scientific expertise. The 'system' reproduces itself in ever more rapidly evolving cycles of restructuration. 'Sociological knowledge spirals in and out of the universe of social life, reconstructing both itself and that universe as an integral part of that process.'[15]

It is precisely to the extent that the epistemology of contemporary social theory waivers in this limbo between embodiment and abstraction that Baudrillard has placed the semiological approach in the service of a critical interpretation of contemporary culture. But in order to achieve this, Baudrillard had to purge structuralism of its claim to uncover an ideal systematicity; he had to reinterpret this claim instead as a response to the ordered abstraction of commodity culture and the self-regulating impersonality of systems of exchange and of signification in complex, late modern societies. In this sense, the formal elements of structural analysis – the arbitrary nature of the sign, the constitutive status of the system (as opposed to its user), and the manipulation of discrete, fungible terms according to the rules of a code – appear in Baudrillard's analysis as embodied features of commodity culture and contemporary social experience. In *Le système des objets* Baudrillard proposed these aspects of the sign as historically relative characteristics of the object emerging in the age of standardized production and mass consumption, whose consequences for the experience and meaning of social life could in part be deciphered through semiological reconstruction. This meant that Baudrillard would treat the structure of the sign, its systemic autonomy, and its tendency to favour metonymic relations of signification (space over time), as properties of modern culture rather than as preponderant features of all societies. This is how the sign became for Baudrillard a kind of structural model of reification (*FCPES* 163), and why structuralism presented itself in his work as both *interpretans* and *interpretant*. Baudrillard was not concerned with structuralism only as a particular doctrine or method, but also as a cultural expression of the generalized appeal of social theories stressing the determining powers of form, structure, system, order, regularity, symmetry, homology and identity.

CONCLUSION

> The past went that-a-way. When faced with a totally new situation, we tend always to attach ourselves to the objects, to the flavour of the most recent past. We look at the present through a rear-view mirror. We march backwards into the future. (Marshall McLuhan)[16]

In a sense, then, Baudrillard's early studies offer an interesting variation on the dialectical hermeneutics of modern sociology, particularly Habermas's theory of communicative action and Giddens's structuration theory. There is no doubt that in the period 1968–76, Baudrillard would have accepted Giddens's sharp differentiation between modern and traditional societies wholeheartedly. He would also have accepted the hypothesis that modernity functions like an emergent property whose tendency to run away with itself in severe dislocations is precariously contained within a larger dynamic equilibrium. But Baudrillard would soon part from any 'optimistic' currents associated with the defeat of objectivism in social theory (dialectics, hermeneutics, reflexivity), arguing that the sociological recuperation of the subject and of the historical agent draws retroactively on a nineteenth-century fantasy of rational action and coherent social praxis. As Marshall McLuhan often reiterated, we have a strong tendency to perceive the present through the 'rearview mirror'. There are practical reasons for this (we cannot learn empirically from the future), but in social thought, hindsight is frequently delusional because it draws inferences from bygone conditions. The tragedy of critical theory is that its own demystification of the ideological structures of domination (or, in Habermas's case, the ego-psychological critique of 'systematically distorted communication') has effectively unravelled the slip-knot of revolutionary action. Insight produces adjustment, correction, compensation, revision, and much further research – but very little 'action', certainly nothing so grandiose as a world-historical praxis. From a technological point of view, the hermeneutic recovery of the subject is obviated by its own condition, Weber's formal rationality, whose very success lays a foundation for the operationalization – the objectification – of reflexivity. What makes it possible for us to begin to grasp the way in which we have so far 'made' our own world also reveals that the process of 'making' necessarily escapes conscious awareness until it is practically made and done with. 'Postmodernity' might well be defined as the consequent understanding: that our conscious interventions, based on 'theory', are usually either ineffectual or disastrous, rarely what we had hoped.

Whether this historical experience will serve ideologically to legitimate formal rationality further, or to discredit it, is impossible to foresee. Baudrillard's assumption, which, with *Symbolic Exchange and Death*, takes him right outside the mainstream of critical social thought, is that this decision is now outside governance. The self-regulation and 'control' implicit in electronic technology already functions well beyond the purview of any imaginable praxis, other than the possible expression, in some unpredictable form (not necessarily irrational), of all those ambivalent 'passions' of the 'symbolic' which cannot be contained and integrated into the 'system'.

Giddens's double hermeneutic has only come to our attention because it is already history. Every culture is a construction of practical social knowledge, but the modernist dream of a practice which can actually plan moral transcendence of the given is an illusion generated by the increasing pace of change, which seduces us into mistaking partly successful prophecies for substantial historical projects. The dynamic function of knowledge production as a basis for informed intervention is now known to us precisely because its mythic power has been demystified. The promise of emancipation through knowledge has already been superceded by its technologically enhanced autonomization: our knowledge is not really ours after all, but a hybrid formation increasingly dominated by nonhuman and nonsubjective components. Human knowledge is in fact becoming a programme designed to recycle itself automatically, effectively imposing a higher order closure of the structuration process. The self-conscious participation of the increasingly knowing Hegelian subject never catches up with the regulatory functioning of the system.

IV

From history to metaphysics

12

Symbolic exchange as a critical standpoint

Baudrillard's reading of the contemporary forms of modernist culture and society achieves a kind of climax of internal consistency in the *Critique* (*FCPES*) and *The Mirror of Production* (*MP*) which, after *Symbolic Exchange and Death* (1976), it will never have again. Some commentators have attributed the subsequent *virage* to a failure of moral insight or of political commitment on Baudrillard's part. A more charitable explanation would be that he lost faith in the claims of intellectual movement politics, which want to be academically respectable and revolutionary at the same time. He had pushed the theoretical models of society received from sociology and critical theory as far as they would go, and was no longer interested in producing variations on their familiar shapes and themes, or reinventing the wheel (an occupational hazard of dissidents like himself).

Baudrillard's attraction as a social philosopher lies in his capacity to relate the formalized abstractions of the civilized habitus to the mysteries of social being. We have already seen in his work how social observations throw as much light on the problems of theory as the theories throw on the problems of society. Baudrillard appropriates the academic languages of social theory – even the technical languages of molecular biology, wave mechanics, catastrophe theory, chaos theory – and applies them illegitimately, collapsing the normal distance between the signifier and the signified, the sign and the referent, so that abstractions and intellectualizations are pressed into dimensions of lived experience, words become things, models become material infrastructures. If Baudrillard is unconcerned by the usual distinctions between word and object, theory and praxis, this is not because he cannot tell them apart, or wishes to subordinate one to the other, but because he senses vividly how social life itself is 'theoretical', as 'abstract' as the social science which tries to distil it into formal models. Plato thought of society as an imitation of nature, and of art as a corrupting imitation of that.[1] As we have already seen, Baudrillard is a perverse Platonist who treats theory as a social enactment in a world where social action is itself an artform. Not just theory, but society itself, strives for an effective simulation of the social; and so there is no reason why social philosophy should not also try to learn by approaching the problem of human organization as a problem in art history or aesthetics.

This way of looking at things is of course unstable, and the question arises concerning what, if anything, furnishes the gravity, the seriousness, of Baudrillard's work. If there is a credible answer, it lies in the enigma of Baudrillard's concept of 'symbolic exchange'. The latter evolved from an attempt to develop and refine the standpoint of critical social thought through an ingenious synthesis of Mauss's sociology of the gift (as developed in part by Lévi-Strauss) with Bataille's notion of expenditure: *la part maudite*. This project has blossomed into a full-blown 'philosophy' of symbolic exchange, issuing in contestatory concepts of seduction, fatality and the principle of evil, whose relation to Baudrillard's earlier work is sometimes difficult to discern.

All critical social philosophy finds its form of truth in some notion of 'resistance', or failure to conform to institutional norms. If one believes that everything is relative to institutions (and most of us do when it is convenient), then one can explain all of one's intellectual misconceptions, miscalculations and exaggerations as forms of 'resistance'. Who can demonstrate with certainty that anyone is being deliberately wrongheaded? In societies where the thought-police have been beaten back by liberal law, we try in principle to make sense of everything, no matter how 'deviant' it seems. We approach all thought sceptically, equipped only with abstract paradigms of discourse as an organization of errata, of originality as a misappropriation of influences, of thought as a web of overextended metaphors, and some judgement of what *might* be true, a Pascalian wager, which is always a mixture of personal vision, bias, intellectual labour and critical intention.

The philosophy of symbolic exchange is an enactment of this radical, resistant strain of scepticism. It seeks the metastable form of an erratic and deviant posture, to sustain an atmosphere of irresolution and tension. With the possible exception of *Le système des objets* and *La société de consommation*, Baudrillard is rarely analytic, although his approach is phenomenological and descriptive rather than synthetic. His misuse of metatheory as a description language has the paradoxical effect of decomposing the object. He throws all the pieces up in the air, where they seem to hang, miraculously, in dynamic equilibrium, offering no hint as to how they will fall. In its various guises – death, seduction, virus, evil – the metaphysical principle of symbolic exchange is the distilled essence of conceptual *anomie*, the rhetorical evocation of the ontological excluded middle: an absence or an anxiety which can be found in phenomenology and existentialism, Nietzschean pragmatism and Nietzschean romanticism, structuralist formalism and dialectical historicism, Eurocentric elitism, deconstructionist feminism, popular culture, primitivism and exoticism.

In certain respects, symbolic exchange can be compared with *différance*, *differend* and *chora*. All these poststructuralist terms express an ambivalent affinity with Heidegger's narrative of Western culture as a search for the 'real' at the expense of true Being. But in defiance of linguistic formalism, symbolic exchange is rife with analogic continuities, idiosyncratic interiorities and emotional expressions. It is experience-near, though in a highly politicized way, which makes it reminiscent of those 'situated knowledges' and 'strategic essentialisms' with which North American poststructuralists have practised a kind of conceptual reverse discrimination. Everything to do with signification and action is placed on a continuum and reduced to its unconscious phallogocentric meaning as rape and murder. As Roland Barthes argued, 'language is fascist', but in the medium of symbolic exchange, it is still possible to mean 'without the *techne* cutting through the *physis* with a name blade'. It is possible to be a woman without having an identity, except virtually, as 'a reading effect, a woman-in-effect that is never stable and has no identity'.[2] It is possible to be aggressively active without being an agent or doer, because 'the "doer" is variably constructed in and through the deed';[3] to be observant without raping nature, because the feminist eye does not 'fuck the world to make techno-monsters'; and to put science in the service of morality because 'only partial perspective promises objective vision'.[4] From these privileged, supranormative standpoints, one may take an essentialist position towards everything without being an essentialist; one may say what something is without actually defining it; one may make value judgements without discriminating, excluding, harming; one may generate hierarchies of all kinds without being hierarchical – and thus participate in all the benefits of 'Western metaphysics' without being hegemonically Western. How all this is possible has never been explained, but it suggests the standpoint of symbolic exchange. Like 'situated knowledge' it is a way of cobbling together an Archimedian point of reference which is not a 'subject', or a myth about the primacy of 'language'. Symbolic exchange might be described as the 'trickster' version of *différance*, the demonic version of strategic essentialism.

The consistency of the critique of the political economy of the sign depended precisely on the emptiness of the standpoint from which it was conceived. At first, Baudrillard made only passing references to the anthropological literature, and to various social practices, such as the potlatch and the gift cycle, which were said to be examples of symbolic exchange. For a long time, one had to be satisfied with the term 'ambivalence'. The critical analysis of the 'system' was complete because its other was nothing and nowhere, a pure form, like Herbert Marcuse's 'negation', or Heidegger's Being. As the alter of political economy, symbolic exchange is itself an abstraction, a circulating form without any required content. In *Symbolic Exchange and Death*, Baudrillard acknowledged this tacitly mimetic character of his critical standpoint, and proposed to turn it into an explicit strategy of doubling and reversal. Thenceforth, symbolic exchange became increasingly localized and acquired a specific content. As we have seen, it would 'side with the object, take up the cause of the object' (*FS* 190), and thereby transform itself into an odd version of the 'system' itself.

THE SYMBOL VERSUS THE SIGN

In Baudrillard's original usage, the term 'symbolic' never refers to language or to anything language-like (although language may furnish one of the materials of the symbolic). If it has any consistent sense, the Baudrillardian symbolic is related to the problem of affect – emotion, feeling, mood, meaning: what he termed *ambivalence*. This was certainly the case in the early work, where symbolic exchange was posited in opposition to the structuralist symbolic (Lacan, Lévi-Strauss); it was not a sign system or a Law or a formal principle, but a kind of affective interchange or dynamic intensity. The concept of symbolic exchange would therefore appear to be an attempt to integrate the concept of social form with an expressivist concept of meaning, as an emergent process of the body.

It helps to keep in mind that for Baudrillard, *meaning* is not the same thing as signification or sense. The gift is, in its purest form, 'meaning', that is, something unique and irreplaceable, which cannot be substituted because it has no equivalent. It is something whose very existence symbolizes the interaction which it occasions, and which likewise could not have come into existence without the interaction. There is no signifier or signified in the proper sense of those terms, since the meaning of the gift *is* the social action, its context in the relationship it creates. The gift is not a sign because it cannot be separated from its context, and transferred to any other: it simply embodies its own meaning, which is nothing other than the way the bodies of the giver and receiver have come to exist in relation to each other. It is an act and a process of imagination, which dissolves when the social relationship it symbolizes ceases to exist in the minds of those who experienced it.

If we think of symbolic exchange very broadly as the process in which this kind of meaning is generated, then we can see why Baudrillard opposes symbolic exchange to the very different process of signification. Signification is always 'produced', that is, assembled out of relatively autonomous elements which are interchangeable and independent of context. There are no constraints on the production of signification, since it is never tied literally to any particular time or place. Moreover, any signification can be reproduced, replicated, transported, and substituted for an equivalent. It does not produce meaning, therefore, but signs, whose signification is not linked to the moment of their emergence, or to the conditions of their articulation, but to their 'position' in a larger 'system' of signifying elements, a system which anyone can enter, but no one can leave. Thus, we can see how 'meaning', or any symbolic object, would be destroyed as soon as it becomes a discrete and arbitrary element in a system for the production of signification.

> The object-become-sign no longer gathers its meaning in the concrete relation between two people. It assumes its meaning in its differential relation to other signs. Somewhat like Lévi-Strauss's myths, sign-objects exchange among themselves. Thus, only when objects are autonomized as differential signs and thereby rendered systematizable can one speak of consumption and of objects of consumption. (*FCPES* 66)

THE DEIDEALIZATION OF SYMBOLIC EXCHANGE

Anything can be symbolic in the interpersonal sense described above, since anything may come to embody the emotional 'meaning' of an interaction, a chance moment, or a relationship, which can never be fully articulated or explicated. But this account of symbolic exchange as a processual embodiment of affective intensities implies some sort of phenomenology of relationships between individuals (which Baudrillard would only begin to supply later, in his treatise on *Seduction*). It is difficult to imagine how an entire society could be organized around the exchange of such symbols, since the very fact of social organization – as in the Kula cycle, or the potlatch – implies premeditation and compliance, and therefore some kind of representational function which in the final analysis must be arbitrary, and thus subject to the logic of equivalence and substitution. Yet Baudrillard associates these indispensable mechanisms exclusively with the production of signs, and not with symbolic exchange.

There is no doubt that this represents a serious contradiction in Baudrillard's thought. In retrospect, it seems that he could only avoid it so long as he kept the concept of symbolic exchange inexplicate. As we have seen, the whole structure of his critique of the sign depended on a certain 'emptiness' in the conception of the symbolic, which he later relinquished. When he did so, Baudrillard dissolved the ideality of symbolic exchange, and radically changed his conception of culture. It is now possible to see how his idealization of symbolic exchange masked the individualistic temper of his thought (which emerges in his taste for Baudelaire, Nietzsche, Segalen, Canetti) by fostering a somewhat utopian vision of the primitive group. This penchant for rosy readings of the anthropological literature was due less to his predilection for Bataille, whose Romanticism is decidedly demonic, than to the influence of Marcel Mauss, whose bland holism is typical of the Durkheim school.

If one wanted to show how systems of gift exchange in Melanesia, or of potlatch in British Columbia, were truly symbolic exchanges, and not merely collective simulations of experience generated by the production of signs (as in the object system), one would have to show how such organized and prescribed relationships nevertheless manage to embody a meaning which directly expresses a privileged moment, a moment which is not merely constructed as a representational effect through the deliberate manipulation of a pre-existing cultural code or system of signs. In other words, one would have to show how the meaning of an *event* has constitutive priority over the signification of a *structure*. (In Saussurian terms, this is analogous to the issue of whether *parole* [speech] has primacy over *langue* [system].[5])

Mauss's idea was that certain societies are capable of existing as 'total social phenomena' wherein 'all kinds of institutions find simultaneous expression: religious, legal, moral, and economic'.[6] One might interpret this to mean that the entire culture, which confers meaning on every object and every act, is itself the embodied expression of a privileged event. Perhaps this is the sheer intensity of the affective moment in which the society itself came into being. Recall Lévi-Strauss's comment, in his introduction to Mauss, that 'language could only have been born in one fell swoop. Things could not have begun to signify progressively.' If the beginning of a culture – let us say the culture of an Australian aboriginal tribe – were like this epiphanic origin of language, it would then be possible to argue that nothing in that culture would be arbitrary except perhaps the constellation of phenomena at the moment of its creation; everything which follows that event simply lives out its 'meaning', through the integrated expression of the culture, in all its aspects. Whether such societies ever existed (or have been dreamed up by holistic Romantics), it is hard to imagine how they could survive contact with external cultures. To sustain such a tight unity of form and content, the universal and the particular, these purely synchronic organizations would have to be perfectly adapted to a very stable environment, since they can only exist by blocking the effect of time as the emergence of the unpredictable and the individual. The society's quest for identity with itself through the infinite repetition of the constitutive cultural event (the established structure) would certainly discourage new interpretations, and thus seems likely to falter in the face of unassimilable elements.

Descriptions of such logically impossible cultures abound in our literature. They are powerful symbols of the enigma of social being, and Baudrillard does not hesitate to play them off against the comfortable realism of Western culture. But as we have noted, his interpretation of the social enigma has become less idealistic, more attuned to the demonic. It should not be a surprise that the most 'primitive' of these enigmatic cultures, those, like the Yanomamo, which ritualize violence, or those, like the K'ung!, which give ontological priority to the dream, are the societies whose disappearance has been most celebrated in the popular imagination. Something of the flavour of Baudrillard's ambivalent idealization of such cultures is conveyed in his comments on Bruce Chatwin's book about the Australian walkabout:

> The strangest feeling one is left with after reading Bruce Chatwin's *Songlines* is a lingering perplexity about the reality of the 'lines' themselves: do these poetic and musical itineraries, these songs, this 'dreamtime', really exist or not? In all these accounts there is a hint of mystification; a kind of mythic optical illusion seems to be operating. It is as though the Aboriginals were fobbing us off. While unveiling the profoundest and most authentic of truths (the Austral myth at its most mysterious), they also play up the most modern and hypothetical of considerations: the irresolvability of any narrative, absolute doubt as to the origins. For us to believe these fabulous things, we need to feel that they themselves believe them. But these Aboriginals seem to take a mischievous pleasure in being allusive and evasive. They give a few clues, but never tell us the rules of the game, and one cannot help getting the impression that they are improvising, pandering to our phantasies, but withholding any reassurance that what they are telling us is true. This is doubtless their way of keeping their secrets while at the same time poking fun at us – for in the end we are the only people who want to believe these tales. (*TE* 136–7)

To summarize: symbolic exchange seemed at first to have a utopian dimension, implying a belief in the possibility of social harmony derived from Romantic readings of Mauss and Malinowski – the timeless equilibrium of the Kula cycles in the Melanesian Pacific – and perhaps something like the expressive immediacy of Lacan's 'parole pleine', or of Rousseau's festival. While apparently joining Rousseau to denounce historical civilization as a perversion, however, Baudrillard has demonstrated no particular faith in the innate 'goodness' of human nature. In this respect, he is Nietzschean (and Freudian) to the core. But it was not until *Symbolic Exchange and Death* that the dark side of symbolic exchange came into clear focus, where it has remained, and grown steadily darker.

THE SOCIAL, THE SOCIETAL AND THE CULTURAL

> [F]rom each point on the surface of existence . . . one may drop a sounding into the depth of the psyche so that all the most banal externalities of life finally are connected with the ultimate decisions concerning the meaning and style of life. Punctuality, calculability, exactness are forced upon life by the complexity and extension of metropolitan existence. . . . These traits must also color the contents of life and favor the exclusion of those irrational, instinctive, sovereign traits and impulses which aim at determining the mode of life from within, instead of receiving the general and precisely schematized form of life from without. (Simmel)[7]

In *Symbolic Exchange and Death*, Baudrillard sets out to show that the discourse of modernity is flowing towards death, a death from 'theoretical violence' necessitated by the principle of reciprocity in symbolic exchange; moreover, he attempts to show that this fatality at the heart of conceptual systems can be seen to prefigure, perhaps even to reflect, the social extinction of culture. A brief excursus on the meaning of the terms 'social', 'society' and 'culture' will help to illuminate these statements.

In the conditions of modernity, the social, or the property of sociability as such, can no longer plausibly refer to the collective activities of an entire society, since the latter is essentially a euphemism for the political entity of the nation state: a geopolitical organization which is too large, too complex and too abstract to warrant the attribution of specifically *social* characteristics (unless one is a Comtean positivist or a national liberationist). The rather misleading concept of a 'social system', therefore, connotes very little that is recognizably *social*, and may thus be designated by the term 'societal'. The societal is not a clearly bounded phenomenon, but is anchored in a variable arrangement of models and paradigms, or as Giddens would say, a system of time-space constraints (customs, traditions, rules, laws, knowledges, technologies).

Sociability, on the other hand, is not directly rooted in the received or imposed societal models and structures, but emerges idiosyncratically in the forms of intersubjectivity which evolve from infancy. These fragile and volatile forms are cautiously extended to wider circles of acquaintance and more complex ('institutional') forms of interaction, often with partial retreats, or without success at all. It is on this uncertain trajectory that the 'social' acquires its traditional association with immediacy, intensity and personality. Of course, the relationship between the social and the societal is always a relative one. The 'social', with its emphasis on the interaction of internal worlds, and on the narrative construction of interpersonal continuities of relationship, gradually shades over and disappears into the 'societal', which is essentially Durkheimian in character (and therefore qualitatively different from the social in the sense that I have defined it). The social is the proximal realm of *ad hoc* semantic experience, organized around moments underdetermined by the 'rules' of behaviour. The societal, on the other hand, is the distal realm of 'abstract systems', 'collective representations', codes, structures, norms, constraints, all institutions which are usually confused, in social scientific theory, with the concept of the social. In modern parlance, the societal consists of the 'languages' of collective *order*, of Baudrillard's object system, and the political economy of the sign.

Given this heuristic distinction, Baudrillard's seemingly preposterous and paradoxical declaration of the 'end of the social' (notably in *In the Shadow of the Silent Majorities*) makes perfectly ordinary sense. When he speculates that there may indeed be no such thing as a 'social' relation (*Shadow* 70–1), that the 'social' is nothing but the organized and mobilized residue of symbolic exchange (72), he is referring to what we have agreed to call the 'societal'. When he theorizes the immense chasm separating the political class of professionals and intellectuals from the societies they claim to 'represent', or interprets the historical evolution of modern politics from Machiavelli to the media (15–19), he is describing the systematic accumulation of these self-governing societal forms, and their gradual (now decisive) disconnection from social relations (the proximal realm still organized around the body).

What makes Baudrillard's argument so complex is his recognition that this distal realm of structures, languages and abstract environments is acquiring, through the penetrating integration of the technosphere, a social power of immediacy (hyperreality) sufficient to challenge the body as the site of symbolic expressivity (the social). Premodern symbolic cultures were all based on a dimorphic interpretation of the body. They consisted of elaborate instruction manuals for interpreting and living the content of life and the cosmos in a dichotomous existential mode. Modernity has reduced the binary structure of primitive thought to the purely formal principle of the digital code, under whose regime every mythic opposition can be neutralized into an infinite gradation of differences on a continuum. Hyperrealism arises from the fact that the digital reconstruction of events is often more coherent and more convincing than organic body perception normally permits or expects. Without technology, the body cannot generate a sufficient variety of experience, above or below the biological parameters of the senses, nor a sufficient distance from experience, to override the fundamental organizing principle of all animal social behaviour – which is to ascribe moral content (modelled on edible inedible, friend foe, fight flight, dominate submit, good bad) to any perception of contrast notable enough to invite deliberation. The philosophical and social dualisms of mind body, white black, good evil, male female, subject object are all residues of this primitive mode of mapping (Lévi-Strauss's 'pensée sauvage'), and they are vulnerable to modern technology. Technology (writing, psychoanalysis, film, information processing) imposes a safe enough distance from experience to suspend the categories of purity and danger, and permit (hyper)realistic re-examination.

Binary oppositions have often been described as forms of oppression belonging to modern Western civilization. In fact they are anachronisms left over from traditional symbolic cultures. The great mythic dualities are already in the process of being neutralized and marginalized by the digital formalism of liberal law and information technology. Duality no longer has any credible content for us, except in art, entertainment, and the politics of race and gender, which are the remnants of traditional morality in the modern age. Apart from these simulative forms, dualism is no longer lived out; it has been almost entirely reduced to the abstract, formal or diacritical differences between on off, true false, public private, present absent. The actual content of culture has been reduced to an endless continuum of equivalent ethnicities, sexualities, genders and identities, whose significance lies in the play of marginal differences which govern the world of sign objects. Baudrillard's vision of the social (i.e. societal) as the 'accumulation of death' (*Shadow* 73) is best understood in this context, and will be explored further in Chapter 19.

So far as the term 'culture' is concerned: it is hard to resist the observation that in the context of modernity, the broad, holistic definition of life as a system of existential dualities, which was carried along for a while by cultural anthropology, reaching its apogee in the structuralist revolution, now refers mainly to the most mediated and homogeneous aspect of our experience, namely, what the Frankfurt School described as the 'culture industry' and the world of mass communication – 'le degré Xerox de la culture' as Baudrillard has called it (*TM* 17; *TE* 9). Culture in the more local but still collective sense (as it might have applied to the Azande or some other 'tribe' or 'people') is simply no longer available to us in any cohesive and stable form. It is true, as the Anglo-American 'cultural studies' school of Marxism insists, that intensive collectivities can develop around 'popular culture' themes, that no degree of disembedding can preclude 'appropriation' by actual people into shared and defining experiences. But this kind of quasi-voluntaristic, 'cultural' intersubjectivity is highly volatile, and essentially individualistic in form. The group identity that may result has reference not to a life but to a phase, not to a 'community' but to a statistical or demographic 'cross-section', and is essentially adolescent in character (though it may occur at any time in the life span).

The other way in which the culture of modernity may have intersubjective meaning has to do with the opportunities created through distanciation, the openings formed within the anonymous societal matrix of hypermediated culture, for the cultivation and perpetuation of infantile forms of experience, which are extremely rich and intense, but normally coopted by traditional, more obtrusive forms of life. In archaic societies, the societies of symbolic exchange (which may be good examples of the 'panoptic'), eccentric self-development and exploration is supposedly more constrained, perhaps quite rare.[8] In the ancient empires of Asia and the Mediterranean basin, however, such postmodern scenarios of 'decadent' self-development were certainly fostered by combinations of wealth and cosmopolitan education – though not on the scale of contemporary modernity. As we shall see in the next chapter, the 'exoticism' of these parasitical urban cultures serves as a strategic model for sublimating the 'primitive' social symbolic of the infant body into the highly refined societal forms of civilized culture: what Baudrillard describes in terms of seduction, and the ritualized 'play of signs'.

SYMBOLIC EXCHANGE AS AFFECT

Particularly since *L'échange symbolique et la mort*, Baudrillard has confined his analysis of social processes to the abstract forms of culture, as is evident in the way that the play of the sign begins in his work to eclipse and finally to replace ideas about social relations, conflict and politics. In light of the foregoing, it is easier to see what might be meant by phrases like 'the black hole of the masses' or 'the end of the social'. From the beginning, Baudrillard has foregrounded the modernizing effects of abstraction and globalization, more recently discussed by Giddens as processes of 'disembedding' and the 'colonization of the future'. It is not at all implausible to think of the cultural experience of late modernity as an attempt to negotiate the widening gap between the social and the societal, between forms of intersubjectivity retracting into the sphere of the individual, and forms of society detaching from the sphere of intimacy altogether and panning out into various encompassing, self-governing, regulatory systems. (Of course, the traditional, social scientific and common-sense theories of 'society' continue to have their relevance: how else can one grasp the otherwise inexplicable right/left moral fervour generated by the decline of the coal industry in Britain, or the panic about 'national identity' and 'foreign investment' in regions such as North America, where these concepts are now virtually meaningless?)

If this 'postmodern' frame of reference is accepted, then we have a way of positioning the central theme in Baudrillard's work: from *Le système des objets* to *L'illusion de la fin* it has been about the splitting off of the affective part of social life from the societal dimension, and the ways and forms in which affects may resurface in the societal, with the inevitability of the 'return of the repressed'. Here, it matters little whether affects are conceived as part of some core sociability which is subsequently selected and moulded by 'culture', or whether one adopts the extreme constructionist and neo-Lacanian view, so popular today, that emotions are cultural by-products, entirely incommensurable and therefore deceptive as evidence of the human. Either way, Baudrillard's thesis that modernity systematically sharpens the split between affect and societal form can still be supported. The argument is that 'society' has become an increasingly system-like abstraction striving towards structural closure and 'perfection' in part by off-loading its affective social content: the so-called death of the social. The remainder is an unstructured, unintegrated 'mass', a split-off bundle of 'imploding' forces whose relation to the 'system' is precisely that of the 'repressed', poised for return.

In the early writings reviewed above, this perspective took the form of the political economy of the sign, where it was sufficient to theorize the 'ambivalence' of symbolic exchange as the 'other' of the value/sign form: as nothing more precise than that which exchange value excludes from the intersubjective mediation of objects. In this sense, the affective dimension of the primitive societal could be seen as something still intimately related to the social domain of affective, interpersonal being. It would then appear that we have stripped this away, leaving a husk of functional societal calculation, the 'passion for the code' and the manipulation–consumption of signs. The traditional societal forms of affective reciprocity and reversibility (what Victor Turner called the 'liminal' dimension of 'communitas') – feasts, festivals and rituals – are privatized, 'personalized', and stuffed back into the secretive individual 'unconscious', whose social aspect only survives in the form of the neurotic 'symptom'.[9] Baudrillard's critique of structural linguistics (*FCPES*) and of anthropology as ideology (*MP*) would then follow in logical order, since, as Eric Wolf has argued, semiolinguistic ethnographic models are really projections of our own social simulations back onto the primitive 'mind'.[10]

Baudrillard's conception of the symbolic as a reciprocal emotive form of sociability culminates in his famous critique of Western 'productivism'. Certainly radical, but with its echoes of Heideggerian antitechnological ontology, it is not so very different from the insights of an earlier hermeneutic sociology, which preached the incommensurability of cultural 'life worlds', as the following reflections of Peter Winch suggest (recall Mauss's 'total social phenomenon'):

In Zande magic . . . [social scientists] can see . . . only a misguided technique for producing consumer goods. But a Zande's crops are not just potential objects of consumption: the life he lives, his relations with his fellows, his chances for acting decently or doing evil, may all spring from his relation to his crops. Magical rites constitute a form of expression in which these possibilities and dangers may be contemplated and reflected on. . . . The difficulty we find in accepting this is not merely its remoteness from science, but an aspect of the general difficulty we find . . . of thinking about such matters at all except in terms of 'efficiency of production' – production, that is, for consumption. This again is a symptom of what Marx called the 'alienation' characteristic of man in industrial society, though Marx's own confusions about the relations between production and consumption are further symptoms of that same alienation.[11]

In *Symbolic Exchange and Death*, however, Baudrillard truly begins to enter a post-Marxian universe, what he had earlier called the 'cybernetic imaginary', the third order of simulation, where it is no longer possible to adopt a position marked by some term for the thing external to the system, a 'natural', outside the simulation process. Symbolic exchange, now understood more explicitly as the core of death, disorganization, or undecidability in every human construction, has become part of the system which abstracts it. Symbolic exchange no longer opposes, but interlaces, the play of signs. And the meaning of affect shifts in Baudrillard's discourse. It is no longer in the name of symbolic exchange as a primitive origin that Baudrillard writes, it is no longer the exclusive reference to ambivalence which supports his analysis. Not the concept of the affective, the symbolic, the ambivalent, but Baudrillard himself – his own ambivalence – grounds the project. This marks his definitive withdrawal from a critical sociological posture, and the emergence of something more like Bataille's 'expérience intérieure': 'les états d'extase, de ravissement, au moins d'émotions méditée. . . . Le rire dans les larmes. – La mise à mort de Dieu. . . .'[12] It is the accomplishment of Baudrillard's 'transcendental immersion', the hurling of the discursive self into the abyss of *Oublier Foucault, Simulations, Seduction, Fatal Strategies, The Ecstasy of Communication*,

America, *Cool Memories*. Baudrillard explores n trust and fear, but jealousy, envy, hatred, co euphoria, shock, disorientation, disappointment, r gloom, destructiveness, remorse, hope, curiosity. Th tone of his writing frequently relents, yielding a cube of c ment floating in a warm pool of grief and nostalgia. The worl out of its social scientific box and becomes phantasmagorical, vio-lent, paranoid, extreme.

THE SOCIAL POSITION OF AFFECT IN THE THREE ORDERS OF SIMULATION

> There are three orders of simulacra, running parallel to the successive mutations of the law of value since the Renaissance:
> – The *counterfeit* is the dominant schema in the 'classical' period, from the Renaissance to the Industrial Revolution.
> – *Production* is the dominant schema in the industrial age.
> – *Simulation* is the dominant schema in the current code-governed phase.
>
> The first-order simulacrum operates on the natural law of value, the second-order simulacrum on the market law of value, and the third-order simulacrum on the structural law of value. (*Death* 50)

Symbolic Exchange and Death attempts to trace and to characterize the progressive abstraction and generalization of affect through the 'three orders of simulacra': the repressive desublimation, or fetishization, of 'death'. Reciprocity is no longer simply an innocent exchange of the gift, but a challenge, a sacrifice, a mortal duel, a fatal reversal. The correlative of the discrete charm of the bourgeoisie was a noble savage; but the perfect operationality of the digital universe of cool simulation implies a much more catastrophic exclusion: what might be described as a 'pure culture of the death instinct', to borrow a phrase from Freud.[13] If the Azande have a symbolic relation to their crops, and the Nuer to their cattle, which binds together their personal relations, their morality, their spirituality, all in a transparent whole, the Azande or Nuer individual is bound there also, with his crops and cattle, in 'unbreachable reciprocity'. Baudrillard warns: If we start dreaming . . . of a world where signs are certain, of a strong 'symbolic order', we should have no illusions. Such an order once existed, but it was composed of ferocious hierarchies; the transparency of signs goes hand in hand with their cruelty. (*ESM* 78; *Death* 50)[14] It is of little consequence whether we interpret the blood and mutilation of ritual, sorcery and rivalry in 'stateless' societies as inscriptions of a

Durkheimian social order on the body, or as psychodynamic expressions of envy, fear and desire. The element of paranoid violence in the symbolic is proximal, vicious, terroristic – certainly projected, but not so disavowed, as is possible in the impersonality of digital systems and remote societal structures. In modern societies, with the dissolution of the feudal order and the 'emancipation of the sign', the consequences of affective proximity are progressively diluted and deferred in the widening scope of abstract systems, whose operational perfection is based on a 'profound denial'.

The sequence 'ritual–law–code' summarizes the developmental passage of the societal dimension in modernity (RLC 97–107). The affect-binding sacrificial rite, the cyclical rhythm, the festal reversibility of order and structure – all this ritual gives way to the intellectual dynamic of natural (or divine) law and transgression, to philosophically ordered, societal forms of religion and social exchange governed by the absolute: the principle of good and evil. The relation of affect to the social order starts to become one of psychic representation and repression, rather than public expression and constraint. Baudrillard correlates this 'first-order simulacrum' (or primary simulation) to the late Renaissance, linking it in art historical terms to a fundamental, governing distinction between the natural and the artificial, the authentic and the counterfeit. The dominant schema roughly parallels Foucault's 'Classical *episteme*', with its emphasis on representational correspondences, natural signs and verisimilitude.[15] But the 'stucco angel' is soon replaced with the 'Industrial Simulacrum', whose more explicitly conventional, commercial law of value we have already discussed (*Death* 50–7). The functional principle of this schema still refers formally to the properties of a subject, though no longer the Divine Creator (or humanistic subject) of a universe of natural law, where everything interconnects through metaphor and similarity. In the mechanical world of production and reproduction, the paradigmatic agent is a partial producer of relative values operating through media of conversion and equivalence. Relations are serial and metonymic, like the functional sequences and controlled repetitions of industrialized manufacture. According to Foucault's archaeology, this is the age of history, biology and economics, the era of the invention of 'Man', who will one day 'be erased, like a face drawn in sand at the edge of the sea'.[16] In Baudrillard's view, this has already happened; or at least, (re)production has been superceded by absolute simulation (the third order of simulacra, or tertiary simulation) in which the classical metaphysics of representation (epistemological, political, aesthetic) has given way to the hyperreality of the *code*, the pure fungibility of signs, in which the subject no longer represents, and is no longer signified: the subject *is* a signifier, or even just a signal generated by the digital scissiparity of a cybernetic matrix, like DNA (*Death* 57–61).

'Today, abstraction is no longer a question of maps, doubles, mirrors, or concepts, and simulation no longer relates to a territory, a referential being, or a substance. It is the generation by models of a real without origin or reality: the hyperreal' (*SS* 10). With the 'precession of simulacra', there logically follows a draining of the social into the societal forms of regulation and reproduction. We discover again, as in a spiral, the same strategy of critical analysis: the repressed content – the social – reconfigures as the legitimating projection of the repressing form. Like the referential quality of the signified, and the natural aura of use value,

> [the social] serves as a universal alibi for every discourse, no longer analyses anything, no longer designates anything. Wherever it appears it conceals something else: defiance, death, seduction, ritual, repetition – it conceals that it is only abstraction and residue, or even simply an *effect* of the social, a simulation and an illusion. (*Shadow* 66)

Baudrillard still writes in terms of the social; but given the deritualization and disembedding of its cultural content, he can only lament its passing as a significant other. Society ceases to be the locus of an objective crisis, and the concept of the social has become little more than an alibi for politics and social theory. Social science reads more and more like the institutionalized version of the Machiavellian factions, vying for control of the political (societal) agenda.

> Out of this involutive sphere [of the 'mass'] which is opposed to all revolution from the top and refuses to play the [political] game, some would like to make a new source of revolutionary energy (in particular in its sexual and desire version). . . . They would like . . . to reinstate it . . . as historical negativity. Exaltation of micro-desires, small differences, unconscious practices, anonymous marginalities. Final somersault of the intellectuals to exalt insignificance, to promote non-sense into the order of sense. (*Shadow* 40)

After the splitting off of affect and the final separation of social being and societal form, there really is nothing left to discuss but theoretical models and their correlative violence, a kind of pataphysics in which the analysis finally disappears into its own chronic self-preoccupation, not really a social crisis, but the crisis of theory itself: a sort of precession of poststructuralism.

13

The metaphysical ambience: a prelude to fatal strategies

We have the feeling that philosophical discourse is exhausted, that it can only reproduce itself in different forms, in different combinations. What does this closure consist of? . . . it's nothing like death, or the end, but an opportunity. And if this is called philosophy, then I think that philosophy not only has a future but that it *is* only if there is a future, if non-anticipatible events lie ahead. . . . That's what provokes thought. (Derrida)[1]

My aim has been to show how art has been the means to philosophy at both ends of its history. . . . [I]n transforming itself into its own object, it transformed the whole of culture. . . . Asked what artist we might breed for, my answer is, those with the keen sense of play that survival in the artworld now demands. The more important question is what philosophers to breed for, and my answer is, those who can give us the philosophy that art has prepared us for. (Danto)[2]

Although Baudrillard has been deeply influenced by Marx, Nietzsche, Sartre, and many other seminal thinkers (notably Bataille), there is woven into the background of his thought a kind of metaphysical ambience which is characteristic of his time, in significant measure due to his own influence on it. The following is a blended narrative exposition of this ambience – poststructuralist or postmodern – loosely combining strands from Kojève (Hegel), Heidegger, Bataille, Horkheimer and Adorno, among others. Virtually any passage of Baudrillard's writing can be related back to the themes compressed into this chapter.

IMMANENCE OF BEING

Man is part of an immanent immensity; but the advent of consciousness allows Man to posit the dimension of experience as a mere property of his existence rather than as the substance *tout court* of Being as such. Thus, sentience attenuates, or splits, into the form of a polarity, an opposition in which an observing ego, a kind of prosthetic 'identity', hovers between some residue of the immanent self and a world of discrete, functional objects. The latter is the profane world of practical reality. The positing of the object establishes this practial plane of existence as the domain of consciousness, but in so doing, it also makes the problem of transcendence inevitable. Prior to consciousness of the object, there was no subject, only the Bergsonian flow of immanence, 'durée', the animal in the world like water in water;[3] but on the plane of practical existence, the object in a sense *transcends* this flow: it is raised up through abstraction, delimited, or, as Saussure said of the linguistic sign, 'découpé'. The object has become clear and specific, a figure of consciousness, and in that way *alien* to the undifferentiated continuity, or Husserlian *hylé*, of the self immersed in pure immanence. This object of consciousness is the seed of manufacture and science – Heidegger's dreaded 'technology', and the awful, degraded quality of politics. But first it is the point of human emergence. One might think of it as a kind of primary repression, but in that perspective, it is also the beginning of the end of Man. For it is starting from the axiom of the object as the figure of consciousness that the human subject can be seen as the secondary effect or the by-product of the profane world of practical life.

The doctrine of intentionality holds that there must be a subject in order to posit an object, and the mysticism of quantum indeterminacy supports this notion. But in a deeper sense, no subject can be posited without an object: the object creates the space-time of thought, and its ontic discreteness (its 'readiness at hand', as Heidegger might say) serves as the model for the social individual, as both agency and entity – as a thing that wills. Because the thing that wills cannot exist without the object, the individual subject must labour to sustain the object, must will and intend the object, trimming its borders, and cultivating its abstraction, merely in order to survive (as subject). This is, at bottom, an anal project, which Freud described, in *Civilization and its Discontents*, as the essence of civilization, like the Tuileries.

Thus, in a crucial sense, the intentional subject serves the object world even as he or she subdues it into neat rows of edible produce. Human servitude is never merely passive: the subject stalks the object, kills it, dresses it, and consumes it. Eventually, with the command structures of the neolithic revolution (agriculture-based settlements), the subject begins to sew and reap the object, to represent the object, and even to store it and to circulate it. The subject always possesses and destroys the object it serves.

According to Kojève, Hegel saw this pattern of dependent consumption as the very movement of human desire, which is *negation*. 'The I of Desire is an emptiness that receives a real positive content only by negating action that satisfies Desire in destroying, transforming, and "assimilating" the desired non-I.'[4] To understand Baudrillard, however, we should bear in mind that Hegelian negation was long considered the essence of critical thought. Dialectical negation was the power of the subject over the facticity of the object. It constituted intelligent judgement. This interpretation of Hegel presupposed a subject-centred view of the world in which the subject is a primary substance which 'posits' the object and then 'contemplates' it, and then finally negates the object as a mere projection of itself. But on Bataille's account, following Nietzsche, the object is only posited by consciousness to the extent that the object creates a mental space for the subject. And if we follow Kojève, the subject does not produce the object: before anything else, the subject *consumes* it. Therefore, where negation appears to produce contradiction, to generate movement and differentiation, this is only true in a secondary sense. For there to be differentiation and production, a prior moment of consumption is always required, and production is always a form of consumption.

This corresponds to Baudrillard's main thesis on early modernity, namely that the Enlightenment attempted to mask this relationship, to invert it so that production would precede consumption in the manner of cause and effect (1973). He calls this a 'second-order simulacrum'. In fact, as Baudrillard argues, there is no relation of cause and effect between these terms, although consumption, like entropy, may be more powerful in the long term. In protest against the influence of Hegel, Gilles Deleuze tried to define Desire as the opposite of dialectical negation, embracing the myth of production as pure positivity and phallic presence.[5] Baudrillard had always wanted to follow up his *Mirror of Production* with a *Mirror of Desire* that would comment on this move, but he wrote *Seduction* instead (*Live* 58). He knew that social criticism, such as his own, from the point of view of 'symbolic exchange', or that of Deleuze, from the point of view of 'desiring production', is basically a sophisticated (disembedded or deterritorialized) modern form of consumption.

But this 'positing or production of the object', saturated though it is with myth and self-delusion, has had far-reaching consequences in human history. Horkheimer and Adorno called it the 'dialectic of enlightenment'. The price of the ego is the suppression of the self, the renunciation of Bataille's immanent continuum – what Heidegger called 'the forgetting of Being'. According to Horkheimer and Adorno, this positing of the object by the ego is 'a denial of nature in man for the sake of domination over non-human nature and over other men . . .'.[6] While appearing to control the practical world, the human being secretly toils in servitude to the discrete object which he or she manipulates. Again, the abstraction of the object sustains the abstraction of the ego. But the ego denies even this primary repression of immanent Being, and tries to displace the domination of the self in an orgy of domination over nature. The history of modern Europe seems to demonstrate that Enlightenment Reason will always in its ultimate effects reproduce the demonic forces it sought to master, because Enlightenment is in its essence only the symptomatic modern expression of *instrumental* reason, which objectifies nature (posits the discrete object) in order to consume and destroy it, whilst all the time remaining a slave to it, repressing in its name the internal 'instinctual' nature of immanent being.

In *The Phenomenology of Spirit*, Hegel understood subjectivity in precisely this way: as an ambivalent struggle between mastery and slavery as conditions of sentient existence. In that sense, the famous 'master–slave dialectic' is a paradigm of psychic conflict as well as a model of social history. What connects Baudrillard to Hegel, through Bataille and Thorstein Veblen, is the fact that this battle is neither for survival nor for property, but for prestige pure and simple. For Baudrillard, as we have seen, invidious distinction always takes precedence over needs and use values in social life. Hegel's Desire 'negates' the 'thing' quality of the given, yet finds in the thing it destroys its only mirror: it sees in the thing how it goes beyond the thing, how it differs from what it is. But this self-reflection is the mute and blind opacity of a thing; it is not true 'Self-Consciousness'. It there are two things in the world, Desire and the Thing, Desire wants something more: the mirror of Desire itself. To *transcend* the 'thingish' quality of the ego, Desire desires another's Desire, the Desire of the Other, as Lacan would say.

> [T]o desire the Desire of another is in the final analysis to desire that the value that I am or that I 'represent' be the value desired by the other: I want him to 'recognize' my value as his value. . . . In other words, all human, anthropogenetic Desire – the Desire that generates self-consciousness, the human reality – is, finally, a function of the desire for 'recognition'. . . . Therefore, to speak of the 'origin' of Self-Consciousness is necessarily to speak of a fight to the death for 'recognition'.[7]

But there is a catch in this logic; for if the victor is to secure the other's recognition, he cannot kill his adversary, since that would extinguish the very Desire he desires. The alternative is to enslave him. The loser survives as the Slave, but not primarily in order to provide the Master with the fruits of his labour; much more fundamentally, the Slave supplies the Master with prestige. Otherwise the Master would have finished him off. Of course, along with prestige will come economic and political power; but (as Baudrillard points out) the latter will be meaningless without recognition, which is *symbolic* power.

There have been many interpretations of Hegel's 'master–slave', the most notable being Marx's theory of history as class conflict. The emphasis on the symbolic dimension of the conflict owes much to Lacan and Bataille, who attended Kojève's lectures on the eve of the Second World War. The symbolic line of interpretation culminates in Baudrillard's *Symbolic Exchange and Death*, which substantially completed his reflections on political economy and sociology, and set the tone for the rest of his work.

According to Baudrillard, the historical evolution of Capital and wage labour has not fundamentally changed the underlying symbolic structure of human society; although it did succeed in masking that structure sufficiently, during the great era of industrialization, to make the rediscovery of the symbolic in the 'post-industrial' age something of a surprise. The period of urban industrial 'massification' generated a strong atmosphere of economic realism, in the sense that planning and organizing the production and distribution of goods seemed to be central functions, powerful expressions of what is most fundamental to existence in the real world. Politics could be about something 'real', something other than the status function of an hereditary elite manipulating the symbols of power. The illusions of tribal and religious societies had been swept aside by the Enlightenment, to reveal the objective basis of 'material' human history. And now for the first time, the previously diverted majority could assess its real economic interests, and debate its real future, and work for real change, on the basis of objective knowledge about what actually counts in the material world.

It is certainly possible to argue that the industrial age is still with us. In Baudrillard's perspective, however, the objectivist constellation of social thought described above – in which politics was based on a conception of real universal good – was already under some strain in the nineteenth century: the 'simulacrum of the second order', the 'order of the real', was perhaps too logical to withstand the pressure of its own critical energy. We have already become tangled up in third-order levels of simulation, the order of the hyperreal, although it is easy to believe that we still have some strong connection to the previous order. We are deceived by the fact that the symbolic content of the hyperreal is largely derived from the previous simulacrum, the fading universe of ideology, solidarity, revolution, liberation, and the satisfaction of needs and desires. The hyperrealization of the second-order values and projects is certainly evident on the discursive plane: the naturalism of Rousseau and Marx has fallen into disfavour, yet the ideas of liberty, equality and solidarity burn brighter than ever, like supernova. The discourses of the real do seem to be turning more and more inwards; and the terms of the Enlightenment no longer have any index of justification outside themselves: they can only will themselves into 'virtual' being through Constitutions and referenda (see Chapter 22). There is widespread distrust, if not outright repudiation, of the traditional constituents of the real: the substances, essences, references and foundations that once grounded the terms of debate. Yet all these avatars of 'reality' persist as frank constructions, rotating in permanent orbit.

How does the symbolic re-emerge from behind the occluding presence of the real? Baudrillard suggests the example of work. In the present 'simulacrum of the third order', work is one of the rapidly dissolving touchstones of truth. Not so long ago, in the heyday of the second order, labour was the essence of the real, a sort of materialist eucharist in which tangible 'nature' was transformed through efficacious techniques into solid value. But (as in the current period of history) labour was not always so 'concrete'. It was typically an aspect of bondage in the classical world, and of course, a Judeo-Christian curse for the sins of the pre-Lapsarians. In Europe, it gradually became an ascetic ideal, an inspired act of devotion rewarded with spiritual privilege and social status. Soon, the power of labour outstripped the power of God to build paradise on earth. Marx's proletarians were the true creators of human well-being. What made them social heroes, in spite of their immiseration, was the realness, the fundamental, bottom-layer concreteness, of the labour with which they literally shaped the material world. The Stakhanovite vision of Stalinist propaganda reflected the fact that Hegel's slave was expected eventually to surpass his master through labour: the labour would temper his character in the direct struggle with nature, and realize his inner potential through the expressive act of self-objectification. The vulgarity of this socialist realism should not blind us to the fact that all the modern democratic elites practise the same morality, deriving from their professional skill and devotion to work the prestige and status afforded in classical times to the leisured classes.

Baudrillard's interpretation of work turns on the radical intuition that the moral significance of work in modern societies has a parasitic relation to the traditional symbolic social form of gift economies. Through its measure as value in exchange, work masquerades as a term in a reciprocal relationship. In fact, this impression of reciprocity is only an illusion, but not for the reasons that Marx gave. The deception of the worker does not lie merely in the concealed extraction of surplus value (the worker gives more value in labour than he or she receives in exchange value), but more fundamentally in the falseness or non-reciprocity of the symbolic relationship which work introduces into the social body. According to Baudrillard, the Trojan Horse or virus of the capitalist labour relation lies in the value relation generally rather than its particular form as surplus value (see Chapter 14). Surplus value involves a numerical inequality, but value as such introduces a basic alteration of social being. The reason is that the value form imposes an abstract (but ideologically naturalized) form of obligation on all the members of society. The concept of value is an abstraction from the symbolic obligation to return the recognition implied in the gift. As a free floating sign liberated from the nexus of symbolic exchange, value permits arbitrary manipulation of the principle of reciprocity so as to induce, but not to share, a bond. This is the form of the contract. It transmutes reciprocity into the concept of equivalence. Equivalence is potentially free of the symbolic social bond of mutual recognition, because it can be centrally organized and accumulated, and distributed as a form of obligation which does not recognize the personal being of those who enter into relation with it. Everyone who enters into a relationship of exchange with the value form exits the House of Being and commits himself to a relationship of obligation with a Stranger who has no Name and who cannot ever be repaid.[8]

For Marx, the master takes more value than he gives, which implies that value is something that we could all share equally, if only we chose the right kind of political economy (socialism). For Baudrillard, the master gives more value than can ever be returned, which implies that political economy is the institution of non-reciprocity itself (modernity). For Marx, as is well known from his description of the relationship of exploitation, the master capitalist uses Capital to suck value from the worker. For Baudrillard, there is no relation of exploitation; there is a redefinition of social being. Value itself becomes the master, an otherworldly being, a societal projection which accumulates outside the range of social encounter and interpersonal recognition.

In *Symbolic Exchange and Death*, Baudrillard illustrates this point of view through an analysis of the political rhetoric of 'job creation' and the 'gift' of work. The State will *provide* you with a job, the Corporation will *offer* employment to the community. According to Baudrillard, all this is a sham, because it can never be reciprocated. What is offered is not a gift in a cycle of symbolic exchange, but an act of domination in which the recipient is compelled to submit to the controlling logic of the donor, without hope of redeeming the debt. This is the 'vampire' theory of Capital we shall encounter in Chapter 19: to work is in this context to accept subordination, though not symbolic submission to destiny, fate, necessity or desire, but functional submission to abstract systems or the 'state' of things, Capital and the logic of 'growth' for its own sake.

Hegel's dialectic of lordship and bondage held out a false promise: its truth lay in the symbolic moment, the moment of recognition, when the Lord spares his opponent, in order to secure his own prestige. The lie was in the false destiny of the slave, that through work he could eventually redeem himself, and triumph over the Master. The promise of liberation is false because the Master has 'saved' the bondsman's life. This is a gift that can never be returned, except through ingratitude – if the slave turns the tables, and spares the master's life – or through his own death. And that is precisely the symbolic significance of labour in our own time, according to Baudrillard: slow death, the gradual extraction of the spared life, in the name of state and society.

The notion of labour as a stay of execution whose symbolic significance is the recognition of the 'master's' worth and 'power' (but today there is no master, only the 'system' or the 'code' in which we are all immersed together) shows the lineaments of Bataille's economics of expenditure, the conceptions of general and restricted economy. The second-order simulacrum attempts to fulfil the closed system teleology of the restricted economy, in which everything can be accounted for. Exchange occurs only against a standard of equivalence into which everything conceivable is also convertible. The concept of labour within the restricted economy – that is, the *hubris* of the production of objective values – is an idealization of the negativity that founds the ego in its posit(ion)ing of the discrete object: the I survives by 'destroying, transforming, and "assimilating" the non-I'. In short, the materialism of labour is really the idealism of consumption: it is a masking of all that is violent, excessive, destructive and sacrificial in life, the exclusion of death, and therefore of eroticism as well, from the 'normal society' which shuns immanence in favour of the calculated risk of 'earning a living'. Sensorimotor immanence is converted into abstract transcendence, and made practical in the form of universal equivalence.

Of course, modernity has exhibited a crude form of Lordship, which finds a symbolic enemy for ritual execution, and spares the remainder, to work for the state (Hitler, Stalin, Pol Pot). But the modern ideal has been the elimination of Lordship through conversion to the 'invisible hand' of the market, or other impersonally functioning, self-regulating systems, such as electronic security, deterrence, the rule of law and various Constitutions. But even in the absence of Lordship, the logic of bondage persists: 'free' labour remains a form of death; it is a death that is never noticed, because all the sacral elements of destruction through transcendence have been purged, leaving over an objective entropy which is indistinguishable from the natural course of life. Behind the restricted economy, the general economy looms – and this Bataillean figure serves as Baudrillard's 'return of the repressed'.

For Bataille, sacrifice in a general economy is not intended to annihilate the victim, but to destroy the 'thing' quality in the victim, so that the priest or Lord and his audience can transcend the ego of consciousness:

> Sacrifice destroys an object's real ties of subordination; it draws the victim out of the world of utility and restores it to that of unintelligible caprice. . . . Of course, this is a monologue and the victim can neither understand nor reply. Sacrifice essentially turns its back on real relations. . . . It could not destroy the animal without denying the animal's objective *reality*. . . . The return to immanent intimacy implies a beclouded consciousness: consciousness is tied to the positing of objects as such, grasped directly, apart from a vague perception, beyond the always unreal images of a thinking based on participation.[9]

Sacrifice freezes the measurable time of utility in an instant of intimacy, whose 'measureless violence' reveals 'the *invisible* brilliance of life that is not a *thing*', because 'life's intimacy does not reveal its dazzling consumption until the moment it gives out. . . . Death reveals life in its plenitude and dissolves the real order.'[10]

From this perspective, it is not difficult to grasp Baudrillard's point, that wage labour is a compromise formation, in which living, violent and immediate, is given up in exchange for the planned deferral of its final moment. The consequences of the sacred are avoided in return for servitude in the world of piecemeal consumption. Of course, labour itself is a kind of sacrifice, a relinquishment in which living is reduced to practical calculation. But this profane penance is not a sacrifice in the sense of an offering up to some higher, irrational principle, but an attempt to decoy the principle itself. So measured and paced is the loss involved in labour that it turns into its opposite, a gain, through profit and accumulation. Instead of relinquishing what is useful, as in a sort of potlatch, thus confirming a value deeper than domestication, sacrificial labour aims to convert the surplus, the devil's share (*la part maudite*), into excess utility.

The essence of the restricted economy is to harness the general one, to convert the entropy of life reduced to labour into fixed objects and practical values, use values, exchange values, productive technology and capital. The excess utility of political economy can be related to Marx's category of 'fixed capital', that is, to the so-called living labour stored up (and thus 'dead') in physical plant and productive machinery. Marx foresaw that the ratio of fixed capital (dead labour) would steadily increase, until eventually it would exceed, or 'dominate', living labour. He was convinced that this would place a terminal squeeze on profit margins, since he believed that surplus value was derived from living labour alone, whose ratio in the organic composition of capital would inevitably fall in relation to dead labour (science and technology). That trend and the concomitant pauperization of the labour force (in order to siphon off more profit) would lead to 'explosions, cataclysms, crises', for 'Capital works towards its own dissolution as the form dominating production.'[11] At the point of dissolution, Marx believed that the State would take over, and capitalism would become socialism. Through a sort of 'historical somersault' (*ESM* 30), production would somehow turn itself inside out, the State would wither away, and all the accumulated dead labour would rise up and join the living in a celebration of wealth and freedom.

In fact, real wages under capitalism have steadily risen, and the crises, traumatic as they have been, do not compare to the sheer disaster – in every conceivable measure: economic, social, environmental, cultural, spiritual, and legal – of the fully funded experimental alternatives undertaken in Marx's name. Yet Baudrillard, deeply sceptical about socialism, was nevertheless prepared to accept Marx's central hypothesis that 'capital works towards its own dissolution', though on the quite different grounds that it works too well. The problem with capitalism is not that it fosters contradictions, but that it eliminates them; not that it fails to produce what it promises, but precisely the opposite: Capital delivers the goods, usually on time, and generally in sufficient quantity. Baudrillard states the problem in mythic and metaphoric terms, with the justification that there is no rational and determinate account of the way in which rational systems are affected by the irrational elements they attempt to exclude. As the system of political economy grows top-heavy with dead labour, its sheer maintenance requirements begin to exceed the available resources, and to devour its own capacity to sustain living forms.

The limit of the system is not mere inefficiency, not 'human error', nor some fantastic, sacrificial suicide, such as may have afflicted the Mayan civilization, or the Xosa tribesmen who declared war on their white rulers, and destroyed their own cattle and crops in the belief that this would raise ancestors from the dead to fight as invincible warriors in the great battle of liberation.[12] The limit of the system lies in the very perfection of the system itself, since this perfection is congealed with the deferred and repressed death of practical reason, with its frightened ego, clinging to the consciousness of the discrete object, deferring the moment of truth, when all founders in the passionate embrace of the 'accursed share'.

The concept of fatality which Baudrillard will develop in the wake of these arguments can refer, as do the connotations of the word itself, to injury and to fate in the sense of destiny. Our excursion into heterological metaphysics so far makes it clear that the sense of fatality in our culture has been shaped in part by the Hegelian concept of work, and its inflection by Marx. To complete our preliminary metaphysical portrait of the age, we must now turn to the speculation of Heidegger, who is the preeminent intellectual authority in this century to endorse the theme of technology as human catastrophe.

Heidegger's whole philosophy depends upon the hypothesis that an unnatural split occurred in human thinking between 'Being', in the ontological sense, and beings (or mere phenomena), in what he calls the 'ontic' sense. He thematizes this split as the destiny of 'Western metaphysics', which has 'forgotten' the 'question of Being' (i.e. the ontological) and lost itself in the myopic scrutiny of mere things. Heidegger sometimes characterizes this whole Western trajectory as 'productionist metaphysics', a conception which is clearly developed in *Mirror of Production* and *Symbolic Exchange and Death*, whose general arguments we have just been reviewing. Indeed, for Heidegger, Hegel and Marx discovered not the progress of *Geist*, or of humanity through production, as they each in turn had claimed, but rather the accelerating pace of the degeneration which has been unfolding ineluctably since the 'self-concealment of Being' in Plato's 'ontic' metaphysics.

Heidegger's thesis has proved extremely resilient, capable of spreading with minimal cultivation, in part because any possible objection to it can be refuted on the grounds that it is only an ontic consideration, perhaps valid, but certainly irrelevant (such as the problem of Heidegger's espousal of Nazism); whereas the truth of Heidegger's thought lies precisely in its grasp of the *ontological* dimension, the question of Being, which lies beyond such mundane concerns. If the epistemological split between Being and beings is challenged, we are simply referred back by Heidegger scholars to the 'history of Western metaphysics', as expounded by Heidegger himself, whose authority on this point is unassailable.

The 'question of technology', as Heidegger puts it, should not be approached in terms of particular techniques, but of the *Gestell* in which 'Western metaphysics' plays out its Lapsarian programme, from Plato to the present, in the form of planetary domination by instrumental reason. This scenario can be related to Nietzsche's story of nihilism, but retold in such a way that Nietzsche's 'will to power' itself represents a culminating moment of metaphysics on its way towards pure willing, the sheer will to will, or instrumentality as an end in itself. In its most dire contemporary version, the ends of humanity have been reduced by nihilism to non-negotiable copulation with technology, where the terms are set by the technological programme itself, and human societies serve as the 'sex organs' of the machine world (McLuhan). For some, there is a hopeful moment in all this, for it permits visions of the parthenogenetic omnipotence of the 'cyborg', a kind of prosthetic political agency capable of transcending all the bad things about the Western culture which produced it;[13] for others it ends disastrously in the apotheosis of the automated killing machine and the destruction of the planet.

14

Metaphysical accounting: the costs of value

Value is residue. . . . It is this remainder that we accumulate, we speculate on the remainder, and that is where the economic is born. (*Death* 200–1)

Baudrillard's attempt to draw an analogy between the system of objects and linguistic philosophy was not unique in the post-structuralist era, but it was arguably subtler and bolder than many such attempts. The point of his analogy was not to preserve and strengthen either Marxism or structuralism, but to dissolve them into something other than themselves, into a 'différance' whose terms of equivalence (linguistics, sociology, political economy) were symbolically cancelled. Instead of reproducing Marx's critique of political economy in structuralist terms, as did Althusser, Kristeva, Goux, and many others at that time, Baudrillard dreamed up a whole new 'critique of the critique' in which the categories themselves were radically transformed.

In *For a Critique of the Political Economy of the Sign*, Baudrillard adumbrated a theory of modernity as a 'system of generalized exchange' in which all of human history appears as a progressive, increasingly rapid translation of embodied experience into terms of value which can be converted, exchanged, processed, consumed and reproduced – a kind of 'liberation' of existence, permitting unrestricted selection and transformation of elements from a universal combinatory of possible phenomena.

The media of this generalized system of exchange are the forms of equivalence which cover any particular field of existence, permitting combination and conversion of any values in that field. In the domain of political economy, the form of equivalence is exchange value. In (Saussurian) linguistics, it is the signifier. In electronically mediated communication – telegraph, telephone, radio, television – it is the message, measured in units of information, which in turn can be measured in bits. In biology, it is the nucleotide sequences which make up the genetic code in DNA. Baudrillard hypothesized that all these forms of equivalence are gradually converging, that they are already beginning to intersect with one integrated circuit, and that this coaxial movement has appeared early, and symptomatically, in the convergence of the commodity and the sign – yielding the 'political economy of the sign'.

The rise of the political economy of the sign in the nineteenth century was accompanied by the projection of a kind of utopian model of life which envisioned an indefinite reappropriation of the forms of experience converted by the economy into equivalent values. For example, political economy traditionally saw exchange value as a convenient measure of the real utilities (or use values) made available for the satisfaction of real needs. But, according to Baudrillard, the utopian versions of political economy are based on a misunderstanding. The need and the utility mediated by exchange value are not original patterns of experience or authentic natural values whose essential being or original social meaning will be recovered once the intervening form of equivalence is stripped away. They *are* themselves reductive abstractions of experience, inseparable from the forms of equivalence necessary for the institution of a system of convertible values. Without the system of exchange value, the concepts of need and use value would be almost meaningless.

The same general consideration applies to the categories of structural linguistics and information theory. As language philosophy has tended to show, the 'exchange value' (readability, iterability) of the signifier depends a great deal on convention. But this celebrated feature of language – what Saussure described as the 'arbitrary' relationship between the signifier and the signified – conceals a much deeper indeterminacy at the heart of language. The common-sense view has been that the problem of conventionality more or less stops at the level of the sign: either the signified (the value transmitted by means of the signifier) limits the caprice of the signifier, by locating a feature which transcends cross-linguistic variations; or, if the arbitrariness of the signifier infiltrates the signified somewhat, by carving up the 'real' in arbitrary ways, then the authentic underlying values circulated through the language system can be determined through specification of the referent, which supposedly can be located outside the logic of the sign. (Saussure's example of this problem was to compare the French 'mouton' [both an animal and an edible meat] with the English 'mutton' [one would never serve roast sheep for dinner].)

Of course, if the arbitrariness of the signifier can extend to the whole of the sign, engulfing the signified as well, then the relation of the sign to the referent may also be susceptible to the indeterminacy of conventional systems, rendering perception itself arbitrary, and 'reality' a matter of convention. Although Baudrillard developed specific aspects of this familiar argument into a general theory of simulation, his original point was to *distinguish language from meaning* (a quite different and not so familiar argument). He wanted to show that modern semantics has involved us in a kind of formalist delusion which has nothing to do with meaning but serves instead to underwrite the reduction of language to an abstract system of value, just as utility serves as an 'alibi' for the system of exchange value in the commodity system (*FCPES* 143–63; *Death* 6f.). The signified and the referent are no more authentic than needs and use values. For Baudrillard, it is misleading to think that one can appropriate 'meaning' by converting the linguistic sign value (which is arbitrary) back into an authentic experience, or that one can reappropriate natural semantic values by neutralizing the language medium. The concept of 'signified' (or 'referent') cannot be separated from its role as a 'functional simulacrum' serving the progressive abstraction of formal language systems.

For Baudrillard, the semantic dimension exists in the moment or process of its destruction. This view is hard to grasp, and we shall be returning to the point frequently. Meaning in the sense which Baudrillard distinguishes from information and 'semiolinguistic' signification (as he initially opposed the symbolic to the sign), only arises in a highly restricted context which is immediately subject to cancellation. Anything else (such as the 'unlimited accumulation' of signs, for example through systems of writing, the stockpiling of 'information' in databanks, and so on) does not involve meaning so much as production and signification, which tend to exclude meaning, in the same way that the object system disembeds the symbolic object and converts it into the formalized media of equivalence characteristic of 'sign-exchange value', or the generalized commodity system.

In the Baudrillardian universe, the semantic dimension, or meaning, has nothing to do with the real or the artificial, the conventional or the natural: it is at best a kind of illusive emergent property, an interplay of experience and affect, which Baudrillard describes as the 'ambivalence' of social bodies in 'symbolic exchange'. Among these ambivalent social bodies we shall discover, with Baudrillard, the trembling body of *jouissance* (which is not the same as 'satisfaction' or 'gratification' – Lacan), the violent body of sacrifice (which is not the same as moral responsibility – Bataille), the unconscious body of seduction (which has nothing to do with discovering the real desires of the true self), the futile body of destruction (not consumption), the tormented body of loss (as opposed to accumulation), the fatal body of perversion and distortion (not liberation), and, implicitly, the *foetal* body of the prelinguistic infant in aesthetic encounter with the alterity of its own carnal experience.[1]

Interpreting the concept of value in its most general and inclusive sense, we might then say that, for Baudrillard, modern history organizes and rationalizes experience, as we live and destroy it, encounter and lose it, into an objectified system. The system translates 'moments' of experience into a form which can be preserved, studied and accumulated. The value forms converging into the general system of equivalence convert aspects of human sociability (e.g. perceptions, sensations, affects, transferences) into modalities which are easily stabilized, transported and exchanged. (For further elaboration of this point, regarding simulation as a system of cultural communication, see Chapter 20.) From this point of view, signification and utility can be interpreted as correlatives of the formal or technological exteriorization of the semantic body. It follows from this kind of reasoning, at least as a possibility, that the ultimate historical result of the translation of experience into value may well be the disembodiment and deplanetization of the human species, as described, for example, in William Burroughs's vision of human evolution from the worldly medium of time into the 'virtually weightless' condition of outer-space, out-of-body extension.[2]

A certain affinity between Baudrillard's theorizing of 'ecstatic' forms of reification and the ethos of 'cyberpunk' and the cyborg has been well documented in recent studies.[3] Nevertheless, as Gane has argued, the association (in the English-speaking world) of Baudrillard with postmodernism involves 'something of a misunderstanding'.[4] Baudrillard was at first less interested in the progressive potentials of rationalization and liberalization (which Marx recognized) than in the consequent suppression of ambivalence and the destruction of symbolic exchange as a form of life. He has continued to see the archaic influence of these symbolic forms (the obligation to cancel accumulation through reciprocal exchange or ritual destruction[5]) as the only means of escaping the logic of value, of 'exterminating' the terms which make up the polarities of the sign (the signifier and the signified) and the commodity (exchange value and use value). The spirit of the *hau* principle, with its magical, Talion-like rule of symbolic reciprocity and reversibility, still dominates his thinking. For Baudrillard, in contrast to the linear directionality of Western time, all that is done can and must be undone (including his own theories). He has never abandoned the sophisticated wisdom underlying symbolic exchange, which both Mauss and Malinowski considered universal, at least for 'primitive' societies. According to this,

> all 'goods' were potentially malign and would work against their possessors unless they were forever in motion. The 'goods' did not have to be edible, or useful. People liked nothing better than to barter useless things – or things they could supply for themselves: feathers, sacred objects, belts of human hair.[6]

Originally, symbolic exchange had the Nietzschean significance for Baudrillard not only of taking us beyond the modern 'law of value', but of a 'revaluation of all values'. However, in his estimation, although there has been a general disruption of rationalized value systems (for as Nietzsche argued, truth is a self-dissolving concept), the revolutionary transvaluation of values never took place. The passage beyond the 'law of value' led only to a kind indeterminacy, in which 'there is no longer a reference, or a coefficient of value', but a 'monstrous proliferation', an 'epidemic' in which value is completely 'fractalised' (SD 22). The feared convergence around a centralized code of value is counterbalanced by an ironic dispersion of value. Consequently, Baudrillard's strategy has evolved in such a way that he no longer wishes to oppose value with the symbolic, but rather to enter into the spirit of simulation itself – the fatal strategy – not to propose alternatives, which are simply swallowed up in the general 'indeterminacy', but to 'get into synchony with these processes, including in one's writing' (SD 22). Thus, paradoxically, in this curious and roundabout way, Baudrillard's radical anti-sociology does begin to fall into line with the *laissez-faire* position of liberal postmodernists like Richard Rorty or Gianni Vattimo, for whom it is important for philosophy today to recognize 'that the perspective of reappropriation has been used up' and 'that nihilism is our (only) chance'.[7]

V

Fatal strategies

15

The impossible object of morality

We cannot live without objects, and in a sense the private domestic relationship with things must in all societies be as essential as dreaming for the maintenance of psychic equilibrium:

> It is certain that if we could deprive someone of that game of evasion–regression played out through the possession of things, if we could prevent him from holding his own controlled discourse, conjugating himself, outside of time, through objects, the destabilizing effect would be as immediate [as in R.E.M. sleep deprivation]. (*SO* 116)

Why try to pretend that this is not so, or that it is only a temporary condition, the fault of alienation, the consequence of an improvident organization of the material world? Kant said that things were merely a means, whereas humans, by virtue of their Reason, are ends in themselves. He imagined a state of perfect morality – the 'Kingdom of Ends' – in which objects never created a gap between subjects: no subject would treat any other subject as a mere means, but only as an end in him or herself. But the world dreamed of by morality is always compromised by our dependence on the real world of things, and by the fact, as Baudrillard expresses it, that 'We cannot live absolute singularity, that irreversible state whose sign is the moment of birth. It is this irreversibility of birth toward death that objects help us to resolve.'

The inevitability of 'heteronomy' lies in the impossibility of rendering the world transparent to the self as a pure expression of subjective being. Objects will always intervene between subjects, and the problem of how to organize them 'fairly' is in principle irresolvable – except in the technological imaginary (which has replaced the revolutionary imaginary as the new historical promise of an absolute human subject). At the level of abstraction on which these philosophies and *Weltanschauungen* operate, pure subjectivity and pure objectivity express the same wish for an impossible transparency. The obduracy of the 'thing world' embodies an inevitable division within ourselves (interiority) and between ourselves and the world around us (exteriority). Objects will always separate us from ourselves, while at the same time introducing into our relationships 'an irreducible element of non-relationship to the world' (*SO* 127). Like the repression barrier (or in Lacanian terms, the 'bar' which divides the signifier from the signified), they connect us to what we are not, and isolate us from what we are.

The classical account of this dilemma is not to be found in Freud, however, but in the philosophical theory of alienation. The concept of alienation is usually traced to Hegel, whose broad theme is the consolidation of the absolute subject through an appropriative synthesis with nature. But the idea of the soul's haemorrhaging in the fallen world of objects is everywhere in the world's religious cultures. In Europe it achieved a concentrated secular expression well before Hegel in the folklore of alchemy and particularly in the myth of Faust. If the subject cannot escape the 'material world' (as all the world's variety of ascetics preach), then perhaps the subject can dominate it, harness it, divert its power to human use. In a sense, perhaps that power does essentially belong to the subject; as Marx argued, it is nothing more than human production in its process of historical development, during which it naturally becomes separated from itself (capitalism), like Hegel's 'other', and then reunited with the subject as the final expression of its essential 'species' being (socialism). The reunification of the subject occurs through reappropriation of the object, the overcoming of alienation through the self's recovery of its objectified essence in labour.

> It is just in his work upon the objective world, therefore, that man first really proves himself to be a *species being*. This production is his active species life. Through and because of this production, nature appears as *his* work and his reality. The object of labor is, therefore, the *objectification of man's species life*; for he duplicates himself not only, as in consciousness, intellectually, but also actively, in reality, and therefore he contemplates himself in a world that he has created. In tearing away from man the object of his production, therefore, estranged labor tears from him his *species life*, his real objectivity as a member

of the species and transforms his advantage over animals into the disadvantage that his inorganic body, nature, is taken away from him.[1]

As the history of the twentieth century has shown, the effort to sustain this illusion that there is a 'real objectivity' for the species to recover inevitably leads to a reign of terror. The Frankfurt School Marxists soon realized that the 'domination of nature' inevitably entails the domination of man.[2] Too rigorous an attempt to control the world of objects seems to lead to a strange and paradoxical fatality, whose classic form is tragedy, *hubris* and the peripety of the will, and whose repetition, as Marx foresaw in the *Eighteenth Brumaire*, is usually a farce or an unconscious parody. In effect, the fatal strategy, which Baudrillard described in 1983, but which he had already foreseen dimly at the heart of the object system:

From the moment that an entire society begins to articulate itself through models, and to converge with them to the point where objects take on as ephemeral a status as words and images; when production contrives systematically to destructure these models into series, and the series into marginal differences and combinatory variants; when through the systematic inflection of the series, the entire edifice becomes paradigmatic, but in an irreversible order (the scale of status being fixed and the rules of the game being the same for all) – in this state of controlled convergence, in this organized fragility, in this perpetually destroyed synchrony, negativity is no longer possible. There are no longer any open contradictions, no more changes of structure, no more social dialectic. . . . Such a society, launched on the course of technological progress, performs all revolutions upon itself. Its expanding productivity never opens out into structural change. (*SO* 184)

Of course, this engulfing of negativity and conflict – what the late Herbert Marcuse called 'the one-dimensional society' – by no means guarantees stability. The fatality of the object system remains opaque and ambiguous; and if indeed sumptuary society neutralizes all prospect of structural change, fantasies of breakdown and failure loom all the larger in the cultural imaginary. The real myth of the 'Civilization of the Object' lies in its anxious moralism (that is, its *politics*), its prophetic self-denunciation, the compulsive 'surreification' of objects and of consumption to the point where they take on an absurdly demonic value. As we have already noted on other occasions, Baudrillard serves himself up as his own best example:

Let us say that this counter-discourse establishes no real critical distance: it is as immanent to the sumptuary society as any other of its aspects. Negative critique is like the second home of the intellectual. Just as medieval society stabilized itself on the opposition of God and the Devil, so we find our equilibrium in consumption and its denunciation. But it was still possible for real heresies and black magic sects to organize themselves around the idea of the Devil. Our magic is merely white, because in abundance there is no more heresy. Such is the prophylactic whiteness of a saturated society, a society without fear of heights and without history, without any other myth than itself.

But here we go again, offering the same morose and prophetic discourse, caught in the trap of the Object and its apparent fullness. We know that the Object is really nothing, that behind it, the emptiness of human relationships converges, like a rough sketch of the immense social mobilization of productive forces reified therein. We await the brutal irruptions and sudden disaggregations which, in equally unforeseeable fashion as May '68, yet just as surely, will break up this white mass. (*SC* 116)

ALIENATION IN COLLECTING

These images of chronic instability in a morally rigid and frightened culture are reminiscent of the classical description of obsessional self-control. Baudrillard has turned out to be quite a connoisseur of compulsive modalities: the collection, the gadget, the robot, the auction, obesity, voyeurism, terror, obscenity, fashion – the 'passion for the artificial' (*Death* 94) – and the fetish – 'the passion for the code' (*FCPES* 92). His analysis of the collector's psychology in *The Object System* provides a kind of introduction to the many other discussions of the fantasmatic drive for transcendence and control, culminating in the curious *Please Follow Me.*[3]

Every object is in essence a vehicle of some kind of transformation (*SO* 8), generally either of the world, or of the self. From this point of view, the object has two possible functions: to be 'practised', or to be possessed. The first involves the practical totalization of the world by the subject (Marx's project: production); whilst the second has to do with an enterprise of abstract self-totalization in imaginary isolation from the practical world (consumption). At the extreme, these two functions of the object are embodied by the machine at the functional end (culminating in the digital LED display control panel), and at the other, by the pure object, the thing-degree-zero, emptied of its function, abstracted from its intended use, which takes on a strictly subjective value: the collector's object (*SO* 104).

Anyone familiar with Bruce Chatwin's charming little novel, *Utz*, or the subsequent film by George Sluizer (1992), will have an idea what Baudrillard was trying to convey in *The Object System*. Like Kaspar Utz, Baudrillard's collector of objects represents a kind of limit case of the psychology of consumption. In a sense, the collection is a form of protest, a retreat to the margins of the object system (the obsessional tends to be passive aggressive). The collector establishes a privileged domain of value, by means of which he is able to repudiate the cynical and hypocritical discourse of the world. In the case of capitalism, for example, he shuns its phantasmagoric illusion of 'personalization', personal service, personal relationships – the whole insulting apparatus of 'glacial sollicitation' (*SC* 252ff.) epitomized in the 'Thank You – Have a Nice Day' message flashing on the banking machine monitor at the end of every solitary transaction. Like Kaspar Utz, the obsessional recoils instinctively from this cold mother into his masturbatory chamber, where he houses his collection of objects, the series of which begins symbolically with the very thing that she once denied him. Kaspar Utz has failed sexually: his visit to the local brothel was a humiliation; then the Stalinist terror took hold of Prague. His one passion is to build his collection of Meissen porcelain, which the State grudgingly allows him to keep in his apartment until his death. This concession to the privacy of the possessive individual is granted on the assumption that Utz's obsessionality will never allow him to rebel, or even to defect. The communists are quite comfortable letting him travel to the West each year; they allow him just enough latitude to improve his collection, of which he is much more decisively a prisoner than of the police state itself.[4] We find Utz precisely where Baudrillard would have predicted:

> Because he is alienated and dispersed in the social discourse whose rules escape him, the collector seeks to constitute another discourse which would be transparent to him, for in the collection, he controls all the signifiers, and the ultimate signified is at bottom himself. Unfortunately, the collector is bound for frustration: believing that he has transcended discourse, he fails to see that he has merely exchanged the openness of an objective discontinuity for a discontinuity which is closed and subjective, where even the language he uses loses all general value. This totalization through objects always carries with it the mark of solitude: it lacks communication, and pines away for it. (*SO* 127–8)

FETISHISM OF THE COMMODITY

The fetishistic logic of the collector takes us still deeper into the mysteries and paradoxes of the modern object. If it is indeed the case, as Baudrillard says, that we are the prisoners of the object world, we can also find there a strange kind of freedom if we submit to its peculiar and alien forms – that is, if we agree to adopt fetishism itself as a wilful strategy. This deliberate alienation transforms the passivity of the exploited producer – whose projected soul was thought to animate the object system – into the active perversion of the aesthete, whose sensual submission to the inhumanity of the object delivers the body from the prison of the soul (*FS*).

The aim was not, at first, to subvert Marx's critique of political economy. Baudrillard was only trying to radicalize it, to extend it into the domain of the sign. But in discovering the sign at the heart of the commodity, he realized that the logic of fetishization extended beyond the consumer's relation to the object, the surface effect of misrecognition and reification. Much more crucial was the illusion that the surface of the commodity was a cover, that something is concealed (and therefore alienated) in the commodity, something human and hidden waiting to be recovered. It is this effect of the play of signs, that the surface is *only* a surface, that there is more behind it, that we must try to see *through* appearances to find reality, which constitutes the practice of fetishism. The true fetishist is not the consumer, but the social critic – the antifetishist – who actually believes in the projected universe of values which offers to be recovered and reinhabited. The fetishist wants to go through the mirror to find the alter ego on the other side, the hidden world of depths promising reality, identity, satisfaction, justice and success. Thus fetishization is not just a misconceived relation to the object; it is the whole ideological process of capitalism and its critique, which through the structural articulation of the commodity as sign, and of the sign as commodity, expresses the essential form of the production process itself.

As we shall discover in *Seduction*, it is the absoluteness of the fetishist's obsession with surfaces – with everything that conceals and represses – which liberates him from the illusion of value (if from nothing else). Through his exploration of empty forms and decontextualized abstractions, the fetishist originates the idea of negative freedom. He or she knows that liberty is not a value to be realized, but a void whose condition is the destruction of value. The nihilation of value, especially moral value, is the ultimate expression of a pure symbolic power. The radical strategy is therefore not to recover the truth (or truth-value) which political economy is alleged to have 'repressed' (alienated). Precisely the opposite: it is to make a mockery of these 'alienated' values and thus to undermine the whole system of values as such. One does not transcend capitalism by retrieving the utility concealed behind the veil of fetishism. On the contrary, the appropriation of utility merely confirms the naturalness and the rationality of the social order built around the commodity. Instead, the commodity must be pushed to its limit-state of absolute meaninglessness and uselessness, the pure form of exchange value, which Charles Baudelaire seemed to envisage as a function of modern art (*FS* 116–19). Baudrillard is insistent on this point. Every successful act of consumption, every realization of a desire, is a projection of the productivist system of values. Conversely, every disappointment, every frustration, every failure, every loss, every fall through the cracks is an escape, perhaps thereby contributing in some small way to a new tendency, a new pataphysical law: the *falling rate of satisfaction*, which like Marx's economic law of the falling rate of profit, indicates a fundamental contradiction at the core of a world of positivized values (*FCPES* 204–12).

Thus, the negation of exchange value is not utility, but futility (*Death* 95). The cover of Abbie Hoffman's yippie best-seller in the late 1960s exorted the reader to 'steal this book'. But it sold at the publisher's list price nevertheless. One cannot 'liberate' use value by giving things away for free, or by distributing them according to need, as the communists pretended to be able to do. Use value is unintelligible without exchange values (*FCPES* 205): functionality, efficiency, cost-effectiveness, productivity, rationality, fairness, are all largely meaningless outside a capitalist frame of reference. These values did not exist prior to the age of political economy and its critique, and we have not devised an alternative form of organization which would give them a more substantial meaning than they already have as the legitimation categories of modern industrial civilization.

What, then, can be the revolutionary potential of 'desire', or 'desiring-production', in the economic order which now prevails? According to Baudrillard, none. The liberation of desire is one of the great twentieth-century delusions, for capitalism *is* the revolution of desire, in a very real sense. One cannot speak of the 'liberation' of desire apart from the great object system of consumption, which is nothing else if not a permanent revolution of desire, an endless reproduction of the moment of its liberation. It is, after all, only in modern societies that the formal emancipation of consumption has been pushed to this point, where everyone is free to 'express' their own sexual identity, to manipulate the signs which produce and reproduce their own sexual desire, and where there is actually a public debate about these things, so that everyone can feel that their personal satisfaction is an issue of great political significance, that their desire is being denied because not everyone is willing to endorse it or to applaud its public performance.

The very fact that we can speak of desire in this way, as a force of production or of truth, still to be tamed, or yet to be released, suggests in fact that the great discourse of desire, from advertising and fashion to the psychoanalytic proclamations of radical theorists, primarily concerns the history of an abstraction. Desire in this vague, chthonic, sense, is a fetishistic cultural construct,[5] like 'interest' or 'utility', whose traditional modernizing function has been to generate a naturalistic referent for the sign-exchange economy, and its permanent revolution of value.

Baudrillard's reflections on these issues culminate in *Symbolic Exchange and Death*. In *Seduction*, he abandons the socioeconomic frame of reference which had governed the first ten years of his writing, and reinterprets the same problem of the perverse structure of desire in the quite different register of the personality, and the interpersonal relationship. As he later hinted in *America*, *Cool Memories* and *L'autre par lui-même*, he had by the time of *Seduction* already entered a kind of 'Hell'. But in Baudrillard's case, Dante's inscription, 'Abandon Hope, All Ye Who Enter Here' would refer not to the theological Inferno, but to its modern equivalent, Politics, which like Orpheus's Eurydice, perpetually dissolves under Baudrillard's backward glance.

Baudrillard's analysis of desire begins with the attempt, in 'Fetishism and ideology: the semiological reduction' (1970), to account for its 'perverse structure' in the generalized system of exchange value (*FCPES* 88–101). The question is framed in terms of Marcuse's theory of 'repressive desublimation', the idea that capitalism remobilizes repressed instincts as motivational systems functionally integrated with the *status quo*. As was his usual method then, Baudrillard tried to yoke the analytic language of structuralism to the synthetic categories of critical theory. In the fetishism article, originally published in *La nouvelle revue de psychanalyse*, he resorts to what may very well have been Lacan's deepest insight into Freud: that the most interesting sense of our Western concept of motivation is desire, but desire itself has little or nothing to do with personal wishes or the concrete 'things I want'. It has to do with something intermediate, something which only exists *between* the self and the other, something which dissolves rather than confirms ego-identity. If it has a 'force', if it 'arises' from anything, then perhaps desire comes from the *lack* of identity – from not having one, from not being one, and from the inevitable failure of one's attempted identity. The standard Lacanian metaphor for this condition (the human condition of living the gap between reality and fantasy, suffering the difference between what we are and do, as distinguished from what we can imagine being and doing) is borrowed from Freud, namely, *castration anxiety*, whose meaning and scope the Lacanian tradition has helped to widen over a range of issues from birth trauma, and separation from mother, to anxiety about death.

Thus, Baudrillard's concept of desire is rooted in Marx's theory of commodity fetishism, as interpreted through Lacan's reading of Freud (which in turn is rooted in Kojève's interpretation of Hegel's master–slave dialectic). For Baudrillard, Marx's theory of 'fetishism' was a variant of rationalism, because it naively posited the meaning of the object as a property of the subject. The subject's desire for the object is tautological: it is the legitimate historical search for the original identity of subject and object, the reintegration of production and consumption as the single moment of the subject making the world and knowing it as the object of his or her own desire to make it. Thus, it presupposed an original or potential unity of consciousness, undivided by 'external' (unconscious) forces and things.

Marx had already described religion as 'the opium of the people' – it clouded their perception of reality. The theory of commodity fetishism has its intellectual origins in the same theological doctrines Marx rejected from a 'materialistic' point of view: it expresses a modernist version of the true religion of Jehovah, which condemned the idolatry of Baal and the 'golden calf', the metaphorical opium eaters who worship 'graven images'. For Marx, 'species being' lay in productive labour. That was spiritual reality, an alienated essence, a failed transcendence. It postulates an essential human power (labour) which has been transferred to things (reified: the worship of things, *mana*, fetishes), so that the relationships between things replace the true relationships, thus creating the conditions of false consciousness (everyone joins the wrong religion), of primitive 'magical thinking' and 'alienation' (people are not progressive, not enlightened, don't know what's good for themselves).

The psychoanalytic perspective which Baudrillard adopts does not attempt to understand the fetishistic relationship in terms of a transcendent value or a repressed nature. Instead it explores 'a perverse *structure* that perhaps underlies all desire' (*FCPES* 90). The fetish is not the object itself, but the closed perfection of the signifying system which encodes it. Freud had already anticipated this approach in his famous observation that beings who exude an aura of narcissistic self-sufficiency – beautiful women, cats, contented children – can be irresistibly attractive.[6] The appeal seems to lie in the impression of wholeness and inaccessibility, like a 'smooth body without orifices', which can only be created through the artful manipulation and multiplication of signs. The play of signifiers displaces the anxiety of absence, both expressing and concealing the incompleteness of the body, which itself becomes a kind of part object, a body as phallus (see *Death* 101f.).

There are already hints of what Baudrillard calls the 'perverse structure' of desire in the etymology of the term 'fetish' itself – a whole range of ideas and connotations of enchantment, sorcery and seduction through ornamentation, embellishment and the manipulation of signs. Now connoting a property of mind, a projection, the term originally derived from words about doing, making and artificiality. From this, Baudrillard amplifies his argument that 'alienation' in the fetish does not really involve a relation to things and substances – in other words, to the signified: it involves a 'fetishism of the signifier [in which] the subject is taken in by the factitious, differential, coded, systematized aspect of the object' (*FCPES* 92).

His central example, which is taken up later in *Symbolic Exchange and Death*, concerns the naturalistic ethos of the 'sexual revolution'. Baudrillard was at first primarily concerned to show how the affective dimension of the sexual body is decontextualized and universalized in the generalized economy of the sign. The body becomes a 'charnel[7] of signs', 'a structural material for sign exchange, equal to the sphere of objects, to resolve its playful virtuality and its symbolic exchange . . . into sexuality taken as a determining agency, a *phallic* agency entirely organized around the fetishisation of the phallus as a general equivalent' (*Death* 101). Through the integral articulation of sign and commodity, the body becomes the central locus of cultural idealization, the ideological object par excellence. Like the Lacanian phallus, it functions as the 'privileged signifier', a sort of semiotic exchange value, which grounds all circulation within the object system, 'the signifier intended to designate as a whole the effects of the signified. . . .'[8]

Thus, the body enters into the routine soft core of the health and fitness industry, whose function is to ward off castration anxiety by means of splitting and idealization, by transforming the body through a 'labour of signs' into a simulacrum of the phallus, like a kind of naturalized version of Medusa's snaking hair, surrounded by multiplying signs of living presence. The publicity conventions of naive and sentimental nudity serve to mask the deadliness and violence which always shadow sexuality, and which resurface culturally in the stylized categories of hard-core pornography, the myth of the snuff film,[9] and the discourse of harm, rape and domestic violence.[10] There is a proliferation of rational and progressive erotica (the 'liberation of the body') which resolves the ambivalence of corporeal existence, which is always divided against itself and fragmented by the root indeterminacy of gender and sexuality. Sexual intimations of mortality (the *mise à nu* is symbolically always '*mise à mort*') are abstracted and neutralized in the functionality and rationality of a 'body entirely positivized by sex – as a cultural value, as a model of fulfilment, as an emblem, as a morality' – not in sexuality, but 'the formal democratic lobby' of 'the right to the body and sex', which absorbs the subversive negativity of the body and desire in the system of need and satisfaction (*FCPES* 97–8).[11] 'The myth of the unconscious becomes the ideological solution to the problems of the unconscious' (*FCPES* 100). The effect of dis-closure, of 'repressive desublimation', is created precisely through *closure*, the formal perfection and autonomy of sign systems, 'the semiological reduction of the symbolic' in the socially integrated positivity of 'truth': the unconscious celebrated by semiology and diffused (defused) in the mass media; the body exposed to the heat and light of the vacation sun;[12] or the cool mannequin gaze, which expresses the ultimate fulfilment of the sexual system wherein a 'woman is never more completely herself, and therefore never so seductive, as when she accepts to please herself first, to gratify herself, to have no other desire or transcendence than that of her own image' (*Death* 109). 'Perverse desire and ideological process are articulated on the same "sophisticated" body' (*FCPES* 95): 'the body at last outstripped and submitted to a discipline, a total circulation of signs . . . its wildness veiled in make-up, its drives assigned to the fashion cycle' (*FCPES* 93–4). The intensity of the lived cleavage of the body is neutralized in the discrete separation of signs, which coolly surround the body and close it up like an egg.

If the symbolically naked body is all face, all an expressive play of features, then the hyperrealism of functional nudity destroys even the bourgeois distinction between the face and the clothed body. But it does not thereby reveal the visage of the symbolic body, the 'figure [face] of alterity'. It erases the features, and their otherness, rendering the body symbolically faceless, without expression, clinically 'realistic' (*Death* 133).[13] Within the sphere of sign-exchange value, or the object system whose apotheosis is the human body itself, realistic nudity is therefore not a natural state of the body, but a signified in a sign relation, where dress, reduced from its symbolic ceremonial role, functions as the signifier. Costume has been replaced by clothing, which must signify the body (*Death* 96). Fashion reflects this endless play of signification, the simulation of the body as natural referent, the 'privileged signifier' of signifiers. The body becomes the locus for the negotiation of identity: the site of a personalized 'semiological reduction of the symbolic' which for Baudrillard 'properly constitutes the ideological process' (*FCPES* 98). In nudity, which does not exist except when 'reduplicated by signs' (*Death* 105), there can be no symbolic exchange, for in the ambivalence of the latter, the body consumes the individual and becomes, like goods and women in primitive societies, or like the youthful Aztec bodies ruptured by sacred fire and sword, a sacrifice, or a gift, a pure expenditure.

The idea that I would identify my body as a thing in the world of objects appears, from the point of view of symbolic exchange, as a strange move in an unfamiliar language game. That I would link my identity to this thing, that this thing, me, could be humiliated, insulted, fetishized, that it (or I) could be 'reduced to a sex object' – all of these notions belong to the age of liberation, the capitalist revolution, the ideology of equality and freedom. Bataille expresses this insight as follows:

> The principle of sacrifice is destruction, but though it sometimes goes so far as to destroy completely (as in a holocaust), the destruction that sacrifice is intended to bring about is not annihilation. The thing – only the thing – is what sacrifice means to destroy in the victim.[14]

In terms of Heidegger's 'ontological difference': the point of symbolic exchange, as Baudrillard intends it, is not to signify anything, but to cease to be human, to cease to be an ego-thing in a world of functional objects (*Death* 107), to be exalted into a fantastic intensity of feeling which *dissolves the discreteness of beings back into the 'continuity' of Being*: what Bataille describes as a 'vague sphere of lost intimacy', where the thing-ego is 'lost in the world like water in water'.[15] 'Man is afraid of the intimate order that is not reconcilable with the order of things.'[16] This is why the symbolic is violent, why, for example, the slow semiotic construction of good striptease[17] is threatened by intimations of the symbolic, by the sudden possibility of a voyeuristic instinct to lay bare and rape (*Death* 109). As we shall see later more generally in the case of seduction, the good stripper's deliberate gestures are sacerdotal in origin: she is a priest who ritually transubstantiates the body into the phallus. But as Lacan says, the phallus 'can play its role only when veiled'.[18] The really good stripper holds everything in a kind of balance which finally brings the whole philosophy of European culture to its moment of truth:

There is nothing behind the succession of veils, there never has been. . . . The whole Western undertaking, which ends in a vertiginous compulsion for realism, is affected by this squinting relationship to castration: we pretend we are restoring the ground of things, but unconsciously, we ogle the void. Instead of recognizing castration, we dress ourselves up in all kinds of phallic alibis; then, with compulsive fascination, we seek to set the alibis aside, one by one, in order to uncover the 'truth' – which is always castration, though finally revealed as castration denied. (*Death* 110, 169–70; compare the example of the Japanese vaginal cyclorama in *Seduction* 31–2)

16

Seduction

REVERSAL AND SELF-REVERSAL

Something of this radical metaphysics of appearances, this challenge by simulation, still lives in the cosmetic arts and the glamour of modern fashion. . . .

In opposition to all . . . pious discourses, we must again praise the sex object; for it bears, in the sophistication of appearances, something of a challenge to the naive order of the world and sex; and it, and it alone, escapes the realm of production . . . and returns to that of seduction. In its unreality, in the unreal defiance of its prostitution of signs, the sexual object moves beyond sex and attains seduction. It again becomes ceremonial. The feminine was always the effigy of this ritual, and there is a frightful confusion in wanting to de-sanctify it as a cult *object* in order to turn it into a *subject* of production, or in wanting to rescue it from artifice in order to return it to its own 'natural' desires. (*Seduction* 91–2)

It is interesting to observe how, in the transition from *Symbolic Exchange and Death* to *Seduction*, the significance of the sign suddenly reverses in Baudrillard's thought. The ideological sign-labour of consumption as a conventional force of production within the object system has somehow metaphorphosed into 'radical metaphysics', a *challenge* which 'alone' escapes the order of production. In short, fetishism has become seduction.

The sense of reversal is especially clear if the comparison is made with any of the writings up to and including *For a Critique of the Political Economy of the Sign*. Whereas the sign had been, for the still nominally neo-Marxist Baudrillard, unequivocally the site of exclusion (through abstraction and reduction) of expressive meaning, in favour of codified signification, suddenly the sign seems to offer, from the perspective of seduction, the best available medium for the irruption of the symbolic in the smooth functioning of the 'cool' universe of tertiary simulation.

It is not that the distinction between 'meaning' and 'signification' disappears; there is just less dichotomy between them. More importantly, as we saw in Chapter 12, Baudrillard relinquishes his identification (via the concept of symbolic exchange) with an ideal social relationship. There is no longer a pretence that theory is the opposite of the world's pain and suffering, that the theorist has found the political solution to evil. One might say, indeed, that the shift, most evident in *Seduction*, to the more radical posture of 'refusal'[1] involves, paradoxically, a greater acceptance of emotional 'reality' – a maturation of sorts. Baudrillard certainly lets go of idealization as a defence; and with that development, there is less splitting into moral categories, a much more nuanced sense of the world's complexity, and less projection. The level of prose aggression remains high, largely in the form of an increasingly riotous disharmony with things as they are. But the aggression itself is not disowned (Baudrillard is not paranoid, just defiant). Unless one is a political priest and saviour, who needs everything to be conducted in an atmosphere of high moral seriousness, the later diatribes can seem quite sane at times. They are nearly always informative about the implications of the largely unintended conditions we are creating for ourselves and for our children.

The logic of the switch from morally reprehensible fetishism to rather desirable seduction was outlined explicitly for the first time in *Symbolic Exchange and Death*. Prior to 1976, Baudrillard's work had been characterized by a certain tension between the perverse and the emancipatory impulses. Though he had rejected the principle of production by the mid-1970s, he still tended to define consumption as a 'productive force'. The earlier work struggled with the contradictory implications of the *Grundrisse* (the posthumously published notes for *Capital*), in which Marx oscillated ambivalently (dialectically) between production and consumption, value and need, agency and technology, subject and object, as foundations of historical materialism. With *Symbolic Exchange and Death*, all hope of emancipation is relinquished along with the myth of an active, as opposed to passive, relation to history. The difference can be summed up as an immoderate refusal to accept production as a necessary condition of our existence.

Baudrillard simply decides to regard the world as a place where production is an unwelcome imposter, a most unappealing blight on the order of being. A more radical disaffection with the world as we know it is hard to imagine. Even the most iconoclastic dissidents evaluate themselves primarily in the light of their productivity – their competition to create culture, to generate disturbance, and to 'produce difference'. Baudrillard is no exception in this regard: he 'produces' culture at a phenomenal rate. But his antiproductivist contention is, all the same, carefully thought through, and profound in its implications. Through assiduous avoidance of moral opposition, he tries never to create or to sustain values, but only to destroy them. In this sense, Baudrillard never actually produces anything; rather, he embraces production itself as an ineluctable form, as if he were giving himself over without resistance to a massive flow of production which carries him forward on a great wave of history.

Baudrillard's celebrated ambivalence – his intensified acceptance–rejection of the world as it is – was first systematically expressed in the paradox of 'theoretical violence' proposed in the preface to *Symbolic Exchange and Death*: the project for a pataphysics of the tertiary or cybernetic level of simulation.

> Cybernetic operativity, the genetic code, the random order of mutations, the uncertainty principle, and so on: all of these replace determinate, objectivist science, a dialectical vision of history and consciousness. Even critical theory and the revolution belong to the second-order simulations, as do all determinate processes. The installation of third-order simulacra upsets all of this, and it is useless to resurrect the dialectic, 'objective' contradictions and the like, against them; that is a hopeless political regression. You cannot beat randomness with finality; you cannot beat programmed and molecular dispersion with *prises de conscience*, or dialectical transcendence; you cannot defend against the code with political economy or 'revolution'. All of these old weapons (including those of the first order, the ethics and metaphysics of man and nature, use value, and other liberatory systems of reference) have been gradually neutralized by a higher order general system. Everything that filters into the definalised space-time of the code, or tries to intervene in it, is disconnected from its own ends, disintegrated and absorbed. This is the well known effect of recuperation, manipulation, of circulating and recycling at every level.
>
> . . . This is why the only strategy is *catastrophic*. . . . Things must be pushed to the limit. . . . The only strategy against the hyperrealist system is some form of pataphysics, a 'science of imaginary solutions'; that is, a science fiction of the system's reversal against itself at the extreme limit of simulation, a reversible simulation in a hyperlogic of death and destruction. (*Death* 3–5)

Following *Symbolic Exchange and Death*, these arguments were then rehearsed in a series of trial analyses, or thought experiments, which focused in particular on the problematic status of the social (*In the Shadow of the Silent Majorities*, *L'effet Beaubourg* and *Oublier Foucault*). Baudrillard argued in effect that the 'totally administered society' is a political chimera of both the critics and the apologists for 'capitalism'; its attempted operationalization tends, paradoxically, to dissolve the social body upon which it is supposed to work, to create a nonparticipating mass of depoliticized consumers who become more and more difficult to mobilize in the interests of a determinate power. (We shall examine this contention further in Parts VI and VII.)

Like most of Baudrillard's arguments, the claims made about the implosion of the masses and the end of the social are empirically false. But this fact can be (and still widely is) overlooked by anyone with a sense of humour. There are two good reasons to do so. The first is that the hyperbole is acknowledged implicitly from the outset, as in any worthy satire. The second is that there are few analyses of comparable scope dealing with the sorts of problem Baudrillard has been attempting to bring to our attention. Moreover, the arguments themselves, for all their apparent illogic, achieve an elegance and consistency of intellectual vision which seems appropriate for the cultural moment. Baudrillard should never be taken literally as a prophet. He rejects realism and validity as criteria of his work. But his 'predictions' have a curious way of becoming a little truer every day. Like McLuhan, he has succeeded in reframing as literary commentary much that is marginal in social science, so that now its vital significance can be felt more keenly.

And so it transpired, through the machinations of Baudrillard's deep sense of historical irony, that 'fashion' – that apotheosis of capitalist decadence and cynically masked exploitation – would evolve in his thought from a fetishistic system of ideological control to a radical form of seduction which defies the economic 'reality principle'. As he had already suggested in *Symbolic Exchange and Death*, 'Ambivalence awaits the most advanced systems. . . . The fascination which they exert, because it derives from a profound denial such as we find in fetishism, can be instantaneously reversed' (*Death* 4).

SUBVERSIVE SEXISM

Woman is still the ground of representation, even in postmodern times. (de Lauretis)[2]

And when we have a male in front of us, we could ask: does he have some female in him? And that could be the main point. That's it: reverse everything, including analysis and criticism. . . . Reverse Everything. Make women the point of departure in judging, make darkness the point of departure in judging what men call light, make obscurity the point of departure in judging what men call clarity. . . . (Marguerite Duras)[3]

Thus, with fashion pushed to the extreme and turning into seduction, and *Seduction* metamorphosing into one of the *Fatal Strategies*, we have the first full-dress performance of the pataphysical 'science of imaginary solutions' which Baudrillard had announced in *Symbolic Exchange and Death*. The truly fatal hypothesis of *Seduction* is that (in the Freudian sense of 'libido') there is only one 'sex' – phallic or 'masculine' sex. Any attempt to oppose it on the discursive level of sexuality itself, such as through the construction and naturalization of a 'feminine' sexuality, is implicitly to accept the terms of the phallic order, even to deepen their hold, by reinforcing the binary conception of difference around which 'sex' (i.e. gender[4]) has been organized culturally.[5] It may even serve to revive biological essentialism, as Baudrillard charges Luce Irigaray, and thus to confirm the stupefying notion that 'anatomy is destiny'. Thus, for Baudrillard, the standard discourse of feminism is virtually isomorphic with the political economy of the sign, and its discourse of desire; moreover, it promises quick delivery into the tertiary phase of simulation, where 'all liberations are transitions toward generalized manipulation' (*ESM* 10; *Death* 3).

According to Baudrillard, the only site of resistance to this apparently totalizing discourse (what Judith Butler calls 'the epistemic regime of presumptive heterosexuality'[6]) is *seduction*, whose secret is the 'transubstantiation of sex into signs'. The radicality of seduction lies precisely in its lack of positivity, its *indeterminacy*, the fact that the semiological ordering of sexuality 'constantly fails', as Jacqueline Rose once put it.[7] In Baudrillard's view, sexuality fails because the principle of seduction is secretly at work, deconstructing sexual identity, undermining the positivity of the binary terms of the sex/gender code.

The fatality of this conceptual move, however – its deliberately self-refuting, intellectually masochistic side – lies in Baudrillard's identification of the seduction principle with the stereotype of Woman as 'femininity'. Previously not one to cite Hegel (perhaps the most discredited philosopher in contemporary France), Baudrillard approvingly quotes his apothegm about 'womankind' ('femininity' in Singer's translation of *Seduction*) as 'the everlasting irony in the life of the community'.[8] It is precisely in the booby-trapped atmosphere of feminist debate – where almost anything you say can be held against you – that Baudrillard chooses finally to let himself go right over the top, just when it is most likely that he will be accused of political reaction. The gesture is reminiscent of his choice of title for the little pamphlet about Foucault, describing how we might begin to 'forget Foucault', published at the height of the latter's unprecedented celebrity.[9] He seems to have gone out of his way to ensure that the foundation of his argument will be 'wrong'. It is almost as if he regards plausibility as a weakness in an argument, as if giving complexity its due were a vulgar ruse, like the forger's art, not done for its own sake, but to deceive the buyer. And there is no doubt about it: Baudrillard certainly does not wish to deceive; he wants to corrupt totally. (Presumably on the grounds that deception is at the heart of every discourse – so why mask it?) From this eccentric point of view, his self-defeating posture has a compelling rationale; for if the counterfeit is just a perversion of production (like plausible social criticism, flattering in its imitation of the world), the point of seduction is to lead the world itself astray. So Baudrillard is quite subtle in the crudeness of his argument. He sets out to purge every trace of reflection, consideration, complexity, to present the world in black and white. Yet the exposition of this colour-blind vision intends precisely the opposite effect: to make us realize that the only illusion, in the true sense of a genuine falsehood, is moral judgement itself, white and black, man and woman, truth and deception.

Baudrillard acknowledges that the connection between femininity and seduction is problematic, in need of further exploration; and nowhere does he equate the 'feminine' explicitly with the female. (In fact, his main criticism of feminism seems to be that it makes this equation too easily, thus confusing pragmatic social status with symbolic social status.) But for all intents and purposes, seduction and woman are interchangeable in key passages of the text, seeming to confirm Alice Jardine's remarks about 'the slippage in male theoretical discourse from the *feminine* . . . to women . . . to 'we' ('we Westerners')'.[10]

Nevertheless, Baudrillard's line of reasoning is consistent with the sophisticated contemporary version of Freud, as articulated by a variety of Lacanian and deconstructionist feminists. For example, Sarah Kofman's paraphrase of Freud's 'Femininity':

> What is called a woman's instability is perhaps related to that bisexuality which is so marked in every feminine life, to that perpetual balancing between feminine and masculine. That absence of a stable position makes woman unlocatable, elusive, enigmatic in the eyes of men, who are less subject to bisexuality, to that permanent conflict between femininity and masculinity, since in man the masculine always predominates, since the penis has always been such a leading zone that if certain neuroses or psychoses did not reveal repressed feminine desires in man, one might even wonder what masculine bisexuality means . . . . [W]ith 'woman' men never know for sure *with whom* they are dealing, they try to overcome her lack of 'proper nature' and propriety by making her their property, by deciding, given her undecidability, in favor of masculinity; in short, by endowing her with 'penis envy' as a definitive mark.[11]

Kofman offers us a mythic view of 'woman' as 'unstable'. The passage is even more stereotypical of 'man' as a kind of uncomplicated but insecure tyrant, rather like Baudrillard's parodic depiction of production. The questionable presumption is that 'masculinity' is somehow more firmly rooted in the 'real world', more explicit, less divided against itself, though rather empty at the core. In the world of binary opposites, this image of Man fits neatly with the exotic view of Woman as 'Other'. But like the pairings of the signifier and the signified, or exchange value and use value, in Baudrillard's deconstruction of the sign-object, *both* terms (man *and* woman) are fictions (by virtue of reduction to the discrete). As Baudrillard showed with the political economy of the sign, the abstract articulation of the hierarchized opposition 'exterminates' the many ways in which men and women are different from each other and from themselves. It reduces them to one 'principle of difference', or diacritical mark, which is essentially the form of equivalence (the phallus exchange standard). The co-terminous fictionality of gender – and the impossibility of any sexual fantasy to stand on its own as self-sufficient – are suppressed in the dichotomy between the natural (e.g. the signified, the useful) and the constructed (the signifier, the exchange-equivalent). In this version of the binary schema of political economy, however, it is not clear which term – the masculine or the feminine? – plays the role of nature, which of cultural construction. But it would make some difference politically to determine which term functions as the signifier, which as the signified/referent.

In *Symbolic Exchange and Death*, as we have seen, Baudrillard has it that the 'masculine term' (the phallus) serves as the 'exchange standard', i.e. as the culturally constructed signifier, the principle of equivalence upon which the circulation of 'sexuality' as a sign system is based. The feminine is the signified, the referent, 'the ground of representation', that is, the absent or suppressed term which functions as the 'alibi' (like Marx's use value), for the 'positive' term, the circulating form of equivalence. In the fetish system, of course, the fetish presents itself as the dominant term: full, self-contained, and universal, like Hegel's subject, or Marx's commodity. Such is the mythic phallus of yore. And from the perspective of ideology critique, the feminine pole represents the absent ('alienated') natural ground: the true and authentic foundation upon which the abusive cultural construction of the masculine (the phallus) is based. The revolutionary logic is clear. The suppressed or satellite term must be recovered, and this can only be achieved by sweeping aside the central term around which the system is organized. Just as Marx's utopia was based on the elimination of exchange value, Charlotte Perkins Gilman's *Herland* is based on the elimination of men.

The whole thesis of *Seduction* emanates from Baudrillard's reluctance to resolve the ambiguity of the masculine–feminine opposition in these conventional revolutionary terms. The monstrosity of the latter, a *reductio ad absurdum*, reveals the essential asymmetry between sociability and sexuality which is concealed behind the smooth linguistic logic dominating contemporary discourses on sexuality and power. In the Marxist frame of reference, it was always possible to imagine eliminating the object world, doing away with commodities, obviating money, making everything available, without intermediary (no exchange equivalent, no market, just direct production for use). This revolutionary analysis has been carried over, by analogy, into the critique of patriarchy; but few are willing to spell out the consequences directly as policy. The inhibition has resulted in a massive and euphemistic displacement upwards of sexual politics onto the politics of language and the image. For example, the hated oppressor (not even man, but the 'phallus') is characterized as something which needs to be retranscribed through semiological warfare (not physically eliminated like the market or the ruling class). Gender becomes the object of a kind of Keynesian sexual reform (something to be saved through judicious redistribution of pub(l)ic resources) since it is, after all, constructed, a kind of 'pub(l)ic works project', and presumably therefore deconstructible, through cybernetic mechanisms of cultural and ideological control.

Baudrillard's rebellion against the conventionalizing terms of gender discourse illustrates, once again, that his own extension of the language paradigm into new spheres of social being is not intended as a triumphant demonstration of the 'new methodology' of the structuralist revolution. Wherever he adopts language as a theoretical model, one can be sure that his purpose is to show the violence of the model and the cost of its imposition. Baudrillard refuses to maintain the polite distance between theory (discourse) and its objects (social being) because he assumes that theory will not accept the gap anyway, but dispense with it at the first opportunity. In this context, the hyperbolic pataphysics of *Seduction* are nothing more than an imaginative exploration of the consequences of the self-conscious linguistic abstraction of sexuality characteristic of late modern culture.

The odd thing about seduction, however, is that it pushes the ontological imperialism of language right through the object and out the other side. Radicalized (and 'volatilized'), the play of signs leaves everything as it was. Yet, somehow, everything has been subtly reversed: it has become uncanny. 'Femininity' is no longer the naturalized alibi for an artificial principle of equivalence and circulation (the 'phallus exchange standard'), as it appeared in the light of fetishism. Nor is it an idealized 'refinement' of instinctual nature, the sublimated prize object of cultural transcendence: neither the absent and suppressed term (the 'alibi'), nor the dominant form, but the very incarnation of artificiality, drastically opposed to any normative concept at all, hostile to any kind of articulative logic. Femininity is a total fake.

Like the fetishist, Baudrillard insists that we can look behind the superfices of sexual typologies to find an essential truth (or anti-truth) about the ontology of gender: namely, that all sexuality, male or female, and all gender identity, masculine, feminine, or otherwise, always involves a process of impersonation, a masquerade – a *simulation*, as Baudrillard would say. But this refers to a very particular, quite basic (or 'primitive') type of social-symbolic simulation, in which the element of play always has the upper hand.[12] Seduction *is* that element of play, and so it is the perspective of seduction which allows the theory-voyeur to step back from the gender system, and the 'Mirror of Desire', in order to understand sexuality in a new light. If the fatal strategy has an appeal, it lies in its privileged access to indeterminacy. When one travels this road (neither the path of reality, nor the drive to produce reality, but the capacity of seduction to annul reality, its characteristic 'reversibility'), one encounters some very odd hypotheses indeed.

'Seduction represents mastery over the symbolic universe, while power represents only mastery of the real universe' (*Seduction* 8). From this perspective (or lack of perspective), it can be argued quite confidently that the feminine has always been the dominant form, 'the form transversal to every sex', whilst the masculine appears as 'a residual, secondary and fragile formation, one that must be defended by retrenchments, institutions, and artifices' (*Seduction* 15–16). In a sense, Baudrillard is right (even though he is not making a literal assertion). The fragile, defensive and secondary quality of masculine identity has emerged as a central theme in contemporary discussion, embracing the entire spectrum of feminist gender theory, from Jessica Benjamin to Camille Paglia.[13]

Of course, like the 'natural superiority of women', the hypothesis of male identity diffusion is hardly new. None of these debates is new, which is really the point of *Seduction* (and the fatal strategy): not just to mount a *tour de force* in a debating contest, but to create an inspired diversion, to draw attention to the fabulous inconsequentiality, the utterly arbitrary quality, of the most earnest discussion of our times.

The key to the fatal strategy (the strategy of choosing the wrong side in an argument, but seductively, so that the exquisite misery of losing can be dragged out indefinitely) is not just to defend the object against the subject, as we saw already in Baudrillard's exploration of the social being of the commodity, but to take the object's point of view in a world of subjects – in effect, to *become* the object. Baudrillard does not attempt to win political friends by denouncing the subject–object relationship as a 'structure of domination', or by asserting the epistemological superiority of language as an alternative to 'subject–object metaphysics'. Incorrigible, he does not even pretend to resolve, reconcile or synthesize the dichotomy of the subject and the object. Instead, not at all convinced that anybody has really succeeded in thinking 'beyond' it, he chooses to sharpen the polarity even more. He revels in the illegitimacy of cultural dichotomies, which represent for him the delicious revenge of cruel traditional cultures on the smooth modern continuum of digitality. He *seduces* the reader; he becomes our object, which is precisely the point of seduction: to attract a subject to an object.[14]

The political philosopher Kroker once suggested that Baudrillard was a kind of Lazarus who had succeeded in raising Marx's theory of the commodity from the graveyard of the labour theory of value.[15] The same might be said for the Hegelian theory of the subject, which apparently died with the linguistic critique of substance and essence. Rather than credit Baudrillard for announcing the death of the subject (it was Foucault who did that), we might say instead that through seduction, Baudrillard has succeeded in rekindling the subject by developing a technique, surrealist in origin, of rubbing objects against one another til a spark flies; he shows how the object (to paraphrase Lacan) *represents the subject to another object.*[16]

The fatal strategy of the object, its 'ironic power', is 'not the false as opposed to the true, but the more false than false, to incarnate the peaks of sexuality while simultaneously being absorbed in their simulation'. This is

> the irony proper to the constitution of woman as idol or sex object: in her closed perfection, she puts an end to sex play and refers man, the lord and master of sexual *reality*, to his transparency as an *imaginary* subject. (*Seduction* 15)

To the extent that a 'woman' may dispose of this inverse power of irony through the very fact that there is (or was) a cultural sanction to treat her as an 'object' (i.e. that which represents a subject to another object, e.g. the 'man'), paradoxically, the *woman* becomes a subject in a dead universe. Through seduction, her fatal strategy makes her into a 'strange attractor' (the metaphor which Baudrillard later developed from 'chaos theory' to describe a sociocultural version of the stabilization of causal indeterminacy in a state of dynamic equilibrium). She is an indeterminate effect, an emergent property of ironic subjectivity. But when she is promoted to the 'Western' status of an epistemological or desiring subject, she loses this power of strange attraction and becomes instead just another functional ego in the rational and discontinuous (boundaried and discrete) world of functional things (*Seduction* 15); that is, conventional feminism assists tertiary simulation through its 'promotion' (commercial or ideological, it makes no difference) of woman to subject status. And to that extent, she will be 'subjected' in the Foucauldian sense; another functional ego, another object of a restricted economy in Bataille's sense; and her 'presence', in terms of the Heideggerian ontological distinction, will shift from the *ontological* status of Being, to the *ontic* status of phenomenal existence in the world of technology.

Of course, that is where she really is – in the phenomenal world of technology (and all the rest of it). So why shouldn't she become a 'subject' in that world? It is an odd question to have to ask, yet Baudrillard forces us to ask it. Before attempting an answer, let us review the argument so far in the light of a more formal version of the same question: Why does Baudrillard deviate from his previous strategy, which was to resist the structural opposition of terms (signifier versus signified, exchange value versus use value) and to reintegrate them from a perspective external to political economy, namely that of symbolic exchange? In a sense, as we have seen in *Seduction*, he does just this. But unlike symbolic exchange, seduction is not really external to the logic of the sign. It is the sign's ecstatic form. It is, like *fin de siècle* aestheticism, a pure celebration of the artificiality of the sign for its own sake. If Baudrillard had approached the problem of sexual difference in the same spirit with which he had deconstructed the sign-object, he would have demonstrated the structural character of both terms, opposed to an authentic sexuality. Apart from symbolic exchange, the list of candidates for that role is long: polymorphous perversity, libido, desire, Foucault's 'different economy of bodies and pleasures'.[17] But instead, he radicalizes the opposition of the sexes. Why? Perhaps the reason was to have done with the theoretical *status quo*, to move on to a new stage of sexual 'history'.[18] If the first great modernist moment was the injunction to release sexuality from the constraints of power (the libidinal revolution), and the second was to recognize sexuality as power, and to reconfigure its deployment, then the third would be neither to liberate it as truth nor to deconstruct it as power but to turn it (back?) into a frivolous game.

17

The double

PARALLEL EXISTENCES

In the novel *René Leys*,[1] by Victor Segalen, the narrator (let us call him Victor) is a French national living in the Manchu quarter of Peking, 'this gigantic chessboard of a city' (33). He is a man in the grip of an Orientalist fascination, for whom the Celestial Empire might be described as 'a sort of surrogate and even underground self'.[2] He is full of aestheticizing passion, with a great desire to know the Exotic; but also irked by social envy, bristling with political *ressentiment*. He hates Europe, Science, Naturalism. Everywhere, he sees signs that the forces of homogenization have invaded the body of Chinese civilization. To use one of Baudrillard's favourite metaphors, European modernity constitutes a sort of 'virus' (far more deadly than the cheap opium which the British gunboats once forced into the Cantonese interior, to offset their balance of trade with China). Victor dreams of living as a kind of double of the 'hidden life of the Palace', a 'parallel existence'. Like the Emperor, Lord of the Sun and Son of Heaven, Victor's house in the Tartar City faces south, which gives him 'a sense of having no part whatever in the abject and "unanimous" life of the worms that wriggle and seethe on the dung-heap or the tape-worms that infest the gut' (48). He dreams of the chance to know the secrets of the city 'that I am trying to possess, trying to dominate as much as or more than the Emperor himself' (170). With fascination, he imagines 'inside, deep in the innermost center of the Palace, a face' (18). Victor would like nothing better than an audience in the Imperial Palace. He hires, or entertains, anyone who might be able to provide a hint of what goes on behind the wall of the Inner City, the 'Within'. But his desire is not just to mirror the Imperial State, or to mirror himself in it. He feels himself in exile from what would make him whole. There is a sense, therefore, in which he would exalt the Forbidden City precisely in order to disappear inside it, to merge with this exotic image of the Other: to become 'Oriental' (though not to the extent of becoming a naturalized Chinese, and giving up his European privilege and the due process of Western law) (29).

Sensing that language will make his entry into this world, Victor has hired a tutor, René Leys, a professor of political economy at the College of Nobles, to teach him the difficult Northern Mandarin he will need to 'penetrate the Within' (20). Leys is a rather odd fellow, barely 18, whose way with languages flows easily, like the intuitive gestures of the born mimic. Yet he is surprisingly uncultivated for such a master of tongues: a mere grocer's son, with little conversation or wit, unremarkable but for his extraordinary, somewhat feminine, good looks. 'My tutor would be extremely surprised to learn the true objective of my sessions with him', Victor muses (21). But soon, Victor himself is surprised. For whilst all his conventional sources of information have disappointed him with their banality, René Leys has made an extraordinary revelation!

Leys reveals – somewhat inadvertently, almost by accident – that he is on intimate terms with the Palace. More: he was a playmate of the late, lamented Emperor, Kuang Hsu. They would play a form of 'tag', but when the Emperor was about to be caught, he would just sit down wherever he happened to be. The women would get on their knees. 'Do you think a single one of them would have dared to remain standing when the Emperor was seated – even if he'd just sat down anywhere?' (49) Victor is impressed. Such detail 'bears the stamp of the eyewitness'. But each new revelation comes as a kind of peripety, dissolving Victor's conventional assumptions about the Imperial Court. It turns out that the Regent is an able man, not the politically compromised fool he is made out to be. He is concerned for his citizens. Leys and he sometimes escape the palace walls at night for revelries in the Chien Men Wai!

Victor is perplexed by the extraordinary privilege which has been conferred on the young Leys. To explain his dazzling rise in the Imperial favour, Victor develops a sexual theory: René Leys is after all a very handsome, even beautiful young man. Perhaps he is the Prince Regent's fancy? There is circumstantial evidence of such a disposition on Leys's part. He seems very 'chaste' with women. But just then, Leys reveals that the Empress Dowager, now 38, the widow of the late Emperor, has taken him as a lover. The sums he must pay the eunuchs to gain access to her chambers are astronomical. And the Regent, meanwhile, has made him a present of one of the royal concubines. Whenever the story seems too wonderful to be true, there is a new piece of news. René Leys is in fact the

Regent's chief of secret police – not only active in palace intrigue, it seems, but a cornerstone in the defence of the realm, a bulwark against rival lords and republican rebellions. Victor cannot believe his good fortune in finding this marvellous informant. Indeed, sometimes he literally cannot believe his ears, but every seeming contradiction dissolves in the instant it is raised by the unprepossessing Leys.

Unfortunately, it soon becomes apparent that the Regent's administration is in considerable disarray. The aftermath of the Boxer Rebellion has not been auspicious for the Manchus. Leys is consumed in his secret police work, often away for whole nights on mysterious errands. The treacherous Yuan Shih-kai, notorious for his betrayal of Prince Chun's reforms, is once again on the rise within the government. Sun Yat Sen, the Harvard-educated, republican reformer, is leading the Kuomintang rebellion in the South. Three provinces have been declared independent republics. The Celestial Empire seems to be falling apart! What is the plucky little René up to? Victor is distraught, but cannot reason with the boy. At Leys's insistence, Victor agrees that the Dowager may take refuge in his house. A yellow silk handkerchief will be dropped by the door, to herald her arrival. At the third watch, around midnight, she will arrive. But no one comes. Victor is already disillusioned. He confronts René Leys. What proof can he supply of his relationship with the Dowager? The answer is stunning: 'Why – the child' (208). They have a child? Suddenly, Victor is moved to console Leys, who ought to be there at the palace, where he belongs. Leys agrees, but worries over the death that awaits anyone so centrally linked to the Ch'in Dynasty, whose regime is toppling around them. Massacres in the Palace. Falling down wells. Bombs. Victor reassures him. But he warns of another, perhaps more insidious danger, a traditional method in China: poison. They part for the evening. Victor retreats into a kind of manic defensive posture, unable to dispel his doubts about René Leys, yet refusing to give in to them. But the next day, he learns that René Leys is dead. He visits the body in the grocer's house, where it was found. There are no signs of injury. Could the boy have been poisoned? Was it the Dowager herself?

In perplexity, Victor rereads the journal of his conversations with Leys (the basis of the manuscript we have been reading). Gradually it dawns on him that everything Leys had ever told him was prompted by himself, right down to the significance of the hollow sound in the roads near the palace walls (they were secret tunnels, according to Leys). It was Victor who first mentioned the deceased emperor, with whom Leys said he had played; it was he who had first alluded to the Regent, the Empress Dowager, the secret police – and even (most significant of all) the poison! Leys had taken him up on every hint, right to his death, as if Victor had written the script himself.

Note the emphasis, in this narrative, on the 'play' of signs. Seduction lies only superficially in the signs themselves, the 'Son of Heaven', 'Forbidden City', the 'purple walls'. What carries the signs beyond mere *chinoiserie* is the 'superficial abyss' opened up by their reversal, in which everything suddenly turns inside out. Victor seduces Leys to his death with the secret (i.e. unconscious) invitation to tell him the story he wants to hear, to become the object of his 'desire'. Victor does not even know that he is seducing René Leys, and begins to fear, on the contrary, that Leys is seducing him. But all the while, Leys obligingly follows Victor's lead. In his role as the dupe (which we do not fully confirm until his untimely death), however, Leys has also duped Victor, leading him to the 'truth' of his own 'desire', by revealing that the story he has told about himself is actually the story of Victor, a tale of corruption and murder.

In psychoanalytic parlance, *René Leys* might be described as an allegory about the dangers of the 'counter-transference' – i.e. the analyst's transference to the analysand – the *analyst's* 'desire', which inevitably exploits the analysand's desire, which is precisely to be the object of the Other's desire. This is the power of seduction. As Baudrillard says, seduction (like psychoanalysis) is always a dual (duel) process. One tries to make oneself into an irresistible object, but in so doing, one turns the Other into one's own object. Each is the object of the other's transferential fantasy, and the resulting interpenetration of 'floating' signs (which is to say, the intermingling of elements from different scenarios, neither of which has any reference to reality, but only, obliquely, to the illusions of the other), creates a kind of selfless giddiness, a sort of transcendental immanence: the uncanny.

In *René Leys*, we see the first power of seduction, to lead an object from its path by becoming its object, by furnishing, like a work of art, the invitational signs which may serve as links in a narrative which seems indeterminate, yet always has the feel of destiny. It is the meeting of lovers, which plays itself out endlessly in the affair, so long as the moment of encounter is never finally resolved in the closure of productive reason, of action for a practical reason, for an end beyond the pointless pleasure of mutual seduction. This is symbolic exchange, in which everything is symbolic, and nothing is exchanged, because there is nothing, beyond the emergent property of the encounter itself, to change hands. The random secondary effect, the tertium quid, the symbolic, cannot be presented because it is, even as this accidental effect, too primary, too much the basis of the relationship itself. But it disappears as soon as there is an attempt to make it appear as a thing separate from the encounter; it becomes the bastard child which must be taken care of.

'Tell me everything that comes to your mind'; or still more intriguing, 'Tell me everything'.[3] This is the basic initiation of the analytic process, and it is essentially a seduction: not a demand for confession, but a 'challenge', as Baudrillard says, to become an object of pure knowledge. It is impossible not to have this fantasy at the beginning of an analysis, and even the analyst is tempted to give in to it. One wants to know, and one wants to be *known*. But this in turn is a seduction, the teasing out of an auricular desire. In becoming an object, the analysand is 'led astray' (seduced by the analyst), and is thus gradually relieved of the social functions of the ego, and its burdens of self-correction and self-deception. But the analysand, as this object, also seduces the analyst, partly by the lure of his own projection (the analyst is supposed to be the one who knows, as Lacan says), but still more profoundly by finding and secretly fulfilling the analyst's desire. By drawing out the subject's desire (the analyst's transference), the object (the analysand), like Scheherazade, leads the subject into a narrative abyss in which love is never consummated and death is indefinitely deferred. But whose love and whose death? Is it that the analysand must remain forever in need, as if to prove that the analyst loves him? Or is it really the analyst who cannot let go, like the child who wants the bedtime story to last forever? This becomes the issue to 'resolve'.

The Forbidden City is, of course, a simulacrum in its purest sense: an evocation of the Divine Mystery through the simple erection of an interdiction (a wall) which both denies and affirms its presence, forbids and invites empirical investigation; or, in one of Baudrillard's definitions of the simulacrum, 'it is a truth effect that hides the truth's non-existence' (*Seduction* 35). Thus the simulacrum is always the 'veil' behind which the Lacanian phallus, the signifier of signifiers, does its work. But the Purple and Forbidden City is also a simulacrum in another sense: for in its primitive Exoticism, it openly declares what the modernist simulacrum of signs and values tries to conceal through naturalistic conceptions of value, function, signification and desire: that meaning – and by extension, the whole construction of a social world – is essentially an invitation, but not necessarily a friendly one, a subtle, subversive, insinuating, implicating invitation – a *seduction.*

Baudrillard's analysis of seduction finally destroys the innocence of the aesthetic, in the very process of discovering it as the ground of the social. One only has to walk into a good jazz club late at night to understand the indispensability of seduction. The piano and the saxophone weave their webs of notes around the smoky tables for no particular purpose. One pays to get in, perhaps, but the point is not for the musicians to earn a living, or for the manager to provide employment to waiters, or for the public to be entertained. The music just *is.* There is a social history to it, there are relations of production, distribution and consumption, but this whole dimension of primary 'causes' is actually secondary, at least for a moment, to the effect of the music itself, to the emergent property, the sheer marginality and evanescence of an evening's performance. Suddenly we remember that everyone must do something with their lives, and as we sit huddled and sweaty in the dark corner behind the kleig lights, too near the drummer and the blaring speakers, we realize that this is all that the artist is doing: something with her life. What do we do with ours? Even mediocre artists remind us, through the sheer pointlessness of their elaborate constructions, of the difficulty of composing an existence sufficiently interesting to satisfy our intelligence and to contain our feelings. Everyone forgets how hard it is to learn to play an instrument that well, the sheer drudgery of acquiring this power to fascinate, for no purpose at all. The dancer breaks her body, and if we are to believe the extraordinary film by Kaige, *Farewell, My Concubine* (1993), the students of the Peking Opera were brutally dehumanized by their masters. Dynasties break their populations. Seduction is also violence. And if we deny responsibility for our own actions, as so many of us do, then to be seduced is to be raped.

There is no doubt that here Baudrillard has touched upon something which few other writers with social scientific training have been able to approach. It is not a very useful insight, of course. One cannot derive a 'praxis' from awareness of the 'secret' power of seduction in our lives, or from recognition of its 'fatal' consequences. With seduction, one certainly cannot address the questions of causality and blame which social discourse asks. What will make this product sell? Does ballet promote anorexia nervosa? Does ideology prevent the revolution? None of these questions has any compelling interest from the point of view of seduction. Nevertheless, in a certain way, Baudrillard does take us a good deal further in our understanding of the social condition (if only philosophically) than, say, Bordieu's theory of 'symbolic capital'.[4]

Seduction not only leads us 'to the very heart of the center of the Within', in Segalen's phrase; it also misleads us, since the 'within' is nowhere to be found. Seduction simply takes us, for no apparent reason, wherever we find ourselves going, which in principle is impossible to predict. We only think we know where we are going, but this is an illusion which is soon dispelled when we recognize that we have gone past our destination, or in another direction: then we realize that some other principle has been at work which subverts our intentions. If it is not chance, then perhaps it is seduction. The more meaningful our pursuit seems to become, the more our sense of purpose evaporates. We don't know why we are following along. As Baudrillard says, 'please follow me' (*Follow*).

EXOTICISM

> I am come gravely to doubt whether he is able to separate the true from the untrue in his own mind. He may do so in reflexion; he cannot in speech.[5]

The reader who has followed Baudrillard long enough to find Segalen will soon discover that the young tutor in *René Leys* has an historical double, a 'parallel existence', in the form of Maurice Roy, whom Segalen actually did hire to teach him Northern Mandarin, and who did in fact recount the exploits attributed to René Leys in the novel. In effect, there was a 'real' seduction, a seduction of signs, as Baudrillard likes to say, which sends the whole repertoire of fetishistic Orientalism on a journey of its own. Segalen was actually drawn in, perplexed, ultimately disillusioned, and with a little 'polish' he transformed the notes of his conversations with Roy into the novel about Leys. This was in 1911–12. Unlike Leys, however, who died at the end of the novel, the actual Roy outlived Segalen; but he never acknowledged receipt of the novel from Segalen's wife, who sent it to him when it was published after Segalen's death in 1919. Unfortunately, though Maurice Roy actually lived, we have only Segalen's word as to what he said, and whether he lied. Can we trust Segalen, anymore than we trust the narrator who leads René on the path of self-destruction, or René/Maurice himself?

As might be expected, the story doesn't end here. For the reader of Segalen soon discovers that there is yet another historical double, another 'parallel existence', also recorded in some edited manuscripts (unfortunately still unpublished). These are the notorious 'memoirs' of Sir Edmund Backhouse, a second baronet (1873–1944), and renowned British sinologist, the 'Hermit of Peking' (who had not set foot outside China since 1921). He was recognized in his day for his 'genius' as a scholar, and his authorship (with J. O. P. Bland) of *China Under the Empress Dowager* and *Annals and Memoirs of the Court of Peking*. Like Segalen/Leys/Roy, Backhouse had an uncanny ear for the structure and diction of a language. In effect, he was a mimic, and his intellectual reputation was largely founded on this skill. During the last stretch of the Dowager regime, Backhouse worked primarily as an interpreter and translator, also teaching English at the Imperial University in Peking. His autobiographical accounts were written much later, at the invitation of a Swiss professor, Hoeppli, who met Backhouse in Peking in 1942 (two years before the latter died), and was quickly seduced by the sage's wondrous (and debauched) tales of his life 'behind the scenes'. Hoeppli edited the manuscript after Backhouse died in 1944, but felt that a *chronique scandaleuse* such as this was largely unpublishable, even in this era. Just before his own death in 1973, he passed the texts on for bequeathal, preferrably to the Bodleian, which already possessed a large antique Chinese book collection donated by Sir Edmund (he had looted them during the Boxer Rebellion and the 1911 revolution). The manuscripts soon found their way to the historian Hugh Trevor-Roper, who was intrigued by the accounts of the lurid *demi-monde* of mandarins, eunuchs and concubines. They turned out to be a fabrication, of course, and all at the expense of the gullible Hoeppli, who had been utterly charmed by 'the destitute English baronet, with his graceful features, his exquisite manners of a *grand seigneur*, and his strange, hermit instincts'.[6] (Like almost everyone else who encountered Backhouse, including those he betrayed, defrauded or hoodwinked, Hoeppli never suspected his 'incurable love of mystification'.[7]) But from our point of view perhaps the most extraordinary aspect of the story lies in the fact that nearly everything in Segalen's account of René Leys's fantasy of life in the Imperial Court can also be found, *mutatis mutandis*, in the Backhouse memoirs.[8]

What is the point of these stories? Like seduction, they really have no point, outside themselves – not even to provide an illustration of what Baudrillard would do with the concept of seduction. One cannot tell what he might make of them. At best, they serve as examples of the sorts of things that Baudrillard might be curious about. But there is no interest in explanation here. Only a kind of metaphysical attraction to the *exotic* as a sign of the enigma of social being.

Segalen was a serious student of the exotic who, like many of the eccentric luminaries Baudrillard likes to quote (Jarry, Baudelaire, the late Canetti), raised aestheticism into a kind of antipolitics (which used to be called 'decadence'). Segalen was an aesthete in the antimaterialist, Symbolist mould, whose first major influence came from Huysmans. He was an individualist who resisted the concept of the universal, and despised the universalizing tendencies of modernist culture, whose prime vehicle he saw as egalitarianism. He interpreted these generalizing forces in terms of the second law of thermodynamics, that is, the tendency of all energy to 'run down hill', to exhaust itself in the uniformity of heat death, which he found more awful a prospect than nothingness itself: 'un plus terrible monstre que le Néant. Le Néant est de glace et de froid. L'entropie est tiède. Le Néant est peut-être diamantin. L'Entropie est pateuse. Une pate tiède.'[9] Segalen had travelled as a ship's doctor to Tahiti, arriving in the Marquesas three months after Gauguin's death. (Later he would stumble over the traces of Rimbaud in Djibouti.) He wrote about the Maori as 'Les immemoriaux': idealizing the island culture and civilization which was already passing under Western shadows. Later, he lived in Peking for five years, where he met Maurice Roy, upon whose fabulations he based the novel *René Leys*.

For him, the image of entropy in human affairs was already present in what he detected as a declining diversity and a 'Degradation of the rate of exoticism'. He identified this trend with the globalizing process of modern Science, whose future was 'broadly prefigured by the degeneration of ethnographic diversity'.[10] Segalen's strategy for combating this process (in his perception relentless) of homogenization was 'to exalt the partial exotic values that remain . . . exalt the prodigious unknown Past'[11] – in short, the special philosophy of 'Exoticism' whose cudgel Baudrillard has taken up (*FS*, *TE*, *FA*).

HORLA

As we have seen, the concept of the exotic can be related to Freud's 'uncanny' (the *Unheimlich*, whose antithetical term is Heimlich, 'homely' = 'familiar'), and thereby to the figure of the double, so prominent in the world's myths, which has found its way also into

European literature via folklore and fairytale. The theme of the double is inseparable from the theme of the dream, first because the dream always puts the alter of everyday life into play (the day's residues), and vice versa (the dream's residues); and also, more fundamentally, because dreaming itself as a form is always the double of consciousness as a form.

That the dream form is the double of consciousness does not mean that it is the day's imaginary other. That would be to dismiss dream as illusion or falsehood. The dream form is like an indirect, unlabelled narration of thoughts and experiences. In the dream, the latter are not those of the narrator, yet they 'belong' only to the narrator. Bakhtin calls this 'free indirect discourse'. The dream subject and the waking subject are not separate and independent sources of discourse, but they form a kind of counterdependent couple. As Deleuze defines free indirect discourse for film:

> there is not a simple combination of two fully-constituted subjects of enunciation, one of which would be reporter, the other reported. It is rather . . . two inseparable acts of subjectivation simultaneously, one of which constitutes a character in the first person, but the other of which is present at his birth and brings him on to the scene. There is no mixture or average of two subjects, each belonging to a system, but a differentiation of two correlative subjects in a system which is itself heterogeneous . . . far from equilibrium.[12]

Neither is really subject or object, primary or secondary, to the other. Moreover, as Deleuze suggests, following Pasolini, 'free indirect discourse . . . is not amenable to linguistic categories, because these are only concerned with homogeneous or homogenised systems'. The doubting effect of film (and dream) discourse is heterogenous. The film 'language' of images may be conceived as a prelinguistic thought process, which we can relate to Freud's primary process dream work/play/defence mechanisms of condensation, displacement, *mise-en-scène* (considerations of representability), and symbolism – all of which serves as 'doubles' of waking life.

Pasolini writes that every film is at the bottom a 'hypnotic *monstrum*': 'that mythical and infantile subtext which, because of the very nature of cinema, runs underneath every commercial [prose narrative] film which is not unworthy, that is, fairly adult aesthetically and socially'.[13] To use a McLuhanesque metaphor: film is a technological extension of the dream process – again, its double – and thus functions as a kind of exteriorized double in/of collective social space. In Segalen's involutive narrative it turns out that historical discourse itself is contained in a kind of Moebius band of mutual seductions, and parallel existences. The scissiparity of subject, dream, film, doubles again in the film form, at the level of the image content and narrative structure. Film lends itself especially well, through its affinity with the dream work, to redoubling as a narrative theme. This 'parallel existence' was noticed early by Rank, who drew attention, with quaint apologies (film was then still suspect as a cultural form), to the connections between film, dream and psychoanalysis; he used the Wegener film version of *The Student of Prague* as his primary illustration of the double theme in literature for this very reason.[14]

As we saw in Chapter 4, the central metaphor of Baudrillard's early work was the 'mirror', as an image of the doubling relationship of the subject and the object in political economy, and as a point of reference for what is now being superceded in the logic of cultural evolution: that is, the passage from secondary to tertiary simulacra. As he argued in the conclusion of *La société de consommation* (*SC*), the double is the classic metaphor of the subject's alienation, the master trope of commodity fetishism. But as the passage to seduction has shown, the traditional concept of the fetish as an object-for-a-subject no longer applies very readily in the context of the object system. Since the latter is organized as a political economy of the *sign*, the meaning of production and value changes. The naturalism of political economy and its critique is now subsumed in a kind of semiontology of forms, models and structures. This undermines the traditional claim for an originary or authentic subjectivity, once thought to be retrievable through the social, political or economic reintegration of the alienated or doubled self.

Like Rank, Baudrillard cites the silent version of *The Student of Prague* as the most rigorous working through of the logic of the double, but this time as a traditional allegory of commodity fetishism. Unlike Faust, gold is at issue in the student's pact with the devil. Baldwin, the student, is captivated by a count's daughter, whose life he has saved. But he is a penniless and dissipated man, without financial means to enter the appropriate social circles, or to offer his hand in marriage. In his humble lodgings, where he practises swordplay in front of a full-length mirror, he is approached by the devious-looking Scapinelli, who produces gold from his sleeve in an endless stream. 'This is yours if you give whatever I choose from this room', Scapinelli promises. Baldwin agrees on the assumption that there is nothing of value for Scapinelli to take. But Scapinelli beckons him to stand before the mirror, whereupon he deftly coaxes the handsome reflection from its virtual position behind the glass, out into the world; and to Baldwin's astonishment, the devil escorts his mirror image through the door, and into the street.

In the version which Baudrillard summarizes (*SC* 301–7), the student passes from success to success, but soon confronts his own image in flesh and blood. His reflection is pursuing him, and this is not just a matter of social embarrassment; it is a potential disaster. He has promised the contessa he will not harm her fiancé in a duel to take place the next morning. But the mortal deed has already been committed when he arrives at the appointed place – by his double. Things go from bad to worse, until he is nearly driven mad by this haunting self-image, which he cannot seem to escape. He resolves to destroy it. Finally, in his apartment, he fires upon the double in front of the mirror. The glass shatters, and the double evaporates. But it is the student himself who is dying. In his agony he seizes a shard of the broken mirror, and sees his reflection restored to the glass. 'His body escapes him, but for the price of his body, he retrieves his *normal* effigy, just before dying' (*SC* 303).

Baudrillard emphasizes the link between this theme and the great parables of the domination of nature epitomized in the Faust myth. The sorcerer's apprentice reflects the irruption of the market process in the first bourgeois societies of the middle ages and the Renaissance. In *The Student of Prague*, the detached image more specifically symbolizes the rise of Marx's commodity, in which social relations are detached from everyday life, and transformed into the fantastic appearance of autonomous relations between things fostered by the independent functioning of the exchange value system. But already, Baudrillard sees in this a certain 'fatality'.

> [In the objective logic of alienation, developed in all its rigour], we cannot escape what escapes us. The object (the soul, the image, the product of our labour turned object) *takes revenge* on us. Everything of which we are dispossessed remains tied to us still, but negatively, which is to say, it *haunts* us. The part of ourselves that we have sold off and forgotten is still us, or more accurately, our caricature, our fantom, our spectre, which follows us. . . . The alienated man is not just diminished, impoverished, but intact in his essence; he is turned into his own enemy, an evil erected against himself. This is Freud's process of repression on another level: the repressed returns in the agency of repression itself, like Christ's body on the cross, turning into a woman, to obsess the monk in his vows of chastity. . . . The only escape lies in death. (*SC* 305–7)

Maupassant's *Horla* (1887) is in some ways more compelling from a Baudrillardian point of view than *The Student of Prague*, the reason being that the Horla is not an alienated self, but a pure creation of signs, not a cognate being somehow separated (as with the loss of the shadow, or the detaching of the mirror image, or the object of our creation turned against us), but an alien being whose deep personal connection to us is completely inexplicable. Kepler's summary captures this perfectly.

> The 'Horla' . . . drinks water and milk like an animal but is not an animal, crouches on the narrator's breast like the Black Cat but is not a cat, smells the odor of a rose and flips the pages of a book like a man but is not a man, feeds on the life of its victim but is not a vampire. It is the Horla, a new and terrible being, whose emergence means that the reign of man is over.
>
> Without at all knowing why, the narrator salutes the Brazilian three-decker coming up the Seine, and at that instant, accepting the invitation, the unseen Horla that has come with the ship from across the earth fastens upon his life, becomes his inseparable companion. . . . It is not an accident; it is an impulse that the narrator can never explain, as though some force within him, outside the range of his conscious mind, had responded in kinship to a force without. The relationship that follows . . . is one of increasing closeness, very much as though the invisible pursuer were attempting to consolidate their two forms into one. At first, it is only such things as footsteps sensed, not heard, just behind the narrator's own. . . . But by degrees, the Horla moves inside.[15]

Maupassant:

> So, I was a somnambulist, I lived, without knowing it, in this mysterious double life which made me doubt whether there were two beings in us, or one foreign being, unknowable and invisible, which sometimes animates my captive body, which obeys this other, as if obeying myself, and more so, when my soul is numbed.[16]

As in *The Student of Prague*, the only solution would appear to be to destroy the double. The narrator succeeds in luring the Horla, and trapping him inside the locked house, which he sets afire. But why should such a being be deterred by flames? With impeccable logic, the narrator resolves to kill himself instead. 'Après l'homme, le Horla.'[17]

The Horla is certainly a nineteenth-century double (like Segalen's René Leys or the student of Prague); but Maupassant's emphasis on the indeterminacy of the doubling relationship suggests an exception to Baudrillard's claim that simulation and seduction surpass the 'alienation' logic of the double. It seems more accurate to say that in his explorations of third-order simulation, Baudrillard has discovered a deeper dimension of the same theme. No longer constrained by the terms of a Marxian teleology, Baudrillard rediscovers the double in the dynamics of social relationships as they have been reconfigured in late modernity. As the insidious presence of the Horla foreshadows, the double in tertiary simulation takes on a viral form. It might be speculated that this postmodern Horla is linked to some quality of intimate interpersonal relations with interactive technologies. Baudrillard's characterization of the double as belonging to the second order of production reflects his preoccupation with refuting the naive constructivist, or subject-centred, model of the social 'system', with its emphasis on synthesis, praxis and reappropriation (of the alienated substance, or double). Third-order simulation is about discovering the irreducibility of the double. And seduction, as he says, is dual. It is that internal fissuring or doubling of 'free indirect discourse' in which novel beings emerge from an encounter saturated with enigmatic signs.

18

Madame Baudrillard, c'est moi

Song: Education has always been undervalued in the West, hasn't it?
Gallimard: I wouldn't say so.
Song: No, of course you wouldn't. After all, how can you objectively judge your own values?
Gallimard: I think it's possible to achieve a little distance.
Song: Do you? Be a gentleman will you, and light my cigarette?

In the David Cronenberg film *M. Butterfly* (1994), based on the play by David Hwang, Song is, of course, not a woman; she is a man. Like all actors of female roles in the traditional Peking Opera, she is a well-trained transvestite. And she is utterly convincing, a master of the stylized parody approved by Baudrillard, 'femininity as masquerade'. Her French suitor, Gallimard, for some reason, is never conscious of this. Perhaps he is not so much a romantic hero as a fool, like Madame Butterfly herself in the Puccini opera, whose love for an insignificant and inconsiderate American sailor is hardly tragic, at least from the Chinese point of view, but more like the ridiculous delusion of 'a deranged idiot', as Song says of her theatrical predecessor. In fact, like Song, Gallimard himself is a kind of imposter – we might even call him a 'homeovestite': a man with a fetish for dressing up in men's clothes. At any rate, he is certainly a *parody* of the sexually repressed Western male.[1] He is a bit like Utz, in fact, a sort of collector (of Butterflies?), an accountant in the French consulate at Peking, tediously literal about money, who spoils everybody's fun by questioning the featherbedding practices which make life in the Diplomatic Corps bearable. But like a true obsessional, he is drawn with terror towards the deadly game of closure: the object that would complete his collection, and rob life of its purpose (*SO* 103–28). Thus, he is seduced by Song's performance of the death scene in *Madame Butterfly*. Holding the hara-kiri knife, with a superficial tableau of *chinoiserie* swirling around her, like Baudrillard's 'play of signs' (prefigured in the exquisite opening credits, and repeated throughout the film), Song is the perfect fetish object, the ideal enigma for a person – white, Western, male – like

Gallimard. When later Song enquires of Gallimard why, 'with your pick of Western women', he chose her, 'a poor Chinese with a chest like a boy', he replies: 'Not like a boy. Like a girl. A young innocent schoolgirl waiting for her lessons.' Song's comment on this sentiment vibrates with concealed irony: 'I know you are not threatened by your slave's education', she replies, as if thinking of Hegel's master and slave. But it is Gallimard who will learn the last lesson, though it is hard for him at first to grasp. Even after he makes love to Song, he remains happily unaware (or so he maintains) of her magnificent deception – for she never disrobes. As Song explains to the French court, many years later, as a witness in Gallimard's trial for passing state secrets to the Chinese: 'He was always very responsive to my ancient oriental ways of love, all of which I have invented myself, just for him.' In the end, Gallimard has to be *shown* (a bleak scene indeed, which occurs when he and Song, now dressed as a man, are together in the paddywagon, on the way from court).

All the ingredients for a perfect tale of seduction, as an edifying allegory on gender, culture and race are present: the indeterminacy of male and female, the indefiniteness of west and east, the indifference of master and slave. As David Hwang explained in his afterword to the published script of the original stage version, the idea was for a 'deconstructivist *Madame Butterfly*'.[2]

Earlier I suggested that not only the inscrutable Song, but also the earnest Gallimard, had foisted a kind of parody on us. It is really a sort of 'masculinity as masquerade'. If we follow Baudrillard in accepting parody as a legitimate strategy of seduction, then we are bound to admit Gallimard to the rank of seducer, which is ironic, since he is such a dupe. But unlike Song (and much like Victor in *René Leys*) his seductive strategy is *unconscious*, and therefore, in a sense, much more powerful, and much more fatal. As Gallimard himself tells the Consul, regarding the military rout of France in Indochina: 'You don't think those little men would have beaten us without our unconscious consent.' Just as Othello's seeming unawareness of his own murderous jealousy (Iago articulates it for him) seduces us into entering the triangle of dramatic irony, so Gallimard's 'deranged' misunderstanding seduces us into thinking that we know which sex is which. Like Baudrillard's tertiary simulation, the signs no longer hide anything except the fact that there is nothing to hide. We pretend to ourselves that we share a secret with Song, a hidden truth about Gallimard, and about what she has concealed from him. After all, we know that she is a man and a spy, and he doesn't. . . .

On the other hand, at a difficult moment, when they may conceivably be separated forever, she tells him: 'Never forget what our love has brought to life. . . . The days I spent with you were the only days I ever truly existed.' What does this really mean? Is she deceiving him again? Nothing is clear. But we do see that she depends on Gallimard as a pretext for her beloved masquerade (and for her decadent magazines: 'Don't you understand how degrading these images are to women?' her control cadre barks; but luckily they are part of Song's espionage cover). With the intensification of the Vietnam War, and the Cultural Revolution, even the French ambassadors, who represent the oppressor, are forced to leave, and Gallimard with them. But then Song no longer has a licence to seduce. The costumes, the masks, all the brilliant finery of the traditional opera are consumed in the bonfires of the Red Guards (as they are again at the end of Kaige's *Farewell, My Concubine*). What use have they now? Song is assigned to a workcamp for cultural rehabilitation.

As Lacan says, 'Les non dupes errent.' This can be heard in at least three ways: as 'the Name of the Father' (le nom du père), the *no* of the father, but also: 'Those who are not duped are wrong.' There is a case to be made, if not in the name of the father, then on the Baudrillardian grounds of seduction, that in our temptation to take a 'deconstructionist' approach to *M. Butterfly* (as the playwright invites us to do), we, too (like the non dupes), err.

Lacan's Law of the Father translates essentially into the idea that what saves us from psychic oblivion is the father's Symbolic disruption of the child's fusional identification with the mother. Lacan was himself a great seducer,[3] who like the deconstructionists after him, was an adept at keeping the 'play of signs' aloft. Any paraphrase of Lacan is likely to offend an adherent, but the simplest literal reading of him tends towards the following: the father represents language, culture and civilization – the Symbolic *Order*. If the child is not initiated into the Symbolic, does not come to terms with the 'law of the father', then he or she will remain an unhappy wanderer in the realm of the Imaginary, clinging to a narcissistic illusion of completeness and oneness, forever incapacitated by the agonies of disillusionment guaranteed by the inevitable discrepancy between the world and how we wish to conceive it.

The main assumption upon which Lacan's scenario is based, the idea that the infant cannot discriminate without the intervention of language, is widely accepted, though almost certainly false. The not very original contemporary assumption that there is 'no prediscursive reality', no perception except through linguistically mediated categories, can be challenged on empirical grounds.[4] Still, if one strips away the linguistic paraphernalia, one finds a great deal of hardcore Freudian wisdom in Lacan. And his schematic conception of psychic development finds some qualified support in what we know about emotional development. For example, just as the 'phallus' is not literally the penis, but the 'signifier of signifiers', and therefore not anatomically localizable, so, Kristeva has argued, the law of the father is not necessarily about actual fathers (and therefore not necessarily patriarchal). The 'law' concerns the symbolic third, to which both caretaker and child can refer, as something which they agree exists independently of them, something beyond themselves which the child can use as a probe of the larger, unknown world.[5]

Whatever we make of the Lacanian Symbolic, it is not really Baudrillard's cup of tea, that is certain. And yet there is in his theory of symbolic exchange, a hidden debt to Lacan, which resurfaces in *Seduction*. The latter may be interpreted as a kind of creative misprision, in which everything in Lacan is systematically misinterpreted – though one *fatal* idea is carried over: the necessity of submission to the 'Law'. This inheritance actually has two components for Baudrillard: the law becomes the rule of the game, to which we must all, in the end, give in (no matter how clever we are); and desire becomes the self-defeating, or masochistic, structure underlying all of social being (or awaiting its grandiose schemes). In other words, seduction is an ironic, parodic, postmodern version of the 'Law of the Father', which preserves Lacan's original sense of the Symbol as the 'death of the object', of meaning as a process of forestalling, deferring, distracting, diverting, avoiding, escaping . . . what?

PLEASURE

Like Freud's *Witz*, which is, according to Baudrillard, 'a transgressive reversal of discourse', a kind of 'instantaneous deconstruction' (*FCPES* 184), seduction always works from within the dominant form, using its terms in order to stage a subtle subversion, which suddenly takes over. Just at the moment when it can no longer be resisted, when there is no turning back, it turns us around. There is something in this which can be related to the concept of pleasure as an explosive force. The joke makes us 'explode' with laughter partly because it explodes some conventional bit of reality. This is different from pleasure as satisfaction, which Freud defined as a *reduction* of tension: a deflation, not an explosion. And so in that sense at least, seduction is not related to Freud's pleasure principle (which is really about the *avoidance* of unpleasure[6]) nor to pleasure associated with the satisfaction of *desire*.

Though seduction contrasts with the economic concept of pleasure as satisfaction, it can be related to the idea of *jouissance. Jouissance* is an ambiguous term which has been translated variously as bliss, coming, ecstasy. In *The Pleasure of the Text*, Roland Barthes tried to distinguish *jouissance* from pleasure as equated with satisfaction. There is a passage in which he compared reading to Freud's concept of perversion: this has to do with the fetishist's propensity for a 'splitting in the ego' such that 'castration' (the woman's genital) is both perceived and denied.[7] The fetish-object 're-presents' the (missing) phallus (penis). The *jouissance* of reading lies precisely in the sort of 'fetishistic' construction which constitutes our ordinary suspension of disbelief or suspension of 'reality' when we begin a novel or regard a painting: we *know* that we are entering into a fabricated world: the stage, the canvas, the printed page, the cinema screen. We may 'know' the story, but we read it over, or have it retold. The ending of the play may be predictable, but we settle into an exquisite state of anticipation, which depends precisely on this 'split in the ego', this double state of mind, which lets us know and not know, enjoy and suffer at the same time.

In contrast to the pleasure of satisfaction (though not necessarily 'opposed' to it), *jouissance* is more about *giving in*, submitting to a process whose outcome we probably already know, and perhaps even dread. Baudrillard would add that it is always just there, where we give in once again to the familiar (which is overdetermined by our transference), that the *same* will take us by surprise. (Perhaps this is one of the secrets of ritual.) Every repetition is a trap, a disguise for difference, a staging of the unexpected, which awaits us at every turn. The reason is that when we truly give in to seduction, we also *give up* – power. We agree to relinquish control, or at least we pretend to do so, and this is always delicious.

Seduction is essentially a masochistic posture, even and perhaps especially for the seducer. We know and we don't know at the same time. To seduce is to manipulate, but this immediately opens the seducer to manipulation in turn. Manipulation is not really seduction (in Baudrillard's sense) unless it admits this ambiguity, since without the element of uncertainty, only the victim enjoys the play of signs. If the seducer refuses reciprocity and denies the possibility of reversibility, then the seducer abandons seduction and becomes a machine, like Casanova, capable only of productive accumulation of goods, a technician of 'cold seduction', who ministers primarily to satisfaction, to the need to reduce tension rather than to explode with pleasure (which might be unpleasant).

If satisfaction is the reduction of tension, a form of consumption, then seduction is its heightening. It makes us vibrate and throb with pleasure. When the mother says, 'I'm coming to get you, I'm coming to get you', the infant knows that after a certain delay, she will suddenly thrust her hands into the baby's sumptuous flesh, to squeeze and tickle. And the baby is quite aware that he or she will squeal with delight in response to the mother's sadism. But the baby submits, nevertheless, and waits. The level of arousal escalates, and mother keeps saying, 'I'm coming to get you.' And the baby gives in, and gives up, and waits, and waits . . . and then, eventually – Woops! Gotcha! Cuddles and squeals of delight! That is seduction. But who is really seduced? The infant, who consents to this bizarre ritual? Or the adult, who cannot resist submitting, once again, to the infant's inarticulate pleasure?

ONTOLOGICAL OBSCENITY

We have already discussed the internal link between fetishism and seduction, and the transformation of the former, as the structure of the ideological process, into the very antithesis of political economy, a resistance to its 'operational' ideology, 'a certain kind of abstract, linear, irreversible finality' (*MP* 56). In the ordinary conventions of psychoanalytic discourse, the great 'other' of fetishism is *castration*, as we have seen, which implies that ideology, as operational finality, is broadly rooted in the denial of castration. Baudrillard's definition of seduction as a transmutation of the body into signs suggests that seduction is also a 'denial' of castration. Yet something saves it from becoming 'ideological'. The reasoning seems to be that, unlike ideology, which attempts to rationalize castration away, seduction acknowledges castration, and turns it into a kind of game. Seduction accepts the supremacy of 'castration' – submits to the law, as it were – by refusing any transcendental purpose, other than the 'game', which relieves the threat, without resolving anything.

In this broad perspective, 'castration' is fundamentally our inability finally to possess and to control the object. This inability lies halfway between two extremes: on one side, the fantasy that the object world can be brought to heel and rationalized, which tempts us to operationalize our existence, to become functional beings in a practical world entirely given over to our satisfaction, which always symbolizes the achievement of self-sufficiency and independence; on the other side, the fantasy that in our helpless dependence, in our lack of control, we will be subjected to an overwhelming intensity which will shatter the organization of our subjective lives, and reduce us to pitiable fragments of agonizing pain. We might be abandoned, bereaved, tortured or invaded. Baudrillard's point seems to be that production tries to save us from this fantasy of disintegration by literalizing the other fantasy, the fantasy of self-sufficiency; whereas seduction keeps us poised, for as long as possible, somewhere in between, but much more threateningly close to the possibility of incoherence, failure and loss.

From this point of view, *M. Butterfly* stages the entire drama of seduction, its ambiguity as a point of tension between two extremes; but it also stages the self-deconstruction of seduction. For just as we must submit to the rules of the game, seduction itself eventually fails to produce, and must submit to the higher law, which is loss and death. We are left with what Cronenberg always leaves us in his films, the finality not of production, but of destruction – Maupassant's Horla – or what Leo Bersani described as 'the nightmare of ontological obscenity . . . the prospect of a breakdown of the human self in sexual intensities',[8] from which there is ultimately no possibility of redemption, or rescue. Gallimard dies pathetically in prison, during his re-enactment of the death scene that seduced him, staged as an entertainment for the inmates, not so much a parody of Madame Butterfly, whom he becomes, but an upstaging of the cynical 'deconstruction' of her feelings. For at the very outset, when Gallimard had referred to the 'beauty' of her story, Song had shown how his aesthetic experience is nothing more than the hypocritical prejudice of a Westerner. Gallimard had thought that Madame Butterfly's death was 'a pure sacrifice'. Here is Song's ironic, deconstructive reply, which holds him at mid-distance from her, deflating his self-deception, yet preserving his delusory sense of power over her:

> It's one of your favourite fantasies, isn't it? The submissive oriental woman and the cruel white man . . . . Consider it this way: what would you say if a blonde cheerleader fell in love with a short Japanese business man? He marries her, and treats her cruelly, then goes home for three years, during which time she prays to his picture and turns down marriage from a young Kennedy. Then, when she learns he has remarried, she kills herself. Now, I

believe you would consider this girl to be a deranged idiot, correct? But because it's an Oriental who kills herself for a Westerner – ah! – you find it beautiful.

Through a hidden layer in the structure of dramatic irony, Cronenberg manages to sneak past us (and presumably the playwright as well). He seduces us, through Song, into the comfortable knowing of deconstruction, which demonstrates beyond any reasonable doubt that the tragic beauty of Madame Butterfly is a racist fantasy. But the deconstruction of imperialism, so 'convincing' (like Song's performance of Butterfly), serves only as a screen, behind which Cronenberg is busily at work deconstructing us. For we miss the possibility, which he holds in wait for us, that the real scandal is not racism and sexism – not that China plays the 'woman' to the West's 'man' (as the original Broadway play argued) – but the loss of enchantment, and not just the disenchantment of the 'West', but of the Chinese, and of ourselves as well. Baudrillard would call it the 'extermination' of symbolic exchange, or the loss of seduction, which thereafter becomes the fatal strategy of Gallimard's abject destruction, in which he becomes the Gorgon of castration, the 'black hole' which awaits us when the game is over.

And what of Song? In a way it is s/he who is outduelled in the end, s/he who is finally seduced by her own masquerade, for s/he comes to believe in herself, and to hope for love. But she cannot win the confirmation which only Gallimard, who is entirely her creation, can give. If it is true, as Song quips, that men play women in the Peking Opera because 'only a man knows how a woman is supposed to act', it is also true that the only man Song can love is the man created by the illusion of loving such a woman. By seducing Gallimard into becoming a man who loves, Song creates him as the only sign of her potential existence.

Song: You still adore me, don't you? You still want me: even in a suit and tie.
Gallimard: You're not . . . . You're nothing like my Butterfly.
Song: Are you so sure . . .? Come here, my little one. Ah, my mistake: I am *your* little one. Correct?
[Begins to undress.]
Don't you remember that theatre in China where we met so many years ago? The place where you gave me your heart . . .? I am your Butterfly, under the robes, beneath everything. *It was always me.* Tell me. Do you adore me?
Gallimard: How could you, who understood me so well, make such a mistake? You show me your true self. What I loved was the lie – the perfect lie. It's been destroyed!

Song: You never really loved me!
Gallimard: I'm a man who loved a woman created by a man . . . [unintelligible] simply falls short . . . .

VI

Metaphysical ruins

19

Text, technology and death

The excentric development of our systems is ineluctable. As Hegel put it, we are amid 'the life, moving of itself, of that which is dead'. Once certain limits have been passed, there is no relationship between cause and effect, merely viral relationships between one effect and another, and the whole system is driven by inertia alone. The development of this increase in strength, this velocity and ferocity of what is dead, is the modern history of the accursed share. It is not up to us to explain this: rather, we must be its mirror in real time. We must outpace events, which themselves long ago outpaced liberation. The reign of incoherence, anomaly and catastrophe must be acknowledged, as must the vitality of all those extreme phenomena which toy with extermination while at the same time answering to mysterious rules. (TE 108)

If Lacan's 'Law' always wins because we cannot exist indefinitely in the illusion of psychic self-sufficiency (as if we never had to 'separate' from mother), Baudrillard's seduction always wins because it is the only process which can divert us from the unbearable abjection[1] of our 'useless passion'[2]. We are always potentially alone and without purpose in a world we know, unconsciously, to be a ruse we have created for ourselves in order to distract us from the pain of living our essential condition. When Baudrillard refers with such apparent *naiveté* to the 'primitive', he seems to be saying that there is a way of living (through symbolic exchange) in which we can remain connected to this terrible fatality, without being destroyed by it. If we cannot always remain conscious of what it is we are distracting ourselves from, we can, at least, acknowledge that this is what we are doing – distracting ourselves, distancing ourselves – from the enigma of the unknown, from the intimacy of the 'ontological obscenity' which lies within, from the Horla. Seduction is the double consciousness of fetishism, of the splitting of the ego, in which we acknowledge and disavow the truth simultaneously, through an internal counterposition of checks and balances which keeps us humble, and makes us humbler if we grow more powerful.

It is debatable whether Baudrillard was right to locate the disposition of equilibrium-within-disaster specifically in the 'primitive', to see it as the special property of ritual in tribal cultures (later he would situate it in the exotic and the theory-fictional evocation of 'alterity', e.g. *FA* 81–107), but it is worth noting his view that the underlying motive of societies that turn themselves into historical movements is anxiety and flight: we enter history partly because we can no longer bear to sense what is immediately with us, directly in us. This is what Baudrillard means when, in *Symbolic Exchange and Death*, he extends Foucault's metaphor of the Great Confinement in early modernity from madness to death itself. Instead of this exasperating double consciousness (which henceforth will be defined as neurosis or perversion), we choose the all-encompassing illusion that we are functional beings who produce because we are moved by great purposes which transcend us . . . when really we are just frightened and trying to escape ourselves, but no longer able to bear the tension of sustaining this knowledge in the lived pattern of existence. We flee from presence, which is too horrible to contemplate, and lose ourselves instead in the endless deferments of 'writing', the fine arts of cultivated absence and controlled disappearance. If we are sophisticated, we realize that this is all just an articulate way of diverting ourselves from the inevitable prospect of death.[3] If we are full of 'useless passion' – or passionate indifference – we become connoisseurs of the arts of seduction, or – preferably – of being seduced. Whatever our creed, whether it be Marxism, Functionalism, Structuralism, Psychoanalysis, or the worship of the Virgin Mary, the point is, to keep the signs floating for as long as possible. This does not mean that we should refrain from acting as if life has a purpose – just so long as we do it consciously, for amusement only (seduction) – not because we are trying to prove a purpose (or to deny it). For proof (or the desire for it) is an unfortunate thing which, when final, breeds dangerous forms of certainty capable of producing functionalized murder, where symbolic deaths would have sufficed.

THE MORBIDITY OF THE TEXT

. . . Lévi-Strauss demonstrated . . . Lacan demonstrated . . . that 'meaning' was probably only a surface effect, a shimmer, a foam, and that what ran through us, underlay us, and was before us, what sustained us in time and space, was the system. . . . Before any human existence, there would already be a discursive knowledge, a system that we will rediscover. (Foucault)[4]

The omega point of a system is the point of a pure circulation of energies destined, by the very fact of that circulation, to indifference and death. In such a system, exchange becomes impossible owing to an immanent equivalence. . . . (*Cool* 101)

In 1970, the Nobel Prize-winning biologist Jacques Monod explained that 'pure chance, absolutely free and blind, [lies] at the very root of the stupendous edifice of evolution'.[5] For Monod, and most contemporary biologists, evolution does not stand for the unfolding of some cosmic law of development or the unveiling of a master plan: it simply refers 'to the stunning richness of the biosphere and the amazing variety of forms and behaviour it displays'.[6] So there is a creative force in the universe, like Bergson's 'creative evolution'; but it has nothing to do with Spirit, or with living beings, or *élan vital*. 'Living beings rest on the fundamental mechanism of molecular invariance.'[7] The creative force, evolution, the origin of multiplicity, the progenitor of absolute novelty, is not a living being. It is not an agent, not a subject, not even an unconscious desire, not even the sex drive; it is quite 'dead', an inanimate event; it is simply chance – accident, noise, interference: the unpredictable breakdown of continuity.

Chance, multiplicity, discontinuity: as Monod remarks, these ideas are profoundly 'destructive of anthropocentrism'. Few would deny that they have served the decentring trend in contemporary philosophy, particularly in the works of Lacan, Foucault, Derrida and Deleuze, who have succeeded in setting so much of the agenda in contemporary social philosophy. Monod noted the affinity of creative chance with some of Bergson's ideas, and these in turn resonate with important themes in poststructuralist thought. Paradoxically, the intellectual climate in which poststructuralism emerged was constructivistic and antihumanist at the same time. There was a withering suspicion of 'human nature', natural law, anything hinting at essences, substances or reasons (as if Jean-Paul Sartre had invented all these horrible things himself). Everything human was immediately branded as artificial, arbitrary, false. When a novelty emerged, humanity never got the credit. The source was always something more basic than subjectivity, intentionality, emotion or reason: a play of forces, a relation of power – the flux of desire or *différance.* In other words, as Monod seemed to imply, nothing in the poststructuralist universe is really alive: not in the sense of living, willing, wanting, sensing, feeling, remembering, knowing, believing, hoping, wishing or desiring – *internalizing.* Of course, it is not exactly dead either. With Derrida, we might call it a kind of '*life death*'.[8] Alive in a sense, no doubt, but mainly in the way that a drive is alive, as an instinct without an object. A form of entropy.

Classical psychoanalytic metapsychology suggests implicitly that the concept of the death instinct represents the purest possible form of instinctual activity in that it dispenses entirely with the 'detour' of object relations (which were in Freud's view the most variable and arbitrary aspect of the instinct) in order to mobilize the whole body and every living cell towards the essential aim of all drives, which is satisfaction, or in other words, extinction. In psychoanalytic theory, the correlation between satisfaction and extinction is an ideal one, but inevitable so long as pleasure is defined as the diminution of stimulus innervation, whilst the latter – stimulation – is defined as pain, i.e. so long as one accepts the primacy of the pain ['pleasure'] principle and the constancy principle.[9]

'Beyond Eros, we encounter Thanatos; beyond the ground, the abyss of the groundless; beyond the repetition that links, the repetition that erases and destroys.'[10] Deleuze's interpretation of Freud captures the essence of the poststructuralist project, its molecular machinery of powers and strategies without subjects or objects. It may truly be said that poststructuralist ontology represents the world from the perspective of the death instinct – the metaphysical essence of will and desire, which (according to Nietzsche) can operate only on itself, without any determinate connection to the world of things, the phenomenal realm of effects. In a sense, this is the immanent reversal announced by Baudrillard in *Symbolic Exchange and Death* and *Oublier Foucault*, the 'science fiction of the system turning against itself . . . in a hyperlogic of destruction and death' (*ESM* 12; *Death* 4–5).

The endless 'substitution for itself' of the metonymic 'chain of signifiers', the *desire* as 'lack', of which Lacan so famously spoke, is not related to any object (i.e. a person); it is, as Deleuze surmised, the repetition that erases and destroys, an 'economy of death'. The signifier is the medium of equivalence, the exchange value by means of which an inanimate force (drive, *différance*, desire, capital) is projected into time and space in a process of substitutive reproduction, towards the moment of extinction, the flatness of Nirvana or the 'body without organs'. 'Perhaps,' Baudrillard asks,

> there exists in all organic unity a drive to develop by pure contiguity, a tendency to linear and cellular monotony? This is what Freud called the death drive, which is only the undifferentiated excrescence of the living. This process knows neither crisis nor catastrophe: it is hypertelic, in the sense that it has no other end than limitless increase. . . . (*FS* 31)

> In contrast to the usual assumption that the social incarnates the objective progress of mankind (everything which escapes this progress being merely the leftovers), let us imagine that *the social itself is only a leftover*, and that, if it has triumphed in the real, it is in exactly that form. As an accumulating residue from the dispersion of the symbolic order, as sheer remainder, approaching universality, the social has assumed the force of reality: here is a truly subtle form of death.
>
> If such is the case, we are indeed even deeper in the social than we thought, that is to say, even deeper in pure waste and dejecta, in the fantastic congestion of dead labour, of relationships which are dead and institutionalised in terroristic bureaucracies, of dead languages and structures . . .
>
> Of course then we can no longer say that the social is dying, *since it is already the accumulation of the dead*. In effect, we are in a civilisation of the supersocial, and simultaneously of non-biodegradable, indestructible residue, piling up as the social spreads. (*L'ombre* 76–7; *Shadow* 72–3)

THE HOSPITABLE PARASITE

> We have demonstrated . . . in the development of the concept of capital, that it is value as such, *money*, which both preserves itself through circulation, and also increases itself through exchange with living labour. (Karl Marx)[11]

> The medieval proverb *nulle terre sans seigneur* [there is no land without its lord] is thereby replaced by that other proverb, *l'argent n'a pas de maître* [money knows no master], wherein is expressed the complete domination of dead matter over mankind. (Karl Marx)[12]

It takes only a slight shift in perspective to see Baudrillard's point about the simulation effects created by counterpointing 'natural' and 'artificial' values. In political economy, utility serves as the perfect rationale for the proliferation of depersonalized forms of interaction and exchange. In positivist philosophy, abstract models of reference justify the reduction of meaning (an emergent property of the body) to codified systems of signification. The same may be said of the relation between human agency (i.e. 'the historical subject') and Capital. Indeed, the greatest appeal of Marxism, at least in the decadent West, has never been the lionization of the proletariat, but Marx's masterly personification of Capital as the true revolutionary agent of modern history. This is a case of the serpent stealing the best lines, as in Milton's *Paradise Lost.* Capital, for Marx, is 'a mystic being' in an 'enchanted and perverted world', where 'labour's social productive forces . . . seem to issue from the womb of capital itself'. Indeed, Capital is a sort of vampire, a form of living death which stalks abroad, through the city and the country, sucking the blood of living labour, and converting it into greater and greater accumulations of dead labour, of fixed capital, machinery; nature is captured and stored up in a vast laboratory apparatus where 'science' does its work as the new productive force (thus replacing the proletariat as the hero of the historical drama). In a Baudrillardian perspective, the remnants of living labour serve as nothing more than alibis of this disjunctive synthesis of Capital and science, as does use value for exchange value, the signified for the signifier. After all, was it not Capital, according to Marx, which created the social individual in the first place? But not as the harbinger of a new socialist organization of leisure in a society without the State (that was a ruse). *Social* individuals are really the 'sex organs' of technology, pollinators for the spreading vegetation (rhizomatic?) of dead labour. 'Forces of production and social relations – two different sides of the development of the social individual – appear to capital as mere means, and are merely means for it to produce on its limited foundation.'[13]

In broad outline, then, Baudrillard's understanding of history remains fundamentally Hegelian and Marxist, though with a fetishistic twist: 1) the agent of history is abstraction, capital, science, or what Heidegger calls the *Gestell* (enframing) of technology;[14] 2) the ratio between the living and the dead is changing in favour, not of Spirit, as Hegel thought, but the dead: dead labour (commodities, capital, technology), dead time (records, tapes, disks), dead space (trade routes, pavement, pollution, speed, biospheres or 'bubbles'), dead experience (television), dead perception (virtual reality), dead knowledge (data banks and information systems), dead authority (micromanagement through in-house e-mail, polling, referenda), dead communication (writing and information), dead social life (interactive technology and computer-mediated communication); 3) the object is replacing the subject as the new form of sentient being.

THE CUPIDITY OF TECHNOLOGY

Perhaps, after studying the structures of the animist Imaginary, and then the energist Imaginary, we will have to study a kind of cybernetic Imaginary, whose focal myth would no longer be the organicism or functionalism of the previous modes, but an absolute global interrelationality. For the moment, however, the everyday environment is divided in unequal proportions between the three modes. The traditional buffet, the automobile and the tape recorder coexist in the same circle. (*SO* 142)

Apart from his review of McLuhan's *Understanding Media* (1967), Baudrillard's earliest reflections on technology refer to Gilbert Simondon's little-known study, *Du mode d'existence des objets techniques.*[15] Simondon had written convincingly of 'an objective progress of the technical object' in which,

the real technological problem is that of converging functions in a structural unity and not the search for a compromise between conflicting requirements. At the limit, in this movement from the abstract to the concrete, the technical object tends to resemble the state of a system entirely coherent with itself, entirely unified.[16]

Baudrillard treated this analysis as 'essential' because it describes 'the elements of a coherence never lived, never manifest in the real practice of objects' (*SO* 11). With such a model of idealized forms serving as a backdrop, the cultural-ideological variations of different stages of industrial society could be made to emerge in bolder relief. In particular, Baudrillard was able to exploit the contrast between the highly articulated, formal coherence of pure technical features and the doggerel heterogeneity of actual design and everyday use. If Simondon's formal analysis of 'technemes' allowed one to think heuristically of a formal 'language' of technology, then attention to the way objects are actually received, adapted and 'practised' would reveal, in a sense, 'how the "language" of objects is "spoken" ' (*SO* 15).

Simondon's thesis, however debatable (it suggested an immanent principle of form governing 'pure' technical development), implied an essentially humanistic interpretation of cybernetic rationality. If 'man' was to avert his mythic fate of domination by the machine – the ultimate reification – he must spurn his own temptation to pervert technology into a tool of domination. The rational use of technology implied intelligent respect for the potential of technical forms as open systems. Technology could best render its service as a mediation between people and between 'man' and 'nature' if the advantages of supple interconnection made possible by formal simplicity were not thwarted by instrumental expediency and short-term gains in efficiency.

Simondon's morphology allowed another dimension of critical interpretation to emerge. For example, the ideological imperative of efficiency and functionality could be shown to backfire, at a certain point, on these very principles themselves. 'The more the object is made to respond to the demands of personalization,' Baudrillard explained, 'the more its essential characteristics are encumbered by external requirements' (*SO* 169). The automobile provides the most familiar example, since from a purely technical vantage point, standard automobile manufacture has converted the internal combustion engine into a closed system susceptible to the failure of externally aggregated functions and superfluous automatism: separate heating, cooling, lighting, starting and transmission systems all escape the regulation of the engine itself. The automobile becomes 'logically more simple, [but] technically more complex, because it brings together several complete systems'.[17] Thus, it is not only more difficult and expensive to build, but also to maintain in running order. Given the technical superfluity and formal dissonance of the battery-run starting system – to name only one servomechanistic device added on to automobile design – its consumer success (in place of the handcrank) begs for a certain scrutiny. If, for example, the exaggerated fins and chrome work characteristic of certain periods of automobile construction function as signs of status, modernity, efficiency, power, elegance and various kinds of stereotyped identity, the 'use of a superabundance of automatism in accessories and the systematic recourse to the servomechanism even when physical capacities would hardly be exceeded by direct forms of control'[18] also invites interpretation. These 'connotations of automatism', as Baudrillard describes them, suggest a kind of parody of dualistic rationalism, a sort of rhetoric of the 'ghost in the machine'.

> Because the automatized object 'works all by itself,' it suggests a resemblance with the autonomous individual. We are confronted with a new anthropomorphism. Utensils, furniture, the house itself once bore in their morphology, their usage, clear imprints of the human presence and image. This collusion is destroyed at the level of technically perfected objects, but it is being replaced by a symbolism which is no longer concerned with primary functions, but with superstructural functions. It is no longer the specialized gestures, the energy, the needs, and the body-image which man projects into the automatized object; it is the autonomy of his own consciousness, his power of control, his own individuality, the idea of his person. (*SO* 134)

Whereas artisanal production could permit 'inessential' features to vary with the context of the creator and the user, the peculiarity of commercialized technical development is that it tends to build cumbersome inessentials into the very structure of technology as permanent features (*SO* 131–60, 169). This capability for fixed repetition permits a kind of bias to infest entire classes of objects in a systematic way, lending a peculiar kind of entropic resonance to the ambience of everyday life. There is in modern urban spaces sometimes a haunting atmosphere of lassitude, which affects us at the level of the 'animist Imaginary', through the omnipresence of standardized design in everything from coffee cups and doorknobs to waiting rooms and pharmacies. But this mute, alien presence is soon driven out by the 'demiurge drunk with power' (*Ecstasy* 13) who dominates the energist Imaginary, the Faustian drama of heavy machinery and the internal combustion engine. In the 'cybernetic imaginary', however, this sense of dissonance seems to disappear. The dynamics of social conflict and personal struggle are displaced by visions of a new social order for which there exists no metalanguage, no principle of rational criticism. 'Objects have become more complex than the human behaviour relative to those objects' (*SO* 68). The operative infrastructure of techniques is rendered less and less accessible to the user, who is caught up in the vertiginous illusion of absolute personal control fostered by a proliferation of dials, buttons and registers. It is as if social life had been placed on automatic pilot. 'In this tendency away from a fluid and open structuration of practices,' Baudrillard suggests, 'man reveals what is in a sense his *own* meaning in a technical society: that of the most beautiful multipurpose object, an instrumental model' (*SO* 135). 'Man is rendered incoherent by the coherence of his structural projection' (*SO* 69).

> Barthes had already indicated this for the car, where the logic of possession, and of projection, inherent in a strong subjective relation, is substituted by a logic of driving. There are no longer fantasies of power, speed, and appropriation, linked to the object itself, but instead the idea of potential tactics linked to its use (mastery, command and control, optimal use of options, which the vehicle offers as a vector, rather than as a psychological sanctuary). The subject himself is transformed into a driving computer. . . . The vehicle becomes a bubble, the dashboard a console, and the surrounding landscape becomes a television screen (*L'autre* 12–13; *Ecstasy* 12–13).

Baudrillard imagines a subsequent stage – a sort of VR car – in which the automobile is no longer a 'performing material', but an 'informing network', which would deliberate with the driver (wired in through an 'uninterrupted interface') in the ongoing negotiation of a whole way of life (*L'autre* 13; *Ecstasy* 13).

It may strike some readers that Baudrillard's early account of the 'mode of existence of technical objects' in *Le système des objets* already foreshadowed this concept of 'virtual reality', whose emergence in engineering research has become such an insistent theme in magazine folklore. In *Xerox and Infinity,* Baudrillard describes a kind of collapsing of the subject–object polarity and its spatial coordinates, such that the internal and the external, the proximal and the distal, become inextricably intertwined, as in a Moebius strip: 'The machine does what the human wants it to do, but by the same token, the human puts into execution only what the machine has been programmed to do' (*TE* 56). For Baudrillard, however, virtual reality was never just a question of software and electronic engineering capabilities. Its destructuring effect applies even to traditional technologies like photography, whose possibilities are 'no longer those of the subject who "reflects" the world according to his personal vision; rather they are the possibilities of the lens, as exploited by the object' in a way that 'erases all intentionality' (*TE* 56).

In this we see emerging more than the familiar idea of a cybernetic transformation of the social environment from above (command and control): Baudrillard is reading back into the history of technology an immanent principle drawn from the present, thematizing technology as a kind of 'desiring machine' or 'desiring production',[19] that is, as an evolutionary process in its own right. At first, Simondon's formalism allowed Baudrillard to isolate the internal logic of technology from its ideological manifestations, to facilitate analysis of the latter. But as he went into the ideology more deeply, he discovered the same aporia of 'base and superstructure' which had led to the critique of the 'political economy of the sign'. As Arthur Kroker has argued, technology is not simply a 'glassy background ideology'.[20] It is a process of social structuration in its own right, whose 'ideological uses' may go well beyond the surface layer of calculable choices (should telephones be equipped with video screens or not?) to a core of alternatives impervious to conscious control. This perspective implies that certain technologies may penetrate deeply enough into the human 'sensorium' (McLuhan) to bring about an 'ontological shift', as Michael Heim has suggested.[21] In the early 1960s, Norbert Wiener was already discussing seriously the means by which 'machines' could propagate themselves, and evolve through a form of natural selection, based on variations in the 'operative image' the machine produces of itself. As Wiener pointed out, in defence of the analogy with evolutionary biology, 'even living systems are not (in all probability) living below the molecular level'.[22] Conversely, it can be argued that language capacity, and the human brain itself, are technologies, since presumably they have evolved at least in part for pragmatic reasons.[23] Deleuze and Guattari have proposed the concept of a 'machinic phylum'.[24] Computing, of course, greatly enhances this evolutionary potential of the machinic phylum, since it reconfigures all technology as a single interconnected system, in which even the simplest artefacts become linked to a self-regulating assemblage which runs on information and communicates with itself. 'At a certain singularity [transformation threshold, like the boiling point of water], when networks reach a certain critical point of connectivity, they begin to form "ecologies" resembling insect colonies or even idealized market economies.'[25]

THE COMPUTERIZED BODY (CYBORG) AS A HOPEFUL MONSTER

> They were like creatures that were able perhaps naturally to watch themselves and their relation to the universe; creatures that had not yet been born.
>
> I thought – They are hopeful monsters![26]

> You can talk of things so much that they end up materializing in your life: simulation, seduction, reversibility, indifference. . . . In this way, writing ends up preceding life, determining it. (*Cool* 201–2)

Our present understanding of the human body, from the perspective of molecular biology, may be compared to the relationship between labour and capital, as described by Marx. Like the vampire, capital consumes the living in order to reproduce and increase itself, and so, as Jacques Monod implied, the reproductive code consumes the human body. The lived body (present, concrete, tangible, organic, analogic, continuous, romantic, purposeless, expressive, like speech) is really just an indifferent vesicle (a kind of glorified test tube) for the propagation and transmission of the genes. The genes exist as 'bits' of 'information' (absent, abstract, 'tactile', inorganic, digital, discontinuous, cynical, functional, disseminating, like writing).[27] There is no more cogent metaphor of the societal reduction of social being to digital procedure than this dynamic materialization of formal structural models of language and communication: the schema of a force/time (desiring production, power, *différance*, money, the genetic code) inscribing itself in space, the space of an infinite, indefinitely fungible text (the body without organs, the void, the blank sheet, value, matter). Being becomes the space created by the replication of abstract difference, the *différance* which disseminates and propagates 'toward death'. The double. The Horla.

There is no doubt that such an evolving, ocean-like textual being – a kind of digital *Solaris* – has been growing into existence on the information networks linking the world's communication systems. Envisioned by enthusiasts as a 'parallel universe', a 'realm of pure information',[28] it is usually referred to as the 'Internet', and is said to be expanding at a rate of 10 per cent a month, more than doubling every year.[29] An interesting feature of the Internet is that it seems to function very much like any other abstract system, Capital, markets, writing, the genetic code, by drawing randomly on 'living' particularities in a generalizing, systematizing, metaphorical transaction with the 'dead'. According to the folklore of computer-mediated communication (CMC), the Internet emerged in a truly unplanned manner, rather as if guided by an 'invisible hand', like a river created out of quite distinct tributaries, or a patchwork which suddenly falls together from many different sources, 'a common mental geography, built in turn by consensus and revolution, canon and experiment'.[30]

The nucleus of the Internet is conventionally said to have emerged in the 1960s with a US Defense Department Advanced Research Projects Agency (ARPA) program to redesign computer operation, under the slogan of 'interactive computing'.[31] Its structure is rooted in research on nuclear bomb-proof telecommunications. But like Capital, the Vampire, or any other self-perpetuating growth system, the 'net' is in principle resistant to administrative regulation and control, and very difficult to destroy. It feeds off everything with which it connects, converting all it encounters into self-substance. Expansion is limited only by the absolute parameters of its ecological niche: the continuing supply of labour, fresh blood, electronic interfaces. But if the Internet is a parasite, it depends for its survival on the evolutionary resilience of its host. If the host is the human nervous system, as McLuhan suggested, then the invasion of the Internet will depend on adaptive mutations of the nervous system itself. This 'viral' scenario confirms Heidegger's vision of the historical emplacement of a biotechnical symbiosis (*Gestell*). This convergence exerts increasing pressure on both the human form and the technological forms to evolve – or destroy each other. That would be Baudrillard's hypothesis.

Since the early days of military research on communication between computers, many private and independent groups have converged with ARPAnet, through their separate ways of linking computer technology with telecommunications technology, creating Bulletin Board Systems (BBSs), 'electronic communities' (the California-based 'WELL' being perhaps the most famous example[32]), and other networks, such as 'multi-user dungeons' (MUDs), for instance, LambdaMOO, which is 'a very large and very rustic chateau built entirely of words' and also the home of the celebrated 'Rape in cyberspace'.[33] Like the rhizomatic growing together of local markets in the last century, ARPAnet has converged into a global webwork of abstract, digital systems. As one enthusiast writes:

> [T]ens of thousands of people have been laboring to build the Internet. They have worked alone, in small groups, and within organizations, but always like so many ants in a global anthill. Most of these people are only doing their jobs but, just like the ants, they serve the common good while having no conception of the order and the compelling forces that drive their work. . . . Deep inside us, there is a voice that we hear only subconsciously and only as a species; a voice that commands us to take these computers, connect them into networks, and . . . communicate.[34]

From a Baudrillardian perspective, we might describe the Internet as the technological realization of an old Cartesian dream which, through a kind of *ad hoc* 'grammatology', has, in the Internet, produced a literal mobilization of *res cogitans* in *res extensa*. It is as if Heidegger's sweeping vision of Plato's metaphysics unfolding through the history of technology has come true. That the operationalization of the new 'space of writing' has revolutionary or transformative possibilities seems indisputable; though, oddly, these possibilities are frequently described in antirationalist terms, as if CMC will somehow overthrow mind–body dualism. In fact, at least on a Baudrillardian reading, the ideology of CMC seems to reinforce the crudest, most positivistic assumptions behind the mind–body split – most importantly, the assumption that 'mind' functions separately from 'body', in a wholly different dimension – and that the affective embodied semantic domain of the symbolic can be reduced at will to the neutral logic of signification, without loss; in short, that language and meaning can be translated, for the better, into a smooth combinatorial space of digital signalling and coded interaction. But as Baudrillard points out, language draws its social potential from the symbolic dimension. And as the reader may recall from Chapter 12, Baudrillard's symbolic is not 'societal', but 'social', in the most 'primitive' sense: it is an emergent property of bodies interacting. To strip this dimension of language down and condense it into a functional system operating within a pre-established matrix of coded coordinates is to reduce the social aspect of language to what Baudrillard calls 'sociality'.

'Sociality' bears the same relation to the 'social' as 'formality' does to 'form', and as 'communication' does to conversation: it is 'ecto-plasmic' (*FA* 40).

In a widely discussed study of the social effects of new communications technologies and practices, Mark Poster was one of the first to dwell on this ethereal quality of a computerized intertextual utopia:

> Compared to the pen, the typewriter or the printing press, the computer dematerializes the written trace. . . . The writer encounters his or her words in a form that is evanescent, instantly transformable, in short, immaterial. By comparison, the inertial trace of ink scratched by hand or pounded by typewriter keys onto a page is difficult to change or erase. Once transformed from a mental image into a graphic representation, words become in a new way a defiant enemy of their author, resisting his or her efforts to reshape or redistribute them. To a considerable degree, writing on a computer avoids the transformation of idea into a graph while achieving the same purpose. The writer thus confronts a representation that is similar in its spatial fragility and temporal simultaneity to the contents of the mind or to the spoken word. Writer and writing, subject and object have a similarity that approaches identity, a simulation of identity that subverts the expectation of the Cartesian subject that the world is composed of *res extensa*, beings completely different from the mind.[35]

Of course, there is nothing 'immaterial' about the words on the computer screen, but there is clearly a wish to attain or to possess a bodiless state. As the quoted passage indicates, this fantasy would permit an illusion of identity, an ego experience of effortless thought expansion in an infinite field of spatial coordinates free of obstacles. In the unwittingly Cartesian rhetoric of the 'graph', we achieve the temporary (and perhaps one day permanent) ability to bypass the body, and like Jobe, in Brett Leonard's film *The Lawnmower Man* (1992) entering Virtual Reality, to translate ourselves into pure information, where there are no body doubles, no 'defiant enemies', just infinitely malleable, endlessly reproducible, indefinitely branching 'clones'. The implications are indeed revolutionary; but whether they herald the overthrow of 'logocentrism', or rather its apotheosis, is open to debate.

Utopian excitement about the Internet has reproduced not only the imaginary structures of classical rationalism, but the disembodied delusions of traditional moral reason. It is already part of the ideology of CMC that the neutralized space of communication reduces social oppression by enhancing the conditions of formal equality between the respondents. One of the earliest social experiments undertaken in this vein was the Minitel 'messagerie' in France, a multi-service database which was distributed free of charge by the French government during the 1980s to millions of telephone subscribers. This innovative interactive message service quickly grew into a new 'electronic speech community' whose popularity could be interpreted 'as an extension of the liberal politics of communication'.[36] Mark Poster has gone so far as to argue that on the Minitel messagerie, 'genderless anonymity undermines the Cartesian subject'.[37]

As in Poster's reading of the Minitel, much of the contemporary 'hype' about the Internet seems to be drafted in the language of the poststructuralist critique of Reason. But the idea that a new technology would 'undermine the Cartesian subject' actually draws on the quite different tradition of utopian egalitarianism. The latter is, in certain fundamental respects, antithetical to poststructuralist thought. The appeal of 'genderless anonymity' lies not in the antifoundational spirit of radicalized semiotics, but in a quite different vision of universalization, in which all differences will finally be overcome. As we have seen, significant contrasts can be reduced to the logic of signification, so that they can then be socially controlled. Any remaining differences can be homogenized or neutralized through digitization, in fairness to everybody. The universalizing cultural power of digitization is that it reduces the concept 'opposite' to a pure form without content, comparable to exchange value. The ones and zeroes serve as an irresistible general medium of equivalence.

Like Poster, Baudrillard sees Minitel as a leveller of differences, but not with the same cheerful assent. The deep ontological and epistemological consequences of communication between computers do not lie in the sudden liberation of the intertextual ego. The endless 'grafting' made possible by the technology of hypertext simply parodies the classical archetype of 'mind'. It reinforces rather than undermines the pretensions of the disembodied ego to override the frictions and boundaries of body space by substituting an infinitely accessible mental space controlled from above through a system of manipulable coordinates. Nothing could be *more* Cartesian. In contrast, Baudrillard situates the new communications technology within the more encompassing perspective of civilizing abstraction. For Baudrillard, the 'compunications' revolution is the culmination of a vast historical process of formalization and codification whose gradual long-term effect has been the societal reduction of affect and the marginalization of the body in social space. Baudrillard may be wrong; but his analysis directs our attention to the confusion which may occur when post-structuralist antinaturalism (whose Nietzschean inspiration is individual freedom rather than collective equality) is recuperated by the egalitarian instrumentalism of utopian thought. In a panel discussion with Marc Guillaume, Baudrillard agrees that the anonymity of CMC is an interesting phenomenon, but he advances some doubts:

about this lifting of names, identity, the presence of the body. Are we liberated by this? Yes, we are liberated in relation to these powerful symbolic operators. But in what does this liberation consist? Availability (*disponibilité*), virtuality, but on the other hand, we become complete hostages of the code.

When one is liberated from one's name, one becomes, on the contrary, much more dependent on the mark (*marque*), the sign, on all the signs of coded orientation (*repérage*). From this moment, there is a kind of precession of the code and the digit (*chiffre*). We see this in all the operations of Minitel. . . . All these media require a sort of precession of recognition/reconnaissance (*reconnaissance*) by the code, or of indexation in terms of the code, a precession of reconnaissance over knowing by acquaintance. One doesn't know oneself, and one doesn't really seek to know oneself.

The problem resides in this omnipotence of the code. The code is not only the fact of announcing oneself in a coded name, but also the functioning technological matrix of these systems, which control the mode of appearance and disappearance, of coming and going, which isn't the case in the pure operation of language with the name. The more one is unburdened of the body, identity, name, the more one falls under the jurisdiction of a frightening process of coding and overcoding – but this is not a moral judgement.

Does the other exist in all this? If I make semblance (*faire semblant*) to be an other, then the other is also a semblance, somewhat derived from the code, and perhaps from this moment on, the other is simply confounded with the code. The great other would be this code, and there will be no other. Then it is the code which governs an alterity, but a perfectly artificial one. . . . Moreover, this Other [as code] is unassailable, because it is much more shrouded in secrecy, more deeply buried, than the proper Name. (*FA* 39–40)

Baudrillard's point comes even clearer when we begin to take apart some of the rhetorical constructions out of which the discourse of CMC ideology is constructed. For example, we are told that 'Minitel allows private conversations between two individuals.'[38] This is certainly true. But what does it mean to absorb, as unexceptional, the implication that private conversations might have been impossible without Minitel? One does not have to be as pessimistic as Baudrillard to take his point that much of the discussion of the social potential of the new technology is incoherent. Digital utopianism, though attractive in many ways, seems to be vitiated philosophically by a disingenuous rationalism which tries to evade the problem of the heterotopic *semantic* dimension of the body. By conflating the latter tendentiously with the 'Cartesian subject', egalitarian thought can simply cancel it out of the equation, whilst seeming radical and 'postmodern'. Down with Descartes! Death to the 'unitary bourgeois subject' – through computers!

As we have already seen in our discussion of Baudrillard's earlier work, the hyperlinguistic epistemology of contemporary thought not only expresses but also seems to embody (as in the system of objects) an attenuation of the affective dimension of social life. It delineates a theory of abstraction, a methodology of reduction, and a technique of substitution, which neutralizes the (symbolic) meaning of objects by giving them a conscious and calculated existence. Since the symbolic is essentially the connective social form of subjective internal worlds (the psyche), it should not surprise us that, in Baudrillard's estimation, this functional stripping of the object world also erodes the subject's capacity to 'mean'. The semantic dimension no longer emerges from the body, because everything in relation to which it might emerge is already a plenitude: a 'construction', a 'production', an 'effect'. Thus, Baudrillard's science fiction fantasy is that this digital rationalization of societal space will rationalize human interiority as well.

> Today the scene and the mirror have given way to the screen and the network. . . . We no longer invest our objects with the same emotions, the same dreams of possession, loss, mourning, jealousy; the psychological dimension has been blurred, even if one can still retrieve it in the particular. (*Ecstasy* 12)

The subject omnipotently manipulating significations in a network composed of an infinite textual field of signifiers is him or herself reduced to the status of a signifier, just as the subject of virtual reality is transformed into a virtual computer.

> The private space undergoes the same fate. Its disappearance parallels the diminishing of the public space. . . . The distinction between an interior and an exterior, which was just what characterized the . . . symbolic space of the object has been blurred in a double obscenity. The most intimate operation of your life becomes the potential grazing ground of the media. . . . The entire universe unfolds unnecessarily on your home screen. (*Ecstasy* 20–1)

POSTMORTEM FOR POSTSTRUCTURALISM

> One must go further: culture itself, culture in general, is essentially, before anything, even a priori, the culture of death. Consequently, then, it is a *history of death*. (Derrida)[39]

Judging from Baudrillard's published work, and his interviews, the bitter sentiment of loss expressed in passages such as those quoted above from his *habilitation* reached a feverish pitch during the 1980s. These were forcefully expressed in some allegorical musings on the death of Foucault in 1984, which Baudrillard published in *Cool Memories*. Foucault's death must have been troubling for Baudrillard, not only because of the inevitable envy which such an illustrious career provokes in any academic competitor, but due also to the curious 'parallel existence' of their work since at least the early 1970s. (Both began with treatises on the organization of 'things', and both became obsessed with working out the aftermath of Marxism through an ambivalent appropriation of phenomenology, structuralism and psychoanalysis.) Baudrillard was, in many ways, Foucault's intertextual *doppelgänger*, and he treated Foucault much as the escaped mirror image treated Baldwin in *The Student of Prague*. For Baudrillard, Foucault's death by AIDS must have compounded the irony of his premature passing, since the virus, and the havoc it wreaks at the level of cellular communication, was already one of Baudrillard's guiding images of death's accumulation at the expense of the living body. It must have seemed to him as if pataphysics itself were developing a functional existence in the real.

'For thought, the internal scandal produced by its simulated apotheosis is unbearable' (*Cool* 158), he wrote. In consequence, the subtler thinkers of the 'media era', such as Foucault, Barthes, Lacan, have produced 'a philosophy of disappearance' tracing '[t]he obliteration of the human, of ideology. The absent structure, the death of the subject, lack, aphanisis. . . . A whole generation . . . will have disappeared in a manner wholly coherent with what it described, what it sensed, of the inhuman' (*Cool* 160–1).

Yet this 'inhuman' which Baudrillard discovers at the end of poststructuralism is also in a way the figure of death's inversion: that reversibility which is the power of death, but also of its counterpart, symbolic exchange. Through the fatal strategy, Baudrillard's symbolic object survives its own death in the form of

> the pure object, whose power forbids either possessing or exchanging it. It is something very precious that we don't quite know how to get rid of. It burns, and isn't negotiable. It can be killed, but it takes revenge. The corpse always plays this role. Beauty, too, and the fetish as well. It has no value, but is priceless. It is an object of no interest, and at the same time absolutely singular, without equivalent, and almost sacred. (*FS* 47)

This pure object, the object of symbolic exchange, does not pretend to reduce death in the way 'desire', 'différance', 'power' (and

Capital) try to reduce life to interchangeable components, or 'part objects' in a process of production and accumulation. The Baudrillardian object includes life and death, in the form of *meaning*, not because it yields, at last, to human control, or to the dream of human redemption, but precisely by resisting the subject and the psyche. The object resists the subject and the world of intentions and the depth of emotions because it is different from them, irreducibly and fundamentally different, unique, an *essence*, a *substance*, an *Other*. It is not just formally different, diacritically different, accidentally different, like Saussure's signifier, or Jakobson's phoneme, or Lacan's letter, or Derrida's trace, or Deleuze's desiring machine, or the pixels on the monitor screen, or even Lévi-Strauss's mytheme, it is not a structural, i.e. abstract, difference whose function is to mark the place of substitution and exchange. The object is different in depth, and so it will not yield to circulation in a 'libidinal economy' of substitutions and significations. It does not absorb and disperse, but simply stands apart, utterly resistant to the demands of the Cartesian ego, which (especially when computerized) wants nothing more than a decentred digital field of interchangeable 'differences' into which it can project itself omnipotently, changing identities, positions and genders at will. Baudrillard quotes Segalen: 'If taste intensifies with difference, what could be more sensual than the opposition of irreducibles, the shock of eternal contrasts?' (*L'autre* 71; *Ecstasy* 82). To the extent that the object can resist the appropriative 'subject', it sollicits the person, and opens the space of meaning, the 'ambivalent' dimension of the symbolic.

PARADOXICAL MOURNING

Baudrillard's critique of the political economy of the sign resembles in some respects the psychodynamics of paranoid states understood psychoanalytically. The simultaneity of love and hate in the ambivalent relation to the object produces so much anxiety – the fear that hate will destroy the good object – that love is split off and the object is defended through intense idealization. The ideal object is of course unattainable, but the frustration this causes is compensated to the extent that the hateful and envious feelings are denied internally and deflected away from what is precious. Thus the alibi term in the double structure of the sign and the commodity – what Derrida called the 'transcendental signified' – serves not only to rationalize the dirty anal deadly sinful material functional term, the signifier or exchange value (money=shit); it also creates a defensive split, a duality which obscures the emotional complexity in a relationship, arising from the fact that the object is both good and bad, satisfying and frustrating, loving and hating – in short, our ambivalent feelings for the symbolic object.

Baudrillard's work develops the idea that abstract systematization – precisely the kind of formal idealization so typical of structuralism and its offshoots – is historically irresistible because it diverts and temporarily contains painful feelings of envy (status), jealousy (rivalry), greed, hate and anxiety. When he questions 'libidinal economy' and alludes to a 'perverse structure of desire' (for example in the early article on fetishism), he is surely saying that the commodity and the sign solicit 'desire' and 'communication' as 'simulutions' which conceal but never resolve the dense realities of aggression and fear which always accompany wishing and wanting and willing. We don't just desire the commodity, we loathe it to the very bottom of our souls.

Splitting–projection–idealization–devaluation: while there is a marked paranoid theme in all of Baudrillard's work, so apocalyptic in tone, there is an undercurrent which adumbrates a movement from anger to sadness and from schizoid detachment to depressive concern for the object. A new strategic principle of criticism emerges. If the old principle of 'critique' derived from the notion of satellite values, splitting, idealization and projection, the new 'fatal strategy' of Baudrillard's cultural metaphysics is about the uncanny relationships of the psychodynamic body, *jouissance*, death and rebirth. The title of Baudrillard's most recent book refers to this: *L'illusion de la fin*. We might call its central theme the hypothesis of *dialectic interruptus*. For Baudrillard, our culture has omitted to mourn its losses and disappointments, and thus failed also to go beyond itself and to celebrate what comes as a new beginning. Everything in defensive idealization that isn't carried forward or resolved in relation to the symbolic object will fall into bitter disappointment and endless 'disappearance'. The result is the moral panic of puritanical perfectionism. This fantastic millennarian ideal only exists because aggression and hate were split off and denied, but they continue to work within us as persecution and guilt (the death instinct?). There is a perpetuation of the finale, a failure of 'synthesis', in which the 'culture' endlessly defers the moment of climax in its attempt simultaneously to achieve immortality and to avoid the mystery (of) coming.

20

Simulation

[P]eople are beginning to function as elements in a hypertextual network of affiliations. Our whole society is taking on the provisional character of a hypertext: it is rewriting itself for each individual member. . . . The computer provides the only kind of unity now possible in our culture: unity at the operational level. (Jay David Bolter)[1]

The real object of computers and the purpose of computerization is to extend to the total integrated electronic environment the kind of control and monitoring relationships people experience with their own bodies. (de Kerckhove)[2]

Less well-equipped cultures were inclined to make a truce with nature quite early. Perhaps Western man was not prepared for the sudden capitulation of nature with Sputnik in 1957. When the planet went inside a man-made environment, nature had to yield to art and ecology. (Marshall McLuhan)[3]

The logic of the mind–body split is very difficult to avoid in the sociology of computerization. In general, digitization is seen by the experts as offering the same division within experience which has opened up in human culture around writing in general: the gap between time and space, thought and perception, language and the body. The whole 'artificial intelligence' research program is premised on the assumption that mind is discontinuous with body, that mental acts can be generated from an abstract model. The same kind of dichotomy has been extended into the cultural sphere, where speculations about the social function of information technology usually proceed along anthropomorphic lines. Digital information can be used, through the logic of hypertext, for example, to extend the *distal* culture of writing, of distancing, reflection, and rationality; or it can be used, through 'virtual reality' applications, for example, to extend the *proximal* culture of the senses, of sensory simulation, emotional communication, festival, spectacle and 'experience'. In this vision, exactly as in the classical Platonic epistemology, cognition and perception are rigorously counterposed.

A simulated world, a world of pure perception, can serve to counterpoint daily work in the world of signs [language and thought]. But it should be obvious that

> virtual reality cannot in itself sustain intellectual or cultural development. . . . The world of useful work is a world of reading and writing, and yet at least some developers of virtual reality want to bypass or even deny such symbolic communication.[4]

Much social theorizing about computers presumes that the pluralistic but rationalist values of the literate elite will simply reproduce themselves in opposition to the prereflective culture of emotional involvement and spectacle. Consequently, the debate has shifted to the question whether digital culture will ultimately determine the supremacy of one form or the other: enlightened self-regulation of the people, or totalitarian absorption of the 'masses'.

Baudrillard's concept of simulation as a social process relativizes these stark alternatives by integrating both aspects of digitization: 1) the sense in which we are caught up in more and more abstract systems of writing, distancing us from the emotional immediacy of the body, and from the problem of negotiating the boundary between inside and outside (i.e. writing as the uprooting of the Symbolic and the production of a purely formalistic type of individuality); 2) the sense of simulation as a digitally enhanced, all-encompassing override of sensory experience – of society as a kind of total medium, or generalized hyperrealist surround, which abolishes critical distance and absorbs the individual into a 'mass' or 'black hole' of identificatory fascination. It is true that Baudrillard himself reproduces the mind–body split in his theory of the absolute incommensurability of the political class (who no longer 'represent' anyone or anything) and the societal 'mass' (who cannot be represented, except arbitrarily, through psychotechnical simulation (*Shadow* 38)). But at a deeper level, Baudrillard seems to get behind the rationalist split between reality and appearance, science and ideology, actuality and illusion, truth and perception, mind and body, by positing simulation as a constitutive dimension of society. It is not clear whether he thinks that simulation in this ontological sense is constitutive of all societies, or only of post-symbolic societies such as our own. But he insists that it is the process of simulation itself which lies at the root of the cultural disjunction of mind and body, producing both distal and proximal cultures as its 'privileged' and its 'alibi' terms (mind, language, society or spirit are privileged because they impose order on the natural 'chaos' of the body, the senses, the individual, the passions and appetites). The root sense of simulation in Baudrillard's thought is not deception in relation to reality or truth, but creation, or what Niklas Luhmann has called 'autopoiesis'. As Luhmann points out,

> A communication system is . . . a completely closed system that creates the components out of which it arises through communication itself. In this sense a communication system is an autopoietic system that (re)produces everything that functions as a unity for the system through the system itself.[5]

> [The selection of *information*, *utterance* and *understanding* is] a condition of the autopoiesis of social systems. Whatever the participants may understand in their own self-referentially closed consciousness, the communication system works out its own understanding or misunderstanding. And to this purpose it creates its own processes of self-observation and self-control.[6]

If we acknowledge that social systems are communication systems, then Luhmann's theoretical model of a communication system can be taken as a model of simulation in the Baudrillardian sense. Baudrillard would add, however, that the relative power of such closed societal systems of communication varies with respect to other dimensions of social being. Baudrillard would place much more emphasis on the *tension between communication* (in Luhmann's rigorous sense) *and experience* (which cannot be codified for reproduction, except as an element assimilated to a closed system of communication). The argument is not that we can simply choose one or the other, but that, metaphysically (if not historically), with the increasing assimilative power of communications systems, the social dimension of 'experience' has been progressively squeezed for enabling resources. The trend towards automation of self-regulating societal systems (third- and fourth-order simulacra) attenuates the social space for affect ('ambivalence'). As we saw in the last chapter, it is a question of civilizing abstraction, a long-term, nonconspiratorial process of marginalization, or assimilative exclusion. Of course, though Baudrillard emphasizes the tension between communication (in Luhmann's sense) and the psychodynamic social body, he also maintains that the social body is gradually being dissolved in and through 'communication'. He has never been able to ground any countervailing social principle, to give substance to the potential, implied in his affinity with notions of reciprocal exchange, for a psycho–societal balance which would mitigate simulation.[7] For Baudrillard, it seems, all historical existence is by definition a state of dissociated sensibility, though in *Symbolic Exchange and Death*, like T. S. Eliot or Michel Foucault, he dated the essential split at the end of the Renaissance, in the age of Milton and Descartes. No image or trope in the Baudrillardian corpus expresses with conviction the ideal of a balance or counterpoint of intellect and sense, of reflection and experience, of thought and perception, of language and embrace. Baudrillard manages only to protect a phantom otherness – symbolic exchange, seduction, alterity – whose protean forms permit him to adjust our conception of alternative possibilities in relation to shifting cultural forms and modes of cross-referencing experience. This capacity to keep the utopian signifier floating and free of reference has allowed him, rhetorically at least, to resist the dichotomy between the activist 'morality of meaning' on one hand, and passive, apolitical 'fascination' on the other (*Shadow* 37): between political responsibility and popular culture, between the rational promise of a *social* life and the irrationality of the internal world, between reason and seduction. What is difficult to grasp, because subtle in his reading of the contemporary situation, is that in refusing the choices, Baudrillard has not demanded reconciliation and harmonization, but rather questioned the desirability of reconciliation itself. As we shall see in Chapter 21, resolution or synthesis would, through that utopian 'degradation' of imaginary transcendence into closed reality, eliminate the element of alterity which generates all human experience as a challenge – just as choosing one cultural modality to the exclusion of the other attempts to avoid the trouble of alterity by suppressing it.

In fact, the distal culture of writing and rationality and the proximal culture of bodily interaction have been intimately intertwined since humans discovered ways to count sheep and to keep records of crops and livestock. It seems that the earliest precursor of writing involved a form of concrete accounting with clay tokens – about ten thousand years ago.[8] Number and object were united in the same token so that the resulting signs were rigidly bound to an originary context. But in spite of their limited capacity for recombination, extrapolation and iteration (there were no abstract numbers), the tokens could be pooled as signs of administrative authority over the community. Eventually, the system bifurcated into currency and pictography: money and writing, the two great forms of 'circulating' abstraction upon which the great classical metropolitan civilizations in Asia, the Mediterranean basin and South America, were based. So digital distancing has always been with us, immemorially inseparable from sensory-analogic culture. What the history of communication technology teaches us is that for a long time there has been a gradual and uneven (but then in the last 200 years, rapidly accelerating) process of abstraction, both digital (i.e. alphanumeric coding) and analogic (radio, film), and in various combinations (television, video). At the moment, it appears to us that digitization is the more powerful form of abstraction, but this is not the central point in Baudrillard's argument. For Baudrillard, the 'tactile' and the 'digital' are part of the same integrated network of mutually reinforcing cybernetic technologies, not different stages of technological development.[9] The issue is not the opposition between digital and analogic forms of processing, but the supraordinate power of formal abstraction, latent in all technology, which can be operationalized through any new method of reduction to discrete units for purposes of arbitrary recombination: that is, the ever more enhanced absorption of elements of experience into autonomous self-governing systems of communication – simulation in the broadest possible sense.

It is important to recall that communications systems (in Luhmann's definition) are not closed in the sense that they do not interact with the environments which sustain them; they are closed in the subtler sense that, as emergent processes, they function only on their own terms, independently of the supporting environment. Systems of communication include from outside only what can be converted into the system terms themselves. Cybernetics in the 1950s and 1960s revealed this interesting property of physical systems, and structuralism quickly set about rediscovering the same principles in systems of information and signification. Unfortunately, these intellectual movements were influenced by the classical positivist credo that signifying systems exhaust the semantic domain – that there is no dimension of experience, cognitive, conative or affective, which is not constituted inside these closed systems. Much of the poststructuralist rhetoric about the death of the subject is based on this misunderstanding of organizational structures. In fact, natural systems are never exhaustive. They always function in a larger containing environment; and the same applies to the meaning effects of signification, which draw upon and convert material from a much vaster semantic domain, including the body (which includes the brain), and perhaps some transcorporeal substance of social being as well.[10] Subjects in the nondiscursive sense continue to exist: it is just that they can only be *reported* as already absorbed by more and more powerful 'closed' systems of communication, which select the convertible bits of the subject, presumably leaving the rest to the care of marginalized supporting social environments. In fact, poststructuralism has been dominated by a metaphysical obsession with what might escape these closed systems, what might not be or *cannot* be converted into the terms internally functional to signification. Kristeva's 'semiotic' (which would be Baudrillard's 'symbolic'),[11] Foucault's 'power', Derrida's 'différance', Lyotard's 'differend': these are all euphemisms for nonsystemized, nonsignifiable 'experience'.

These nonsignifiable, incommunicable features are what Michel Serres in his usual elegant way has theorized as the 'Demon' of 'noise' who represents the 'third' which must be excluded in order for signification to occur (cf., once again, *FCPES* 143–63). Applying the systems principle to Plato and Liebniz as prophets of mathematical formalization, Serres explains: 'To engage in dialogue is to posit a third and to find a way of excluding him; successful communication is this third excluded.'[12] There is a moment when the abstract form is recognized and grasped in its generality, and then there is a violent struggle to sustain it as the basis for a new operation of thought. This is civilization as a project of formalization.

As we have already considered, Baudrillard appropriated structuralism as an analog of the civilizing process, of reification as an operational by-product of formalization. Again, Serres conveys the essence of this connection in his own definition of a 'structural analysis':

> One generates families of models with distinctive signifying content which have in common a structural analogon of form; the latter is the operational invariant, abstracted from all content, which organizes them. This process of abstraction is so complete that, once the structure is isolated as such (i.e. the abstract elements and relations) it is possible to discover all the imaginable models it generates; in other words, it is possible to construct a living cultural being by filling a form with meaning (*sens*).

Serres continues:

> To liberate oneself from meaning and to dominate it . . . to generate a being from a formal analogon, to deploy the chain of pure consequences of a given structure and to designate at leisure to which stage of this chain a model corresponds – all this defines with precision what structural analysis can do.[13]

That – and not some new virtual reality technology advertised in the latest trade journals – is essentially what Baudrillard means by *simulation*. Its essential elements can be broken down into four stages of semiosis. There is the *isolation of the object* as a possible field of operationalization, which requires the constitution of a specialized environment, such as a 'discipline', with its own closed system of terms, or a 'laboratory', defined by a rigorously tested parameter of predictable effects. Within this environment, a controlled *decomposition of the object* is conducted, in search of functional elements and properties susceptible to various kinds of manipulation and reorganization. Once the object has been reduced to a more or less satisfactory ensemble of discontinuous elements, there is an attempt to *develop an abstract model* of the essential relations between the elements which have been titrated through the distillation of the object. Finally, the elements are inserted into the model, in an attempt to reconstruct, or *reconstitute the object from the system* that has been created.

In light of this, we should consider once again what Baudrillard (or anybody) might mean by 'system'. The social sciences are replete with the language of systems: social systems, cultural systems, kinship systems, economic systems, communication systems. But the word is nearly always used defensively, as a way of glossing over what we don't yet understand. It reflects an intermediate state of knowledge, an understanding of the 'object' which falls short of operational control: that is, short of the capacity to build an actual working example of the object itself. A system is therefore usually something that we have just begun to grasp in a naturalistic fashion (as did, for example, Smith, Ricardo and Marx the expanding market of an industrializing economy) but still find ourselves quite unable to 'engineer'. In Baudrillardian terms, a system is anything whose alterity (or nonsimulatability) is on the brink of elimination.

Lévi-Strauss's analysis of totemism provides a good example of this intermediate, social scientific stage of simulation, in which knowledge remains at a passive, but still potentially cogent, pre-engineering level of development, well short of Michel Serres's dream of 'construct[ing] a living cultural being by filling a form with meaning'.

1. define the phenomenon under study as a relation between two or more terms, real or supposed;
2. construct a table of possible permutations between these terms;
3. take this table as the general object of analysis, which, at this level only, can yield the necessary connections, the empirical phenomenon considered at the beginning being only one possible combination among others, the complete system of which must be reconstructed beforehand.[14]

Ignorant as we are, however, the real, 'hard', operation-style, engineering type of simulation can already be practised at will 'on' society as a form of quasi-applied social science, so long as one is willing to work without expecting to control and predict specific results too precisely. A general pattern of effects is adequate for most politicians and corporations. (It is also good enough for skilled psychotherapists.) Unfortunately, practical knowledge of social simulation as a form of deliberate intervention is restricted to a few manoeuvres which depend for their effect upon a background of saturation bombing. The advertising business is the classic example – not exactly social engineering in the most sophisticated sense. Oliver Stone's *Natural Born Killers* is a brilliant illustration and exploration of 'media violence' as a pure simulation system almost entirely unrelated to the actuality of human interaction, yet so thoroughly integrated with it in the media texturing of the social world that almost everyone believes it to be a mirror of 'social reality', or even a 'cause' of 'real' violence. Feminist research into violence against women, sexual harassment, pornography and child abuse is an example of the same thing. An organized campaign against pornography and male violence, based on 'expert' testimony and soft social science survey reports, has successfully redefined and recontextualized the ordinary aggravations and arousals of everyday life, so that they are now experienced by large numbers of men and women as the moral equivalents of rape and battery, which are held to typify maleness.[15] If one is willing to run the risk of unanticipated consequences, which may spin off into systems of an entirely contrary nature, as happened for example with the Vietnam War, then social simulation is already an available technology and a going concern.

Were it not for the increasingly complex conditions under which social simulators must work, their success would be no surprise, the reason being that the practice is as old as seduction, or the Babylonian priests who faked divine pronouncements, *Zardoz*-style, with hidden chambers and speaking tubes inside their monumental effigies. Just as everyone is an 'expert' on language, because everyone speaks, so everyone is a politician, because everyone has to manoeuvre and to strategize the complexities of everyday life in a social world. It takes only a little bit of concentration and intelligence to achieve some critical distance from the norms, in order to discover how to manipulate the terms of the general simulation to which everybody contributes merely by agreeing to live at least a part of their lives within the vocabulary of the closed 'autopoietic' systems which were extant when they first arrived on the scene.

A common misunderstanding of Baudrillard's theses on simulation holds that there is no such thing as 'reality' – or that reality has lately been replaced by 'artificiality'. This kind of interpretation depends upon the doubtful assumption that artificiality is the opposite of reality, as if things made are necessarily less genuine than things not made, and that some things are either less real, or not real at all. (We encounter again the Platonic ontological hierarchy of Forms, imitations of Forms, and imitations of imitations.) In *Crossing the Postmodern Divide*, for example, Albert Borgmann tells us that 'Community gathers around reality.' Whatever Borgmann means by 'reality' and 'community', he clearly does not have in mind the contemporary media culture. 'At pop music concerts,' he argues, 'reality is torn apart into a gigantic, intricate staging machinery and an alluring, hypercharged commodity.'[16] The word 'reality' is here pressed into the service of a subjective value judgement which does not justify a concept of the 'real' as a measuring rod or an ultimate point of orientation. What is questionable is not the moral preference for communitarianism and family values (that's Borgmann's affair), but the implication that the traditional, home-town 'community', whose passing he understandably laments, is not also a simulation, another 'consensual hallucination', no different in principle from William Gibson's vaunted cyberspace,[17] or Baudrillard's seduction.

The term 'simulation' does not have the same bearing on the issue of actuality or reality as words like 'fake' or 'replica' or 'imitation' may have in certain contexts. Of course, if we define mother's milk as 'real milk', then everything but mother's milk, delivered in the traditional way, is 'fake'. But we cannot wean forever. A flight simulator is certainly not a fake or a replica, and only in a very superficial sense is it an 'imitation' of flying. It is a real flight simulator. Simulation refers to something deep but calculable in the real construction of actual technical, practical or social 'spaces'. A simulation is not so much an attempt to resemble something in appearance as to *reassemble* it from 'within', algorithmically, rather along the lines of Chomsky's attempt to reconstruct grammar with models of generative 'deep' structure, or the possibilities for 'genetic engineering' permitted by the discovery of the structure of DNA. Lévi-Strauss's combinatorial models of totemism, myths and the like, are crude cultural algorithms of a sort. They hearken the day when perhaps we will be able (as Serres promises) to construct cultures and societies from 'inside out'. Depending upon his mood, Baudrillard seems to think that we have gone a long way to achieving this already.

Perhaps we need a better example of a 'real' simulation, one which conforms in general outline to the scientific spirit of the structuralist model for generating a cultural being from a model.

> [T]he new arrival was by definition an adversary, whatever the label attached to him might be, and he must immediately be demolished to make sure that he did

not become an example or a germ of organized resistance . . . it is from this viewpoint that the entire sinister ritual must be interpreted . . . kicks and punches right away, often in the face; an orgy of orders screamed with true or simulated rage; complete nakedness after being stripped; the shaving off of all one's hair; the outfitting in rags. It is difficult to say whether all these details were devised by some expert or methodically perfected on the basis of experience, but they certainly were willed and casual: it was all staged, as was quite obvious.[18]

With only a little reflection upon Primo Levi's account, one recognizes the possibility that the Nazi extermination camps were cultural systems 'generated from a model' (consistent in form, but with slight variations from Lager to Lager, as Levi says). They were a societal experiment, like any other, with the usual human mixture of planning, improvisation and accident. The only significant difference lay in the degree of closure the cultural system of the camps made possible. The unusually narrow frame of existence permitted the full play of simplification, abstraction and reduction of life forms into social systems. Somewhat comparable phenomena were observable in the remnants of rural life in the former commonwealth dominions, where small populations of cultural outcasts were closeted from the play of the world. In the paranoid structures of small-town life in New England, Ontario or New South Wales, acquired gender roles degenerated easily into farcical caricatures, people actually monitored each other's garbage for evidence of debauchery. Yet even in Salem, Massachusetts, virtually isolated during the time of the witch trials, the system of communication was porous enough to allow relief from the terror of the cultural model: the less frightened part of the semantic body could still escape uncodified to impart an intuition of life in forms consciously unknown, other than the manifest relationships dictated by the system. Not so in the extermination camps, where the self-sufficiency of communication, from the point of view of the interned, was so total that even the most casual gesture had to be received either as a message reinforcing the system, or, if not imperceptible, then maddeningly indeterminate.

'Total communication' has always been a possibility in human affairs. Of course, until recently, its potential has been carefully framed and insulated. We see this in the ancient fascination with tragic drama ('pity and terror'), whose power lay in the relentless unfolding of a situational logic which nothing could finally escape. From the time of Plato's *Republic*, the suggestion that such systems could be administered directly on the social body as considered policy was always doubtful. But the now expanded potential for seamless communication was anticipated in the modernist aesthetic, especially in the literature and theatre of the absurd, where single principal worlds like Kafka's *Castle* or Peter Greenaway's *The Cook, The Thief, His Wife, and Her Lover*, seem to colonize the furthest reaches of all possible experience.

So there have always been systems of tyrannical closure whose purpose was simultaneously to express and to control the primitive anxieties of the semantic body. What seems to set the extermination camps apart – and to make them emblematic of modernity – is not this element of encapsulated terror, but the degree of its administrative premeditation. As always, there is (in Michel Serres's language) the generation of a being from a cultural analogon; but in modern societal life this refers less and less to an emergent property, or even to the lowest common denominator of the group; increasingly, it takes the form of a planned assault. The efficacy of these bureaucratically organized impositions ('cyberblitz') lies, paradoxically, in their capacity to enlist as an ally the same methods of formal rationality which once liberated the social imagination, in the heyday of the Enlightenment, from the tyranny of the primitive symbolic body. One could argue that the instantiation of a formal, quasi-scientific, technological 'feedback loop' brings the development of rationality full circle, in full confrontation with the primitive social body of the unconscious. After a period in which the social significance of the body is more or less reduced to *metaphor* (the ethos of 'transcendence' in Classical, Renaissance and bourgeois culture), the ritual symbolic or seductive body of *metamorphosis* is refound at the extremes of *metastases*, in the digital 'hyperreal', 'fractal', 'viral', 'clonal' bodies of tertiary and quaternary simulation (*Ecstasy* 45–56). This would account for the 'tension of immanence' (*Ecstasy* 55), the intuition of an uncanny affinity, upon which so much of Baudrillard's analysis plays, between the 'cruelty' of symbolic exchange and the 'terror' of third-order simulacra.

In fact, the 'total simulation' which Baudrillard describes is not merely a spin-off from cybernetic technology, but a special kind of refinement of the archaic ritual sense of life, whose ethos is celebrated in his encomia for seduction. Among the Bali, for example, Clifford Geertz found:

> a persistent and systematic attempt to stylize all aspects of personal expression to the point where anything idiosyncratic, anything characteristic of the individual merely because he is who he is physically, psychologically or biographically, is muted in favor of his assigned place in the continuing, and, so it

> is thought, never-changing pageant that is Balinese life. It is dramatis personae, not actors, that endure; indeed it is dramatis personae, not actors, that in the proper sense really exist. Physically men come and go – mere incidents in a happenstance history of no genuine importance, even to themselves. But the masks they wear, the stage they occupy, the parts they play, and most important, the spectacle they mount remain and constitute not the facade but the substance of things, not least the self. . . . There is no make-believe; of course, players perish, but the play does not, and it is the latter, the performed rather than the performer, that really matters.[19]

How do we measure the extermination camps against this utterly cynical acting out of life as arbitrary cultural form? If we take seriously Baudrillard's suggestion that the TV series *Holocaust* is a continuation of the extermination practised in the camps (*Evil* 22), are we not then finally exiled in his world of cool seduction, of terror without pity, where no meaningful choices are possible? Such is the usual reaction to Baudrillard: a reaction designed to expel his provocation like a virus. But the madness of the idea of simulation has an insidious logic which, once encountered, is difficult to shake off. After all, is there not some justice in his claim that 'television is the veritable final solution to the historicity of every event': that the televised 'memory' of our century is simply a way of forgetting *en masse* that we have, in fact, already forgotten how barbaric we really are? And didn't Geertz's Bali devise their own, much more effective 'final solution' ('mere incidents in a happenstance history of no importance') *without* TV?

That Baudrillard leads us to this disturbing thought may be taken as a typical exercise in cultural metaphysics. If we insist on reading him (or any other of the poststructuralists, for that matter) as serious epistemology, then of course we will only have ourselves to blame when we fail to distinguish between the Bali and the Nazis. Yet for anyone who wants to make moral pronouncements, there *is* indeed a cognitive issue, and one sees this clearly in the writings of all those who devote themselves with deep concern to problems like the Holocaust. The ear to whom nothing human is foreign always hears the echoes of Baudelaire's refrain: 'hypocrite lecteur – mon semblable – mon frère.'[20] If we accept that all cultural form is simulation – a dire hypothesis, but one worth trying – then prospective moral determinations – making moral decisions on behalf of whole societies – becomes both too easy, and also very difficult, since all ethical warrant for the very concept of culture has been removed. What else can we do, in a Baudrillardian universe, but explore the variations of 'feel' between different constructions of life, trying as best we can to relate them back to some coherent understanding of what it means to be a person with an internal world? Such an understanding may have been approximated, from time to time, in this or that psychoanalytic exploration of fantasy; but it is almost wholly absent from 'cultural studies' and the social scientific repertoire.

Like Kafka, Baudrillard adopts the view (perhaps just to make us sit up) that the internal world has been colonized and evacuated by the sheer effectiveness of third-order simulation. What is left over after the closed systems, the trials and castles, have processed our experience is little more, for him, than the possibility of a strategic search for evidence of the Symbolic Other, or at least an enigmatic alterity. Such is the vision sketched in Baudrillard's most recent essays (TE, *IF*): the near absolute triumph of culture, its penultimate liberation from the constraints of experience, the achievement of a culture without gravity, a decentred and weightless world of thought, in which all cultural distinctions are recycled in a process of disappearance without end. He places us at the opposite end of the cultural continuum constructed by Western social science. If the Yanomamo of the Amazon basin, the K'ung! Bushmen of South Africa, or Australian aboriginals have been positioned as the 'other' we fear will eventually devour us (as in Peter Weir's *The Last Wave*), then we are the other of this other. It is indeed significant, as Baudrillard argues with so much supercilious cheek in *Simulations*, that our collective alter ego is always a lost culture, a culture we have destroyed, or at least a culture dying from the technological virus, Wenders's 'disease of images'. Our other is always a culture so weighted on the side of symbolic experience and dream that the external world (in the ego-psychological sense) seems hardly to exist at all for its members. But perhaps alterity can only be found inside anyway (or at least, by descending into it, and passing through it). Perhaps we are imagining this cultural otherness as a projection of the interiority which we ourselves are, as Baudrillard claims, about to abandon.

If we can find some sense in these speculative formulations, then we can see why cultural metaphysics so frequently involves an articulation of the uncanny: it is an attempt to bypass ordinary perception on a detour through interiority. Cultural metaphysics is essentially the masked claim of interiority in the age of sociology. Yet the uncanny can only be expressed (or rather, signified) after the achievement of some common projection, some 'system of communication', which is already a question of social simulation.

21

Pataphysics, politics and simulation

VARIATIONS ON THE THEME OF SIMULATION

Simulation is the situation created by any system of signs when it becomes sophisticated enough, autonomous enough, to abolish its own referent and to replace it with itself. (L'espace 157)

In 1976, the developed theory of simulation was first presented in *Symbolic Exchange and Death*, a work that has only recently been translated in full; but the concept did not really begin to gain the attention of social theorists and artists until the publication in 1981 of *Simulacres et simulations*, which was followed by a partial translation in 1983 by the semiotext(e) group. In 'The precession of simulacra', Baudrillard argued that simulation 'no longer' refers to a simulated reality or copied original encompassing the metaphorical relation of map to territory: 'Simulation is no longer that of a territory, a referential being, or a substance. . . . It is the map that precedes the territory . . . it is the map that engenders the territory' (*Simulations* 2). But in the view presented so far, simulation has, in essence, always been like this, at least so far as social life is concerned; for society has never been anything else but a map, or more truthfully, a collection of maps, that we gradually learn to read. We may criticize the maps, even destroy the maps, but always by converting to the terms of the mapping system which constitutes the very society in which we are trying to make our counterclaim. There is always plenty, in everything we say and do, that doesn't get included in the map, that doesn't get converted into its terms – particularly our subjective experiences, which may include observations that cannot be located. These are real and *vital*. But from the point of view of simulation, they are totally irrelevant, because, as Richard Shweder points out, 'If social actors conveyed everything they actually felt . . . the performance called society, or at least the spectacle called civilization, would be very difficult to mount.'[1]

Perhaps because of his misleading phrase 'no longer' (which does for Baudrillard what 'always already' did for Derrida), Baudrillard's neo-Borgesian image of simulation was nevertheless received with great excitement in places like New York, where it ought to have been taken for granted! The puzzlement in the English-speaking world over *Simulations* betrays a certain intellectual unpreparedness. In and of itself, Baudrillard's statement is not so radical. One need only think back to the deconstructionist slogan of the 1960s – 'il n'y a pas de hors texte' – or to Baudrillard's first reflections on modernist aesthetics, such as 'Gesture and signature' and 'Design and environment', where he described a closed semio-aesthetic order of 'functional perfection' and 'cold seduction' (*FCPES* 102–11, 185–203, 188). To some degree, the thrill over the map-without-territory model of simulation probably reflects the unavailability of English translations of the earlier arguments which led to it in the first place.

A taste of the latter can be found in Baudrillard's discussion of 'The precession of consumption' in *The System of Objects* (*SO* 188–9), which already offers some bold conclusions. As in the Martin Amis novel, *Time's Arrow*, the flow of time seems to change direction: consumption precedes production. But this seemingly extravagant claim rests on a bed of explicit socio-economic and historical reasoning whose theoretical context is familiar: Marxist humanism. His propositions are warranted with factual arguments and illustrated with plausible examples. Baudrillard addresses an observable decline in bourgeois patriarchalism, and rather prophetically envisions a concomitant rise in deficit spending, public and private (which at the time he was writing had not really got underway). His central point can be put fairly straightforwardly: that while we still, in a sense, 'work' for what we consume, our relationship to everyday objects betrays a very changed understanding of the relationship between work and ownership (he is speaking of the middle and lower classes here). We are less and less inclined to experience the object environment as the representative result of work. Not so long ago, however, the idea of working towards something – a car, a refrigerator, a home – had deep, moral, patrimonial significance: possessions were rewards, earned before they were purchased as securities against the future. Today, 'objects are there before they are earned, they anticipate the work they represent . . .' (*SO* 188). Possessions no longer constitute private capital, society's recognition of the individual's contribution; they represent the debt we owe society. In abstract form: consumption itself has become a form of 'productive labour', financed by capital.

With this apparent flipping of the conventional relation between the antecedent and the consequent, 'the status of an entire civilization changes along with the way in which ordinary things are experienced [mode de presence et de jouissance des objets quotidiens]' (*SO* 189).

> Filtered and fragmented by economic constraints, the human project devours itself: the fundamental truth of the present socioeconomic order is that objects are not at all for possession and use; they are only here in order to be produced and bought. Otherwise stated, they are not structured in the service of needs or even for a more rational organization of the world; they are systematized as the exclusive function of an order of production and ideological integration' (*SO* 193; cf. *Shadow* 27 *passim*).

Only later (in 'The ideological genesis of needs' (1969), and *FCPES* generally) will Baudrillard directly challenge the failed ideal itself – oddly, to endorse its failure. As we have seen, the idea of structuring objects in the service of 'needs', in the interests of a 'more rational organization of the world', strikes Baudrillard as improvident. It implies a profound misunderstanding of symbolic exchange, a denial of human ambivalence, a flight from the alterity of things, a fear of being seduced. Life without openness to these dimensions of existence is impoverished and puerile. The rational organization of the world according to functional principles is a utopia Baudrillard would rather not see realized any further than it already has been. Indeed, as will soon be apparent, it was the metaphysical intuition that he might have witnessed such 'realization' which led him to conceive the hard version of simulation (the system of signs powerful enough to substitute itself for its own transcendental referent), and which inspired his mischievous notion that becoming real, or 'materializing', is the most degraded form of any phenomenon.

'In the system of objects, as in every lived system, the great structural oppositions are always other than they seem,' he wrote in 1968. 'What is a structural opposition at the level of system may be a coherent rationalization of a conflict' (*SO* 53). Baudrillard still saw the Keynesian function of credit as a 'contradiction' (*SO* 190) in which the real conditions of social production are veiled behind the 'remarkable illusionism' of mortgaging the individual consumer's future – condemning him to future labour to pay off his debts – in order to finance production now for others who are working to pay off their debts and so on, *ad infinitum*. Through the essential abstraction of exchange value, launched on a sea of international speculation in floating currencies, the functioning of the economy has progressively divorced itself from any knowable frame of reference, and deferred all conventional accounting in a kind of perpetual 'flight in advance'. In *Simulations*, a decade later, Baudrillard abandons his scruples about this indeterministic flux. The idea that there is a *moral order* to be discovered behind the machinations of Capital, a moral economy to be recovered through the defeat of capitalism, only lends the dismal science of economics a spurious legitimacy.

> Capital has in fact never been linked by a contract to the society it dominates. It is a sorcery of the social relation . . . not a scandal to be denounced according to moral and economic rationality, but a challenge to take up according to the rules of the symbolic. (*SS* 30; *Simulations* 29–30)

Another early manifestation of the simulation concept concerns the problem of the individual. If the individual in traditional societies is *culturally* constructed, and acts in a symbolic universe, the modern individual is *societally* constructed, and moves within a functional system of norms. Baudrillard's way of tracing this development to changes in the status of the object is already familiar. The Renaissance marks the gradual emergence of the *object* from the symbolic social nexus, its accession to the commutative versatility of signs. (It is worth noting again T. S. Eliot's complaint against Milton's 'dissociation of sensibility' in *Paradise Lost*. Interestingly, Milton was among the very first, in *Aereopagitica*, to call for the liberation of discourse.) This 'formal liberation' of the object and the sign defines the field of modern 'consumption', particularly in the sense that the commodity form ruptures traditional practical and symbolic social constraints on the object, and on the 'practice' of objects. What is more interesting still is that the liberation of the object constitutes the liberation of the subject as well, a certain formal autonomization of the juridico-political individual, whose practices (particularly his discursive practices in the emerging public sphere) are precisely those which the commodity has freed from symbolic constraints. This circular or self-reinforcing transition is complemented by the extirpation of social significations from their referential contexts in social life (a kind of gradual disengagement of the signifier) which generates the conditions for new kinds of reflective social discourses – Marx, Nietzsche, Freud, Foucault, and, of course, the discourses of consumption itself: advertising, fashion, media, aesthetics, and the elaborate articulation of lifestyles (which are by no means uninformative, and often appealing in their rigour).

As Anthony Giddens has argued, the being of the individual in modernity becomes 'reflexive' in an entirely new sense.[2] For

Baudrillard, even the routines of everyday life develop into a form of self-reflection, a '*system of interpretation* . . . in which the individual recognizes work, leisure, family and personal relations in an involutive mode . . .' (*SC* 33; emphasis in original). Everyday life in the modern world is 'triumphant and euphoric in its effort at total autonomy and of reinterpreting the world "for internal use only" '. Consumption serves as the paradigm for a new kind of articulate 'praxis', and everyday life becomes the arena for this uninterrupted appropriative activity, in which the individual metonymically recomposes the world in his own image, from bits of advertising, news, entertainment, possessions and representations of glamour, happiness, wealth, power and, with increasing prominence, externalized, simulated violence. 'From the objective viewpoint of the totality, everyday life appears impoverished and residual', Baudrillard declared twenty-five years ago (*SC* 33); but everyday life is nevertheless regularly replenished with spectacular, sometimes redemptive, intimate images of violence which sustain and justify a 'moral economy of safety' in which 'the society of consumption wills itself as a sort of encircled Jerusalem, rich and menaced . . .' (*SC* 34, 35).

The sumptuary society – or more precisely, the society of fulfilment, success, completion, finality (la société de *consommation*) – is unthinkable without something like Baudrillard's conception of simulation. The energy of everyday life in the postmodern world depends upon a regular experience of collective summing up (*consommation*) in which reality, defined in ego-psychological terms as something external and beyond personal control (like starvation in North Africa), is served up at room temperature. Only the mass media can really satisfy this need on a regular basis, and yet it is the electronic networks themselves, with their time-space override, which create the siege-like sense of the world raging at one's doorstep. The sociological structure of this state of affairs is similar to Freud's 'pure pleasure ego': everything unpleasant must be banished from the charmed circle, but in consequence, the first relation to the object is hate.[3] A profound sense of lassitude threatens the pleasure ego of the postmodern cities; on the collective level, there is a repetitious, masturbatory response to chronic, low-grade anxiety which leads in turn to boredom, and guilty withdrawal. The group morality of activism plagues the public conscience like a ghost, and makes the population susceptible to moral panics and vigilante campaigns. There is an endless cycle of censorship initiatives, and the uproar about various kinds of interpersonal abuse creates an atmosphere of blackmail in public institutions and the workplace. Everyone is more or less forced to put on a bland face, pretending innocence, while seeking larger injections from the media of the 'danger' from which they have happily escaped into their private lives.

What is new about this situation is not that social life tends, in the first and last instance, to be governed by paranoid anxieties – that has always been the case, and is certainly true of the archaic societies which incarnate Baudrillard's principle of symbolic exchange. The novel feature is that such a heterogeneous population as our modern Western collectivities can be galvanized so quickly into the paranoid-schizoid position, without resort to the mechanisms of solidarity and cohesion which once dominated the life of groups and small towns. Of course, this catastrophic facility brings with it an 'imminent principle of reversibility'. The crises often disappear as quickly as they come (usually without resolution), and a semblance of political democracy plods on. All the major passions – love, hate, fear, envy, greed, pity – are leached out of the social body and recycled without intimacy, leaving little else but generalized indifference, or a 'viral' form of hatred which has no object (Vitale *passim*).

Not only from an administrative and political point of view, but increasingly in a personal way, Euro-Americans are adapting themselves to living in 'risk societies', which offer a form of life oriented towards 'the reflexive adoption by laypeople of risk parameters as filtered through abstract systems'.[4] Anyone in these societies who is able to read, and to reflect before acting, necessarily conducts himself as a kind of lay sociologist, ecologist and policeman. Citizens are expected to restrict their public behaviour to more and more precise formulae of human equivalence. The hard-won conventions of political and individual rights (which once referred explicitly to the possibility of private life, personal projects, public actions) seem to be devolving into a corporatist ideology of 'Human Rights', which is a sort of management behaviour code for society as a collective unit.

In the moral economy of safety, sexuality in particular requires a good deal of reflexive calculation. It is a consumer problem in its own right, a test site of personal skills in risk evaluation. There is no doubt that the formulation of prophylactic behaviour guidelines is high on the agenda of the legal and social scientific professions, which are well funded for soft research designed to promulgate the dangers of private life. It is not that we are no longer capable of love, but that we tend to get lost in the plans and arrangements surrounding it. This situation is nicely summed up, as usual, by

Anthony Giddens, who argues that 'sexual emancipation . . . is more effectively understood in a procedural way, as the possibility of the *radical democratisation* of the personal'.[5] Emancipation is of course a wonderfully ambiguous modern term. We no longer have arranged marriages, but in many Western countries, sexuality is nevertheless prey to rigorous campaigns of political recodification. It is true that there can be no sexuality without repression; as Foucault puts it, sexuality cannot be liberated from power, it is a *form* of power. But if restrictions are inevitable, the new ones are no longer social or cultural in inspiration: they are abstractly formulated, theoretical, administrative, *societal*, 'emancipatory'. Neither are they symbolic expressions arising from bodies interrelating in social time (which admittedly can be a nasty business), but modes of signification emanating from media time, which can be very nice; not directly repressive social politics, which have characterized most of human history, but coolly enlightened bureaucratic regulation; not forms of passion, but tactics of communication.

SOCIOLOGICAL APPROXIMATIONS OF SIMULATION

> Imagine for a moment our modern cities stripped of all their signs, with walls bare like a blank mind. And then GARAP appears: this single expression – GARAP inscribed on all the walls. A pure signifier, without a signified, signifying itself, it is read, discussed, interpreted to no end, signified despite itself: it is consumed as a sign. And what does it signify, if not a society capable of generating such a sign? In its very meaninglessness, it mobilizes a whole imaginary collectivity; it has become indicative of an entire society. . . . [This] is mass society: an arbitrary and systematic sign provokes the sensibility and mobilizes consciousness, and in this very process, constitutes itself as the collectivity. (*SO* 214)[6]

In the GARAP image of a single omnipresent sign 'constituting' the 'mass', Baudrillard provides an almost Orwellian epitome of a 'collective representation'. The echoes of Durkheim carry even further, of course. More than anyone, Baudrillard has given a special meaning to Durkheim's definition of society as 'above all . . . the idea it forms of itself'.[7] Indeed, a natural impulse in approaching the theory of simulation is to look for a Durkheimian or Althusserian interpretation; and this would be encouraged by the obvious reference, in Baudrillard's periodization of the orders of simulacra, to the *episteme* theory in Foucault's *The Order of Things*. But as

Marshall Sahlins has pointed out, Durkheim's grasp of the symbolic dimension is incongruent with Baudrillard's. 'Durkheim formulated a sociological theory of symbolization, but not a symbolic theory of society. Society was not seen as constituted by the symbolic process; rather, the reverse alone appeared true.'[8] Durkheim presupposed an epistemological division bètween the order of meaning on one hand, and 'real' social relations on the other, which foreshadows the separation between 'culture' and 'social system' in the British structural-functional school of anthropology.[9] The same may be said of Althusser's concept of ideology as 'the imaginary relation of individuals . . . to the real relations in which they live',[10] which implies the standard distinction between appearance and reality which all of Baudrillardian sociology (i.e. cultural metaphysics) is trying to find a way to think beyond.

Tempting though the classical models of society may be, they are not at all appropriate for an understanding of Baudrillard. This is not to say that he refuses conceptual distinctions and denies the reality and inevitability of organizational hierarchies: the various topologies of social stratification and sectorialization are simply accessory to Baudrillardian classification. They exist empirically – they can be described – but their causal and functional 'explanation' have been bracketed or undermined. What emerges in Baudrillard's thought instead is a gradual overturning of the conventional social scientific understanding of motivation and determination. To paraphrase Foucault, Baudrillard does not deny history and society, but holds in suspense the general, empty category of causality in order to reveal transformations at different levels.[11] If nothing else, a general theory of simulation resists the functionalist (and 'materialist') tendency to accord 'superstructural', secondary status to semantic processes and dynamics in society (*FCPES* 114 *passim*).

Thus, in GARAP and the 'precession of consumption', we find the essential ingredients of the later theory of simulation already in place, and set out clearly in a historical frame of reference which Baudrillard never really abandons. What distinguishes the later work is not so much a change of perspective as an intensified commitment to eradicate all traces of a sociological theory of *ideology* (which perhaps explains why Baudrillard and Bourdieu have become such theoretical enemies). As we saw in Chapter 20, the theory of simulation is an attempt to abandon the mind–body split in sociology, and to absorb the problematic of ideology into a more encompassing metaphysical account of social being.

A VISIT TO UTOPIA

In the mid-1960s, Baudrillard has recalled, the reflexive character of everyday life had seemed to him, his colleagues on the review *Utopie*, and also the Situationists, to set the stage for a genuine utopia, in the Marxist and universalist sense of a recovery of the 'species being' of Mankind.

> Everything led us to believe that things would continue to advance irresistably toward a dedifferentiation of life and culture and that this was utopia: to restore a sort of anthropological foundation, an anthropological movement and energy which led beyond the specialized cultures [of modernity]. It was practically a demand for the repudiation of culture by culture itself, the refusal of all distinctive traits.
>
> All of this culminated, as we know, in the dismantling of the university, particularly through the self-liquidation of the human sciences, and of course, May 68. Not a political utopia, but a utopia surpassing politics and urbanity. Into what? We didn't know. It was a sort of prophecy. (L'espace 155–6)

The utopian politics of everyday life failed, in Baudrillard's view. One can sense this already in the bathos of his portraits of the sumptuary society, with its 'white mass' and its moral readiness to denounce itself at every opportunity. Like so many French academics whose success grew out of that decade, Baudrillard visited North America on lecture tours and teaching appointments, in the *aftermath* of this experience of political stalemate.

> America represented, in contrast, a realized utopia. In fact, this was the real passage toward this indistinction of culture and of life which had been our utopia . . . . Of course, it was not a question there of situationism, or radical subjectivity, but quite literally of simulation, since the realisation of utopia can only be a simulation.
>
> For me, America is the original version of modernity. Because it has not known the primitive accumulation of time, it lives in a perpetual present. Because it has not experienced the slow secular accumulation of the reality principle, it lives in perpetual simulation, in the perpetual present [*actualité*] of signs.
>
> Simulation is a much used term. But we can understand from this [that simulation is] a kind of self-fulfilling prophecy: that is, things no longer happen in relation to a transcendent utopia, a utopia which is always postponed, due to the limitations of time; everything takes place in conditions of total figurability, everything is representable, in the immediate materiality of things. Utopia is no longer the domain of transcendence, it is the domain of simulation. (L'espace 156–7)

North Americans are sometimes insulted by the frankness with which Baudrillard, in *America*, articulated the usual European shock on first arriving in North America (Wim Wenders's *Paris, Texas* is another interesting example). What they don't understand is that Reagan's America was for the French left what the China of Mao suits and the cultural revolution was for the American right – an absurd realization of a tawdry utopian vision of eternity.

For good or ill, Baudrillard's political style has grown steadily more arrogant and glib. Yet (as Mike Gane has well demonstrated in a series of books), it remains revealing and insightful – often more so than a lot of the cagier competition in the field of cultural commentary.[13] Radicals and moderate left-liberals have voiced a good deal of outrage at Baudrillard for his cynical and paranoid view of contemporary American culture. He exacerbates the situation by exploiting obvious clichés of conservative antimodernism (notably the 'mob' of Gustav Le Bon, the cultural pessimism of Freud [who was appalled by America], the 'masses' of Ortega Y Gasset, and the 'crowds' of Elias Canetti), turning them into ironic figures of utopian destiny and flinging them in the reader's face. (Baudrillard is incapable of the bemused detachment of a Tocqueville, though he does borrow the Tocquevillian image of American culture as a desert.) Often accused of self-indulgent nostalgia, Baudrillard's frustration over the mass, unionized 'decompression' of 'May 68' was always clear (*FCPES* 176). But some of his detractors may be projecting their own culture shock, their own nostalgic refusal to accept that what they hoped to realize in America – the experience of action, a sense of the unity of the general and the particular, of participating in a universal history unfolding in the density of real collective time: the whole utopian dream – is already dying in its European birthplace, with little chance of being reborn in the former colonies. (This was why the French intellectual elite turned to *tiers mondisme* in the 1960s and 1970s – a form of self-deception which never tempted Baudrillard.)

FROM VIETNAM TO KUWAIT

I write, she wrote, that memory is fragile and the space of a single life is brief, passing so quickly that we never get a chance to see the relationships between events; we cannot gauge the consequences of our acts, and we believe in the fiction of past, present, and future, but it may also be true that everything happens simultaneously. (Isabelle Allende)[14]

What could exemplify more eloquently Baudrillard's notion that utopia has slipped from transcendence into simulation than the

Euro-American experience of war over the last thirty years? The Vietnam War ended – and the imaginary utopian potential of mediatized culture (crystallized in the antiwar movement) passed with it (*FCPES* 164–84, 204–12). There was no transcendence, only some recognition that the entire bloody exercise made no geopolitical difference, and no real change at home: in very gross terms, neither 'capitalism' nor 'communism' was modified in the slightest. As Paul Piccone argued, in terms which echo Baudrillard's developing analysis of the geopolitical situation in the late 1970s,

> From the viewpoint of the new imperialism based on multinational corporations and cultural hegemony, it was a mistake to try to prevent the communist reunification, since relations of domination would not have changed anyway; only their management would have been different. Instead of the US directly dominating Vietnamese society, this domination would have been indirectly managed by the USSR, itself indirectly tied to the US in a relation of sub-imperialism.[15]

If anything, the stunning American defeat had a contrary effect: it revealed the opposite of everything anticipated by the conventional revolutionary imagination. It was not the American but the Soviet Empire which foundered in colonial wars (Afghanistan) and the contradictions of profit-seeking imperialist expansion (Central Europe). It was not 'capitalism' but 'communism' which immiserated the proletariat, devastated the environment, gutted culture, razed the community, and reduced life to the workhouse and the cash-nexus. For Baudrillard, Coppola's *Apocalypse Now* was really about this political *triumph* of the American defeat:

> Coppola may very well dress up his helicopter captain in a cavalry hat and have him wipe out a Vietnamese village to the sound of Wagner – these are not critical, distant signs; they are immersed in the machinery, part of the special effect. Coppola makes films in the same manner, with the same nostalgic megalomania, with the same non-signifying fury, the same magnified Punch and Judy effect. One can ask, how is such a horror possible (not the war, properly speaking, but that of the film)? But there is no response, no possible judgement. The Vietnam war and the film are cut from the same cloth, nothing separates them: this film is part of the war. If the Americans (apparently) lost the other, they have certainly won this one. *Apocalypse Now* is a global victory. (*Evil*17–18)

The point seems to be confirmed by *Hearts of Darkness*, the recent film on the making of *Apocalypse Now*, and Coppola's own comment that film directing provides one of the few opportunities remaining in the world to behave like an absolute dictator with impunity. His film suggests the 'disappearance' of war in the specific sense that war 'no longer' seems to arise as the product of an identifiable agency, beginning and ending as a determinate historical object. After Vietnam, the proverbial 'first television war', war became an indistinguishable special effect, blended into the media culture, whose correlative psychological response could 'no longer' be moral in any truly compelling sense, but simply fascination and low-grade anxiety. We can safely infer that, for Baudrillard, oppression, resistance and 'critique' – politics *tout court* – are also 'disappearing' with war in this particular sense. That is, they will continue the same as always, or worse; but this familiarity will be deeply infected with our awareness of the uncanny, the *Unheimlich*. Moreover, in the process of disappearing, nothing will ever actually come to an end, nothing will achieve a resolution which would make room for something else; war, politics, criticism, resistance and morality will simply accumulate, indefinitely, to the point of saturation.

Baudrillard's bizarre (but cogent) reading of the Gulf War (very badly received in the English-speaking world, where the intelligentsia still takes politics as a matter of fundamental morality) is filtered through this bitter experience of the 1970s. His analysis has not changed since the original publication of 'La précession des simulacres', in which he discussed Vietnam, Watergate and the Cold War in a tone of cynicism unprecedented in Western political discourse: 'Like the Trojan War, [nuclear war] will not happen', Baudrillard declared then (*SS* 57); adding later: 'we cannot deny it: "in itself" the Vietnam war never happened' (*Evil* 17). Fifteen years hence, he repeated the claim in the form of a pseudo 'prediction', this time with respect to the Gulf War, during which Iraq withdrew its troops from Kuwait (*IF* 93–7). The idea that the war would not, and did not, *take place* (n'a/ura pas eu lieu) dramatizes not only the mediatized indeterminacy of the event, its endless anticipation, and the shocking anti-climax of its alleged occurrence, but also its euphoria, especially for the intelligentsia galvanized in 'opposition' to the war. The whole history of the UN confrontation with Saddam Hussein is seen as a sordid realization of the utopian idea (utopia=nowhere, *Erewhon*, 'le non-lieu de la guerre' (*IF* 96)), the dream of historical transcendence implemented as a slow-motion nightmare of simulation. As with Vietnam, perhaps the Gulf War was only

> a psychotropic dream in which the issue was not politics or victory but the sacrificial, excessive deployment of a power already filming itself as it unfolds,

perhaps expecting nothing more than consecration by a superfilm which perfects the war's function as a mass spectacle. (*Evil* 17)

But in the case of the Gulf, the problem is even more acute than it was during the Cold War. There is no longer any coherent 'position' other than that dictated by the operational logic which was so long deferred, and then finally unleashed in a brief show of lethal force.[16] The context of the events surrounding the Gulf (a context which Baudrillard describes as a boycott or 'strike of events' (*IF*)) did not really allow for a genuine choice to oppose the war (there was no realistic alternative safer for the Middle East, or for the world in general, than facing Saddam down). Even denouncing the media distortions, the censored information, the disinformation, seems redundant, since the only people who will read such disquisitions are people (a growing number) who wouldn't trust *any* newsreport, *especially* if it were filmed 'live'. 'It's not a matter of being for or against the war. It's a question of being for or against the *reality of the war*', Baudrillard declares insouciantly (*IF* 95). By rendering the *non-lieu* of the war transparent, he tries to give the critical spirit a leg up:

One gives the war the strength of imagination, elsewhere than in the 'real time' of information, where it is quickly exhausted as an event. The illusion of the war is made vivid, instead of being diluted in its false reality. (*IF* 96)

As usual, the brilliance of Baudrillard's rhetoric obscures the subtlety of his arguments; the intensity of his images condenses 'vast processes of theoretical labour'.[17] If Baudrillard is in some sense right about all this, then eventually his point will seem obvious (if ineffectual), and soak into the texture of our conventional understanding of ourselves, as so many of his ideas indeed already have done.

VII

Modernism and postmortemism

22

Canada as an unidentified historical object of international significance

Our assumption was that there are no longer any ideas closely connected with the facts (that was the 'utopia' of the 1960s and 70s), no longer any real actors on top of events, or any intellectuals with a grasp of their meaning: there is just a tempest of insignificant events lacking real actors and authorized interpreters. *Actio* has disappeared along with *auctoritas*. All that remains is the present: 'action' occurs only in the film director's sense, or as a sort of 'auction', in which events are sold off at the highest bid of information. Events no longer derive from actions, but from speculation, concatenating through chain reactions toward the extremes of a facticity beyond the claims of interpretation. (*IF* 29–30)

This imaginary state of affairs certainly applies to events as they usually fail to unfold in Canada, which is one of those new 'post-modern' countries. No one is quite sure whether Canada was first conceived by Jorge Luis Borges or by Italo Calvino. It is the sort of country whose federal government feels obliged to rent billboards and newspaper space to advertise the flag. Everything about Canada is vague, ambiguous or unknown. Officially, it defines itself as 'two nations'. This curious fact is declared in a Constitution which begins with a clause exempting the constitution from rigorous application, in case the rights it guarantees become politically inconvenient. As an assurance of ineffectuality, there is also a 'notwithstanding' clause which permits any government to suspend the constitution whenever it sees fit.

It is difficult to convey precisely the atmosphere of a country like Canada because it is in a perpetually uninterpretable state of being. Everything about Canada is undecidable. The actual life of Canadians is dominated by what the historian Daniel Boorstin has called 'pseudo-events' (which used to occur only on late night talk shows in the United States, but now reticulate everywhere, as Baudrillard points out in his study of the 'strike of events' (*IF*)).[1] The 'strange taste of the *déjà arrivé*' (the already over and done with) is engraved on the Canadian national palate, because in Canada, events can only be experienced as a 'retrospective unfolding, auguring nothing significant for the future' (*IF* 35).

The Canadian national anthem is a good case in point. Entitled 'O Canada!' it exists officially in both French and English, and contains the usual impenetrable imagery found in patriotic librettos. Lately, however, authorities have come to feel that it is not always in the best interests of Canadians to perform the anthem while they are present. As an aesthetic decision, of course, this would have been widely applauded; but the rationale was actually political. It was felt that if the national anthem were performed on Jean Baptiste Day, a nationalist holiday in Québec, the feelings of political separatists might be ruffled. Authorities were concerned about what might happen if O Canada! were sung at a baseball game in the Montreal Olympic Stadium. Traditionally, the anthem is played just before the first pitch is thrown. To be on the safe side, the stadium officials decided to perform it an hour and a half before anyone arrived at the stadium. They had hit upon the surest method of political survival in the postmodern world: to stage events in such a way that they don't actually occur in any definitive form.

From a Canadian point of view, this seemingly bizarre situation is normal and understandable (although nobody knows what it means, and nobody can do anything about it). Like Baudrillard's mass, Canadians exemplify the paradox of being both objects of simulation and subjects of simulation: objectively, they exist only as an effect created by Statistics Canada, and countless polling agencies, whose ever more detailed analyses of the national psyche compound the determination of Canadians to withdraw from active participation in the tawdry farce of belonging to the Canadian public. Yet at the same time, Canada has come increasingly to approximate its own image of itself, to the point where its only hope of communicating with itself effectively is to do exactly the opposite of what it is expected to do, as occurred in the Referendum on the new Constitutional Accord in 1992, which would never have been held if Canadians had not seemed so likely to vote 'yes', which in the end they didn't.

Like Baudrillard's masses, Canadians have turned conformity into a kind of 'immanent humour' (*Shadow* 30). Their dread of ridicule drives them to satirize themselves constantly, in fits of counterphobic unpredictability. But somehow, in the next referendum, they will have to find a way to do the opposite of what they are *not* expected to do, if they wish to remain on their course of refractory hyperconformity. Indeed, the political situation in Canada has become so complicated as to appear ridiculous (Canadians' worst fear). Perhaps this is why the current Prime Minister, who has the same name as the hero of *Pilgrim's Progress*, is so widely respected: though something of a laughing stock, especially in his native Québec, he is nevertheless the first decent fellow to come to power in a generation, and he makes it a policy never to discuss issues of national significance.

Much of the confusion in Canada arises from the fact that Canadians refuse to say which of the 'two nations' they actually belong to, and who 'represents' them. The problem is that there is only one Canadian citizenship to go round (another example of the immanent humour of Canadian hyperconformity), and only one kind of Canadian passport, which everybody wants the right to keep, especially if they do not wish to belong to Canada. Perhaps this is because they want to be able to leave Canada an indefinite number of times, and they need a passport to do so. But the real reason may be more practical. If Canada actually ceases to exist as a formal unit, a Canadian passport will be indispensable, since it will permit travel without hindrance between one part of its former self and the rest.

Although Canada is officially a 'duality', the number of possible Canadian nations is far greater, since not only the province of Québec, but *all* the provinces secretly want to become 'independent'. Moreover, the aboriginals are divided among themselves over how many nations they comprise, and whether these belong to Canada, or to some larger aboriginal nation which is also a part of Canada, though not actually belonging to it. Each of this growing number of nations wants to have nothing to do with the others; and each bitterly opposes the attempts of the others to leave.

Some English-speaking Canadians resent seeing the French language on their bilingual cereal boxes; but they grow quite indignant when French Canadians accuse them of philistinism and racism. (It is never clear in Canada who is suffering the most.) The French have come closest to defining a straightforward political position. As Yvon Deschamps pointed out twenty years ago, what Québecers really want is 'an independent Québec within a strong and united Canada'. (M. Deschamps is actually a stand-up comic, but his statement on the aspirations of Québecers is more widely quoted than the words of any politician except the former Prime Minister Trudeau, who declared that 'the State has no business in the bedrooms of the nation'.)

Most would agree that in Canada it is really the aboriginals who suffer the most. The constitutional status of the original settlers, who came across the Bering Straits from Asia many millennia before, is the most imponderable of all. Yet many believe that it will be the aboriginal band councils, ultimately, who decide the political future of Canada. Their near total lack of political clout lends their actions an extra historical weight which other Canadians, floating as they are in the outer space of constitutional law, cannot hope to achieve. Moreover, the aboriginals almost never speak to other Canadians. When they want to stop a dam from being built, or to assert their treaty rights, they go abroad, to confer with foreign leaders. This has a devastating effect on the political scene at home. The result is that on those rare occasions when the aboriginals have intervened directly in the national political process, their contribution has proven decisive. For example, it was the single vote of an aboriginal member of the national assembly in Manitoba which overturned the historic Meech Lake Accord, thereby thwarting the hard-won consensus of the entire Canadian political establishment, and hurling the nation into its present constitutional crisis.

Baudrillard has long maintained that in the twilight of modernity, power no longer works as a 'rapport de force', but rather as a form of seduction, or as an exchange of vacuous and tautological significations (*Oublier*). Canadian nationalist politics are a cogent illustration of this thesis, particularly as they are played out in Québec. One of the fundamental and universally recognized facts about Canadian nationhood is that Québec society constitutes a distinct enclave within the Canadian totality. Of course, this is true of every other region of the country, though Québec is culturally more distinct by virtue of the predominance of the French language. Like any other Canadian region, Québec forms part of the larger Canadian economy, but within a framework of greater political and administrative autonomy than the other Canadian provinces. The result of this unusual circumstance is that in Québec the practice of concocting scenarios for democratic action has developed into an art form. The purpose of all politics has been refined to a point of exquisite abstraction, namely, to be born into history: to transform Québec into a collective subject expressing itself on the historical stage, unfolding its destiny according to a cultural programme which lies somewhere deep in the heart of the within, the organic recess of 'the nation'. In Québec, no political gesture is unrelated to this supraordinate imperative – to define the future of Québec. Every political thought, utterance and action can be linked to one of two, official, master political strategies for the realization of this historical future.

The first strategy is to argue that Québec should be deprived of the extraordinary privileges which it now enjoys in Canada. The method of doing this is to separate Québec from Canada, in the hope of increasing the insignificance not just of Québec, but of Canada as well. This is the well-known egalitarian strategy of the radical 'independentistes', in which everyone's interests will be equally damaged, and everyone will be equally to blame. The second strategy – that of the 'federalists' who wish Québec to remain within Canada – is to demand that the cultural and linguistic distinctness of Québec be recognized, and that Québec be granted relative administrative autonomy, while enjoying an economic association with the rest of Canada. In brief, the first strategy is to give up power completely in order, paradoxically, to win it back, but now in an historical or metaphysical form which had previously eluded the Québec people; and the second is to demand the real power that Québec already possesses. The separatists want to destroy Québec's real power in order to conjure it up again in a form which will be virtually unusable; and the federalists want to use it in such a way as to create the illusion that it doesn't yet exist. The second, federalist strategy is perhaps the subtler. If the federalists who want Québec to remain in Canada should succeed, then Québec will be stronger than ever, because the province will have forced Canada to perform an act of abject self-abnegation, namely, to pretend to decide solemnly and democratically to grant Québec a power that Québec already has. Under the federalist strategy, then, absolutely nothing would change in reality; and yet Canada would have been effectively double-binded into total submission. On the other hand, the Canadian federation may well be strengthened if the separatist strategy succeeds, for then Québec would be so weakened politically and economically that Canada would have to come to its rescue, particularly in order to defend its unique culture from the predatory attacks of the international capitalists.

It should have been no surprise, then, that in successive Québec elections, the separatist party has spent most of its time campaigning on the platform that it is not yet ready to separate, whilst the party in favour of federal unity claims to be in a better position ultimately to achieve autonomy for Québec. The same people will tell you, in the same conversation, or answering the same poll, that they are frightened of the political and economic future if Québec separates, and entirely convinced that separation will make no difference one way or the other. They simply assume that Québec will remain a part of Canada after it separates. This may be one of the reasons why Québec has not yet separated from Canada, for many Québecers have noticed that the closer they come to achieving autonomy, the more involved with Canada they become. This may also be the reason why English Canada wants Québec to stay: so that they can have less to do with it.

The truth of this proposition was demonstrated in the results of the last Québec provincial election (September 1994), in which the federalist party was turfed out, and the secessionists were elected to a whopping majority on a platform to hold another referendum on the independence of Québec. As soon as victory for the independence party was assured, the federalist camp began to celebrate, and their leader was universally declared the moral victor. The secessionist leader, M. Parizeau, was deemed the loser, even by his own supporters, who seemed concerned to deny that their victory really meant anything. There was talk of putting off the promised referendum. M. Parizeau appeared on the stage at the victory rally looking morosely *soûl*. At a loss for words, he asked his wife to speak, and then invited his archrival within the independence movement, M. Bouchard, to join him from the audience. This was widely seen as a rather pathetic gesture, since M. Bouchard is much preferred by most of the secessionists, and everyone knows that these men would stab each other in the back at the first opportunity. (Federalists pray that their opportunities to do so will arise at the same time.) But finally M. Parizeau was able to get his victory speech underway. He compared the process of 'becoming a nation' to a game of ice hockey. Then he mused that the long struggle for independence was at last nearing its goal, which was for the people of Québec to become 'a normal people'. The sudden revelation of a yearning to be normal came as something of a shock to many Canadians. It had always been assumed, by secessionists and federalists alike, that Québec wanted to be 'distinct', not 'normal'. M. Parizeau now seemed to be suggesting that Québecers had known all along that they were already perfectly distinct. But perhaps there was a clue to this secret pining for normalcy in the failure of the 1992 Accord on the new constitution, which had been agreed upon by every elected leader in the country, after being forced on them by the premier of Québec. In that document, Québec's distinctness was explicitly declared in the preamble. But in the following referendum to ratify this agreement, the population of Québec rejected it as decisively as did the rest of Canada.

In 1992, the failure of Québec to wring from Canada the power which Québec already possessed seemed at first to give the separatists a definite upper hand; but this advantage soon evaporated. As the example of the aboriginals illustrates, if one wants to wield power in Canada, the upper hand is the last thing one should seek, since it unfailingly leads to election, which then immediately puts one in the wrong. Freshly ensconced in the seat of power, and firmly in control of the media circus, the new separatist government (the third to be elected in the last twenty years) set out to persuade its citizens of the merits of a separate Québec. Their main argument was that in a separate Québec, there would be a strong economic association with Canada, the Canadian dollar would remain the official currency, citizens would be allowed to retain their Canadian citizenship, Québec would remain party to the North American Free Trade Agreement, and so on. Note that these are all benefits that Québecers already enjoy, and which they are in no danger of losing, so long as they remain in Canada.

In order to promote a genuine debate about separation, the new government initiated a series of pre-referendum panels to discuss the different ways in which Québec might secede from Canada. Because those opposed to separation were given no voice in this process, they automatically won the debate. The whole exercise was a perfect simulation of democracy. But the skill with which the separatist government deployed the strategies of simulation and seduction is best illustrated in their plans for the referendum itself. After all, as we have already seen, it is very risky to ask the Canadian people anything. Not only are they likely to say NO!, they will probably make a mockery of the question itself. As Canadians know from Baudrillard's analysis of polling techniques in general, the political question is always a kind of ultimatum, an imposition of a system of meaning, which contains within itself the desired response, namely that the question itself be taken seriously. As Baudrillard states:

> We live in a referendum mode precisely because there is no longer any referential . . . when democracy reaches a formally advanced stage, it is distributed in

equal quantities (50/50). Voting merges with Brownian motion . . . it matters little whether the existing parties express this or that historical or social agenda – it is even an advantage if they no longer represent anything: the fascination of the game, the polls, and formalistic obsession with statistics, is so much greater. (*ESM* 96, 106; *Death* 62, 68)

When he announced the referendum strategy of his new government, M. Parizeau proudly described it as '*astucieux*', which means 'astute'. But the word also means 'wily, foxy, crafty, cunning, tricky'. The reaction in the press was perplexity. How could the great national leader describe the historical struggle of an oppressed people to realize its cultural destiny as a cynical exercise in guile and deception? Apparently, M. Parizeau had realized that the only chance of winning a referendum on separation was to appear not to want to be taken seriously by the voters. According to this neo-Baudrillardian hypothesis, the Canadian people will agree to anything, so long as they believe that it is politically and historically meaningless; so the separatists have set about making their project for independence seem as shallow and opportunistic as possible.

Their first move was to elaborate a patently absurd and obviously manipulative scenario in which the government would actually declare the independence of Québec without consulting the people in a referendum, as they had promised. This declaration would, however, be purely formal, a meaningless gesture without real force: its sole purpose would be to serve as a pretext for framing the referendum question itself. The latter would be worded so as to inquire whether the people actually agree with the declaration, already passed by the national assembly, that Québec is a sovereign country. The ruse of burying the answer in the question itself was here so obvious that no one could take it seriously.

That the separatists have developed a new winning strategy in which they are deliberately trying to discredit themselves – in effect, that they are trying to seduce the population by appearing pathetic, ineffectual, irresponsible and superficial – seems confirmed by subsequent events. M. Bouchard, the darling of the separatist movement, emerged from hospital with one leg amputated, after a nearly fatal attack of flesh-eating bacteria (*necrotizing fasciitis*). Speaking after three months' silence, he declared that the question on the referendum ballot must be one to which Québecers would be sure to answer in the affirmative, and that the referendum must be delayed indefinitely until a yes vote was beyond doubt. This immediately ruled out any possibility of asking the people of Québec if they wanted to secede. The separatists then openly and officially admitted that they were planning deliberately to manipulate the timing and the phrasing of the referendum so as to deceive a majority into believing that their assent to the question would be without political consequences, a mere statement of the obvious, a pure non-event involving no real secession. It was proposed, for example, that the referendum question be 'Do you agree that Québec should have an economic association with Canada?' And even 'Do you love Québec?' Again, the display of cynicism was so blatant that nobody could take it seriously.

The outcome of this long deliberative process is still unclear, and there is no prospect in the near future of a decision which might undo the political deadlock which makes Canada such a safe and desirable country in which to live. But the conclusion seems unavoidable that actual independence in the real world of nation states is an unenviable fate, and that the people of Québec would indeed degenerate into a 'normal people' if they chose to separate from Canada. Just another nation among nations, no longer shielded by the absurdity of the Canadian polity, the people of Québec Libre might even be forced to speak more English in order to drum up investments from abroad. (France invests primarily in the neighbouring provinces of Ontario and New Brunswick.) It would be as if they had suddenly realized that with autonomy they could only become more and more like the Canadians with whom they differ so profoundly: boring and normal. No longer free to be at odds with impunity, deprived of Canadian subsidies to finance their oppositional cultural campaigns, the cherished distinctness of the Québec people would melt away like the snow in spring.

Canadians are universally envied as great beneficiaries of Enlightenment ideals of peace, reason and freedom. But as Baudrillard has pointed out, when 'everything is liberated, the cards have been dealt, we find ourselves before the crucial question: What to do after the orgy?' (TM 11) Canadians are like the guests who are still looking for the orgy, not realizing that the orgy is over, and they are the only ones left. They have invitations to something, but they don't know where to present themselves. Like Nietzsche's 'last men', Canadians (probably Australians too) have always lived in the twilight which is only just beginning to become visible to their hosts and cultural benefactors in Britain, France, Germany, Italy and the United States. Product neither of tradition nor revolution, Canada is a kind of political transplant – in effect, the first prosthetic nation – created by the decree of a foreign parliament fed up with the administrative headache of running an ambiguous colony. As always, Canadians have turned out to be far ahead of their time; they have never known any political geography but the transpolitical zone of unidentified historical objects. The orgy has finally come to them, but too late!

> In revolutionary theory, there was the living utopia of the withering away of the state: politics would cancel itself out in the apotheosis and transparency of the social. Nothing like this has occurred. Politics has certainly disappeared, but it has not been transcended by the social, it has led the social into the same disappearance. We are living the transpolitical, which is to say, the zero degree of politics, which is also the era of the endless reproduction and simulation of politics. Because everything that fails to carry beyond itself has the right to revival in perpetuity. So Politics will never stop disappearing, and in the meantime it will let nothing else emerge in its place. We are living out the hysteresis (hysteresie) of politics. (TM 19)

But it would be foolish to overdramatize the plight of Canada. Not only are Canadians gaining weight faster than other populations, even Americans; they are also growing more concerned about violence as the crime rate drops, which is an encouraging sign of a lively civic consciousness. Soon Canadians will be completely paralyzed by fear, and will thus have good reason to remain comfortably indoors all year round. This will not only protect them from the harsh winter weather and the relative non-occurrence of violence in the streets; it will also encourage them to continue their pattern of refraining from the domestic violence which has been on the rise statistically. The problem with the indeterminacy of violence in Canada is that no one knows where to flee; the experience of violence is so rare that people find it difficult to judge confidently whether a home or a street is safe. Anything might be violence in disguise. This uncertainty has caused something of an identity crisis among Canadians, who have long assumed proudly that they were less violent than Americans. It turns out that the difference between Canadians and Americans is less easy to discern: it seems to lie in the fact that whereas Americans are generally moved to decisive action when faced with a 'clear and present danger', Canadians are reluctant to do anything until they find themselves confronted squarely by an opaque and absent security (as in the case of the constitution itself).

In spite of the chronic safety crisis in Canada, there has been some good news, but it is not at all encouraging. The United Nations has determined that Canada ranks first in the world on the Human Development Index in 1994. Unfortunately, this little bit of silver lining in the dark cloud has worried Canadian officials even more than usual, because it shows definite improvement over the previous year, when Canada ranked second. Not only does it mean that Canada will have nowhere to go but down on the scale of human development, but as the experts point out, Canada's sterling performance may actually worsen the situation in Canada by masking the real problems of living in it.

The effects of Canada's 'vague and absent security' are particularly acute in its universities, as may be inferred from the fact that so few cases of violence or rape have been reported. This is an obvious sign of academic cover-up, or of repressed memory, which are usually present when there is a real problem. Sociologists concerned about this mounting crisis have interviewed thousands of university students. Their purpose was to determine the incidence of rape when Canadians go on 'dates' with each other, or otherwise have anything to do with the opposite Canadian sex. The sociologists reported a rate of over 80 per cent, a transparent sign that the problem has been underreported in the past. In fact, the problem of underreporting had an impact on the results of the study itself, since the vast majority of the respondents were only prepared to admit that they might have been jostled, or subjected to harsh words spoken in a loud voice. Given the nature of the crisis Canada is facing, the sociologists wisely decided to interpret these results as empirical evidence of widespread violence among courting couples.

Other problems have been discovered in Canadian society at large, which can be traced directly back to the universities, and to the insensitivity, sexism and racism of university professors, who are by far the most dangerous single group in the country (as foreign academics may well have discovered at international conferences). For example, in the early 1990s, there was an unpleasant riot in downtown Toronto. Some citizens originating from the West Indies participated, and much property was destroyed. With a determination to act, the Ontario government appointed Stephen Lewis, the former Canadian ambassador to the United Nations, to conduct a study into the problem of racism. The conclusion of his report was that academic freedom should be severely curtailed in Ontario universities, and that a complaint-driven system of tribunals should be established throughout the educational system, so that teachers, or anyone else, including the janitor, could be summarily reprimanded and punished for saying anything to upset anybody, or writing it on the walls (the insurgency problem of graffiti which Baudrillard has already addressed). Lewis's brilliant (and unexpected) solution to the problem of poverty and racism in

Toronto was at first greeted with enthusiasm. The government demanded that the recommendations be implemented immediately, and institutions like York University embraced it as official policy. But Canadians are a sullen and uncooperative people, like Baudrillard's masses, notoriously incapable of decisive action (except in the face of a vague and remote safety): whenever their ambivalence comes to the surface, Canadians implode – that is, they watch American television (a clear and present danger, to be sure). So the government quickly retreated, and the recommendations were eventually rejected as preposterous, demonstrating once again the intractable nature of the problem of violence in Canadian higher education.[2]

We can see from this that Canada is an example of the universal reign of *deterrence* which, as Baudrillard has shown, 'is a particular kind of action [which] prevents things from happening' (*IF* 32). When Canadians discovered Baudrillard, they realized that the world was just beginning to catch up to them: that Canada was in the vanguard, one of the first truly pataphysical nations. They certainly understand what he means when he describes how the meaning of history eludes him. 'It is as if events themselves were sending out the call to walk off the job', he writes. 'Post by post, they desert time, transforming it into an empty present, where nothing occurs except the visual psychodrama of information. And this wildcat strike of events leads to the lockout of history' (*IF* 32). As we have already noted, deterrence is not just the policy of Mutually Assured Destruction (MAD) which guided international politics during the Cold War; it is the crowd control structure of the Centre Pompidou (*BE*), and of Disneyland (*SS*); and in the wake of the Soviet collapse, it has become the general condition of world events as such, no longer a coordinated policy (agreed upon by both sides, as in the case of the Cold War), but an 'objective irony' in events which compensates metaphysically for the growing impossibility of establishing any critical distance from the events themselves.

> [Deterrence] dominates the present era, which tends less to produce events than to make sure that nothing happens, always with an air of historical significance. Or else what happens occurs instead of something else, which fails to occur. Deterrence affects everything, even war, history, the real, the passions. It gives rise (!) to strange events, which don't advance history at all, but play it backwards, linking it to an opposite curve, unintelligible to the historical sense (since nothing makes sense historically which doesn't move in the direction of history). These strange events have no negative power (progressive, critical, revolutionary), since their only negativity lies in the fact that they never happened. A troubling situation. (*IF* 32–3)

23

The aesthetics of evil

The copy is an image endowed with resemblance, the simulacrum is an image without resemblance. The catechism, so much inspired by Platonism, has familiarized us with this notion. God made man in his image and resemblance. Through sin, man lost the resemblance, while maintaining the image. We have become simulacra. We have forsaken moral existence in order to enter into aesthetic existence. This remark about the catechism has the advantage of emphasizing the demonic character of the simulacrum. (Gilles Deleuze)[1]

I watched . . . *Apocalypse Now.* Such a symphony of sound and color it was, and it sang of the age-old battle of the Western world against evil. 'You must make a friend of horror and moral terror,' says the mad commander in the savage garden of Cambodia, to which the Western man answered: No.

No. Horror and moral terror can never be exonerated. They have no real value. Pure evil has no real place. . . .

Except, perhaps, the art that repudiates evil . . .

It was enough to make an old world monster go back into the earth, this stunning irrelevance to the mighty scheme of things, enough to make him lie down and weep. Or enough to make him become a rock singer . . . . (Anne Rice)[2]

Pasolini's *Teorema* is sometimes criticized for its undialectical 'solution': the bourgeois factory owner (and the rest of his family, each in turn) is seduced by a bisexual angel (Terence Stamp), agent of 'divine love' who confronts the capitalist with the spiritual void in which he lives. In a voice-over, Pasolini quotes *Jeremiah*: 'God you have seduced me, I have let myself be seduced, I am an object of mockery'. The capitalist gives his factory to the workers, leaves his family, but more like Christ than Gauguin, he disappears into the volcanic desert, which is for Pasolini 'the visual form of the absolute, of time outside history'.[3] Pasolini's next film, *Porcile*, interweaves parallel tales of primitive, ecstatic cannibalism and modern bourgeois bestiality. The cannibalism of the pre-historic character and the pig-fucking of the modern, Julian, are both symobls of total parricidal revolt. Sounding oddly like Baudrillard, Pasolini describes the cannibalism of the 'prehistoric' character as 'a semiological system . . . extremism pushed to the limit of scandal, of rebellion, of horror. It is also a system of exchange or, if you prefer, one of total refusal – therefore [it is] a form of language, a monstrous refusal of normally accepted human communication'.[4] The modern hero, Julian, is not so much outside the social world, like his predecessor, as withdrawn from it: the violent sadistic refusal of his counterpart is replaced by a passive–aggressive, masochistic, 'strategy'. Pasolini says (again sounding like Baudrillard) that *Porcile* expresses 'desperate defiance toward all historic societies'. Both 'sons' are destroyed: the prehistoric cannibal is lured by peasants, captured, and staked to the ground, to be devoured by wild beasts. He cries out: 'I have killed my father, eaten human flesh, and I am trembling with joy'. The modern counterpart, whose father has made a business deal with a former Nazi, is eventually killed and eaten (Orwell's *Animal Farm*?) by the pigs he likes to screw.

The tenor of these films is the Euro-American cultural crisis which climaxed politically in 1968. They were made in the same general period as *Oedipus Rex* and *Medea*, which have similar transgressive themes. Like Baudrillard, identifying with the total philosophical rejection which students and 'drop-outs' had staged spectacularly in cities all over the Western world, Pasolini early lost faith in the Left, and in the realism which it had always favoured. His technique in this phase of his film-making becomes manneristic, a 'deliberately clinical style'. He 'erase[s] everything which would recall in too heavy a way the density of the body'. 'Weightless puppets, constrained and imprisoned by precise narrative . . . the characters move mechanically within a frozen world.'[5] This is the atmosphere which Baudrillard (RLC 98; *Seduction* 101) also found in Fellini's *Casanova* (1976): a cold rage against the world, which is reduced to total fabrication, the 'cold seduction' of pure signs at play in a subjectless scene of repetition and death. There is no hope. Only the seductive game of simulation, whose complete divorce from any concept of the real has a demonic, Manichean character.

The allegorical structure of this ironic form of protest gives it an air of theatrical futility. Everything is masked and displaced in an abstract narrative which invites and resists direct political decoding. Like Pasolini, Baudrillard seems to be trying to exaggerate the brutality of the power he confronts by pretending that he must resort to the tactics of the court jester in order to survive as a critic. The implication is that 'power' would never tolerate a directly realistic exposé, but only crush it. In the Western democracies, there is something farcical about this posture. What makes the technique so effective is that it will quickly concentrate and activate any potential for outrage and defiance in the ambient culture.

There is no more compelling illustration of this dramatic effect than the rock performances of the Doors, particularly Jim Morrison's shockingly beautiful impersonations of the devil (the 'lizard king'). Morrison's masochistic self-destructiveness actually heightened his power to reveal and clarify the puzzle of mediatic culture, that concoction of stagnant banality and brutal dynamism. Like Coppola's *Apocalypse Now*, his scandalous degeneration more than represented, it actually seemed to embody, to be, to simulate with intoxicating perfection, the now familiar mixture of middle-class rock'n'roll and napalm.

The climax of Morrison's decline was the 1969 Miami Doors concert, during which he became the suburban dictator, angrily projecting himself into the audience, and denouncing himself vociferously as he merged with the rioting crowd. 'Hitler is alive and well and living in Miami!' he is said to have shouted. As with Baudrillard and Pasolini, only more so, Morrison's moment of direct confrontation seems to refract indefinitely, finally to disappear in the rapid oscillation of provocation and self-parody. The hostile attack cascades and fizzles into comic ravings, absurdly wriggling in the arms of stressed-out security guards. The conundrum is that this feigned masking of rebellious criticism, the deliberate self-disqualification through grandiose presumption, the gambit of pretending to pretend, through the exaggerated manipulation of allegorical allusions and impersonations, can sometimes actually be more threatening and provocative than direct confrontation (or real concealment).

Perhaps the reason for this can be found in Baudrillard's theses on the self-cancelling modality of seduction. But the impression of impotent protest created by Baudrillard suggests an even more far-reaching form of seduction than Morrison's method of mounting and dissolving an attack. Morrison's medium necessarily tied him to surface effects. Baudrillard's seduction, on the other hand, is concealed behind a surface of faked shallowness, a disingenuous disbelief in depths. What is masked is not an assault but a submission – not a Romantic revolt but a mannerist lure. Its purpose is not to exaggerate the unreasonable violence of power, but to emphasize its indeterminacy, its vacuous and absorptive generality. By projecting power dramatically as a form of irrational terror which must be dodged and tricked, the parodic, allegorical, seductive discourse of the fatal strategy actually highlights the sane, conventional realism of the world, making its reason seem all the more absurd, its tolerance only a function of indifference, its authority hollow and illegitimate. Unlike Morrison (or Foucault, for that matter), Baudrillard does nothing to encourage the myth-makers and hagiographers, who want to idealize the irrationality of the poet, to transform his rebellion into a heroic epic. Baudrillard does not need to be arrested and charged in order to make his point. His indecency is much more insidious than that.

As Baudrillard points out, one can find the same kind of perverse symbolic challenge wherever the West confronts its imagined 'other': in the Ayatollah's declaration of the *fatwah*, for example. When the relatively rationalized West finds itself swept up in the mythic roles of master and oppressor, it is at a decided symbolic disadvantage, especially if the 'oppressed' respond by identifying with the mythic aggressor, through a staged impersonation of the devil. Of course, with this strategy, small-scale cultures will tend to implode inwardly and eventually die, like Jim Morrison, or the Ivory Coast Tribe in Jean Rouch's *Les maîtres fous* (RLC 105). But when an archaic civilization on the scale of Imperial China or the Persian Empire is faced with modernization – that is, with the cool rationality of free speech, free thought, free trade and the historicity of sacred texts – the defensive, often masochistic identification with the aggressor can be violent, and the impersonation of the devil may be quite literally acted out.

According to Baudrillard, we can see this kind of drama playing itself out in the new strategic, twentieth-century Islam ('Islam *as it is*, not the Islam of the Middle Ages', i.e. Islam as a form of politicized antimodernism) which is 'creating a vacuum around the Western system' (TE 83–4). The effect of Jihad-style terrorism is like the depressurization of an aircraft cabin at high altitude: a well-placed puncture, and all the Western 'values' are sucked right out into the void. This was in effect how the 'third world', as a kind of excluded middle – the 'Demon of noise', to use Michel Serres's communication term – upset the 'balance of terror' held by the Cold War diapoly (*Death* 68–9). In the wake of the death threats to Salman Rushdie, ritually repeated and renewed every few months from Tehran, the feeling has grown that his real persecutor is the West itself. Expounding with the finest eloquence the highest values the West has been able to cultivate – the moral independence of the individual and freedom of inquiry (not to mention the most gorgeous texture of modernist prose) – Salman Rushdie's appeals have fallen on deaf ears. The Euro-American leaders try to be polite, of course. But Thatcher quickly betrayed Rushdie, with words of sympathy for all the religiously offended; and her minister Sir Geoffrey Howe complained that *The Satanic Verses* are 'extremely rude' to Britain.[6] Some heads of state, like the Canadian

Prime Minister Mulroney, refused even to meet him. In an invocation of mythic powers curious for a former Vichy agent posing as an Enlightenment pragmatist leader, François Mitterand declared that Khomeini represented 'absolute evil'. But nothing has been done by anyone in a position to act on this dire judgement, other than, as Baudrillard points out, to take Rushdie himself hostage, by doing the only thing that anyone can think of doing, which is to keep him under constant protective guard.

As in the Gulf War, there is not much of a middle position to hold, unless one believes that one can, before addressing the immediate crisis, somehow right all the wrongs of Western Civilization, resolve all the historical grievances, so that then the West can defend its principles in good conscience! When through reparation and restitution the West has retroactively practised what it preaches, expunged itself of all traces of evil, only *then* may it defend freedom of expression, civil rights, democracy and the rule of law. An impossible demand, yet the intellectual *ex officio* opposition clings to this impractical view as if by default.

Symbolic violence and defiance reconstitute the psychological conditions of the Cold War diapoly, in which there is only power confronting power, with no intermediate area of play. The aim is to undermine the rationality of the West by forcing its defence to take an irrational form. For conscientious objectors, there is nothing left to do but to pretend that one isn't 'part of the problem' (Evil) but 'part of the solution' (Good), in Eldridge Cleaver's words.

On the Rushdie affair, R. J. Hollingdale commented in the *Guardian*: 'It is a very abnormal kind of war, and one in which our side is likely to be baffled . . . every act one can think of proves futile'.[7] Baudrillard's verdict on this predicament of the West is unsparing:

> We have become very weak in terms of Satanic, ironic, polemical and antagonistic energy: our societies have become fanatically soft . . . . By hunting down all of the accursed share in ourselves and allowing only positive values free rein, we have made ourselves dramatically vulnerable to even the mildest of viral attacks, including that of the Ayatollah. (TE 82)

> We have visited so many germs and sicknesses, so many epidemics and ideologies, upon the rest of the world, which was utterly defenceless against them, that our present defencelessness . . . seems a truly ironic twist of fate. (TE 84)

> Every hostage taking bears witness to the unavoidable spinelessness of entire societies with respect to their less important members. (TE 85)

We are utterly incapable of defending even the most obvious of our most basic rational principles because we are still unable to recognize them as the work of a long historical labour, a legacy of real struggle worth defending. We want them simply to be the only and automatic truths, universal truths which triumph over the myth of good and evil without having to confront the myth (in whose moralism we still secretly believe) on its own terms.

Such is Baudrillard's understanding of the weakness of all democratic politics, delivered with an air of ironic lamentation: 'If only our Western universe were solid, all this [postcolonial antagonism] would be meaningless' (TE 84). But there is nothing at all 'solid' about the 'Western' universe. Its democracy is largely a rhetorical construct. And though rhetorical competition may still be preferable as a political form to the existing alternatives, the would-be Western democracies are clearly choking on their own ineloquent, mass-mediatized torrents of political communication. They are divided to the core by utterly incompatible values: on one side, 'identity', which distils all the irrationality of traditional culture into a nationalistic, administrative, egalitarian essence; and on the other side, 'freedom', the unjustifiable idea of modernity itself.

There are different ways of approaching the culturally delocalized political processes of modernization. But, with few exceptions, as soon as one tries to depart from abstract principle (such as Kuwait's sovereignty or Rushdie's freedom of expression) in order to explore 'complexity', one is swallowed up in endless refractions, a sort of liquefaction in the 'total centrifugal expansion of communication'. As Baudrillard is so fond of saying, irony is no longer subjective, it is objective – it has passed into the state of inanimate things and processes. The Talion principle – the law of moral equivalence, which stamps the character of paranoid individuals and groups – works its way assiduously into the geopolitical fabric of the world and its competing cultures. There is the repeated effect of an immediate reduction of the Symbolic – the great ritual principles of Passion, Seduction, Evil and Reversibility – to an indeterminate pattern of 'viral' contagion. 'Nonevents' concatenate without meaning, as if taking revenge on logic and reason themselves.

The disintegrating stages of this process can be seen clearly in the Tienanmen Square incidents of 1989. As Rey Chow has shown, the logic of the situation was deeply affected by the intrusion of a kind of naive Western 'visuality' – i.e. the media. In a sense, it was the arrogance of our belief that we could act as moral witnesses which did the most harm. Or at least, if we *reflect* on such events at all, this is how we are inclined to think. Our narcissistic fixation before the great mirror of the mediascape inevitably leads us to wonder what role *we* may have played in the events that appear to be unfolding thousands of miles away. Whenever there is a desire to refract a 'third world' disaster back onto the West, this is now the basic critical stance: cast aspersions on the observers – *we* are the guilty witnesses, *we* are the victims of the tragic fall. The principle even applies retroactively as when, for example, the nineteenth-century colonial eyewitness accounts of East Indian live widow burnings (*sati*) are condemned as 'discursive violence that is every bit as cruel and indefensible as the practice that is its referent'.[8]

There is no doubt that the presence of the electronic news apparatus at Tienanmen Square was deeply problematic; perhaps it was never seriously questioned. Of course, it is difficult to see how this Western 'visuality' could have been challenged without betraying the students whose lives were on the line. But that does not alter the fact that the privileged status of the media, their sheer inevitability, fosters a remarkable delusion, as Chow points out: the delusion that the participation of information networks in the social process is neutral, an inert function of a transparent medium, not a dynamic factor in its own right, but an objective recording process. In the broadcasts from Tienanmen Square, 'All sensations merged into the sensation of seeing and the epistemological and moral imperative of watching. It was believed that by watching . . . we would be able to prevent disasters from happening'. Of course, the government of the People's Republic could not possibly see things this way. For them, Western 'visuality was a force', a provocation, according to Chow.

> Interpreting the gaze of the world's media as *daring* them to respond to their challenge, the Chinese authorities rose to the occasion by putting their best foot forward – by showing that they dared kill even their own students and workers . . . . Hence, what was intended . . . turned into its opposite. Visuality became not the policing or investigatory order that it aspired to be but a theatrical order and an exchange – not of gazes but of faces (faces being analogous to honour or pride).[9]

Here we have a brutal fascist massacre of a democratic student movement appealing for reform. But in their repression, do they get even a fraction of the sympathy Western intellectuals accorded the students at Vincennes and the Sorbonne in the Spring of 68? It seems that the mere fact of American televisation makes it impossible for the critical intelligentsia to have a clear response. We seem compelled to apologize for the postcolonial police state, and to cast dark aspersions on the 'West', as if somehow to exorcise the terrible power we fear the TV has over our capacity for independent thought.

The hypothesis that Chinese authoritarianism turned the panopticon against itself and converted it into a theatre of symbolic cruelty would be appealing if it were not so obviously a wish-fulfilling fantasy of the disenfranchised intellectual. It has about the same political credibility as Michel Foucault's celebration of the burning, flaying and dismemberment of Damiens.[10] The symbolic challenge, the apparent resurgence of alterity, the seeming ethic of the face (of facing up and facing down), the putatively Baudrillardian invocation of the principle of evil – including the political cruelty of the massacre and its aftermath – all of this soon breaks down as a model of coherent response in the 'face' of the image virus, and the 'visualism' of the West.

Chow's analysis, concerned as it may be for the fate of democracy in China, simply promotes and continues the massive haemorrhage, in contemporary critical theory, of responsibility for anything that happens anywhere except the 'West' (which, unlike the rest of the world, is always held responsible for its own failures). In the end, one cannot even question the motives of the fascists! Everything about the 'events' of June 1989 dissolves into the *mediations* of the event, just as events would seem to do later that autumn during the fall of the Berlin Wall: that great symbolic dismantling of the Iron Curtain appears to have been precipitated by nothing more noble than 'a colossal misunderstanding' of local media reports in East Germany.[11] As Baudrillard argued after '68 in 'Requiem for the Media' (*FCPES*), there is no way to confront the media effectively, except with themselves, which is ultimately a fruitless exercise. In Tienanmen Square, there was no 'facing', certainly no irruption of symbolic exchange. To be part of the television gaze has nothing to do with panopticism or its subversion; it is merely to be lost in a refracted image of oneself, a mirror identification in which one watches and hears the disintegration of the intentional ego. What is offered is too painful actually to see, which is why it can be shown over and over again, and why we cannot help but look, blankly, faced only with our own distance from ourselves. For we necessarily dissociate the images of the square, of the tanks, and of some poor lost souls whom we cannot save. We amputate ourselves in self-defence, trying to escape this expanded, fragmenting relationship with ourselves, which sucks the capacity to see right out of us, like the vision machine and the video dreamers in Wenders's *Until the End of the World*. In Tienanmen Square, we glimpsed ourselves already succumbing to the 'disease of images', and we look forward to the day when 'the automatic-perception prosthesis will function like a kind of mechanized imaginary from which, this time, we would be totally excluded'.[12] Just some brutal murders, an aftermath of repression, and the recorded nonpresence of the world – for in a Baudrillardian sense we did not watch the events at Tienanmen Square – the events watched us. It was certainly not we who spoke, nor the students, nor even the Chinese generals and their political bosses. The tragedy – if Chow is to be believed – is that this was just another cultural showdown, just another propaganda clash, like Hitler's 1936 Munich Games. In other words, no tragedy at all – just farce: our own self-satirizing parody of concern. If there was a centralizing Western 'logos' at work, perhaps its hegemony lay neither in imperialism or the Chinese bureaucracy, nor any ruling class or bloc, but rather, as Andrew Wernick has argued, in 'the commodity and its structurations as such'.[15] It was the inanimate objects of Tienanmen which spoke to us and for us, the tanks, for example, but especially the Goddess of Democracy (sometimes called the Goddess of Liberty) as an ultimate 'sign object'.

As Baudrillard says, the irony of history has passed into the objects themselves: this is the viral logic of 'the transparency of evil'. The irony has no better exemplar than the image of a Chinese-looking knock-off of the Statue of Liberty towering opposite the absent portrait of Mao which had once dominated Tienanmen Square. The Statue of Liberty as an illegal public monument! But the Goddess was no pure political symbol. She was the effigy of a primitive force recuperated as a promotional form, a kind of ultra-commodity. In Andrew Wernick's phrase: 'a Chinese appropriation of an American appropriation of a French appropriation of a Roman appropriation of a Greek appropriation of an upper Paleolithic symbol'.[14] Made in France, the 'original' American Statue of Liberty was financed in connection with an advertising campaign for the Pulitzer newspapers in the nineteenth century. As we saw in Chapter 7, sign-objects act like Trojan horses, smuggling the codes and the cultural logic of the object system into the body politic of the unsuspecting host. What disseminates is not necessarily an idea (the idea of liberty), or its symbolic negation, but an overriding form – 'not only the universe of discourse that promotion enfolds, but the promotional mode itself[15] – a virus, a ritual *possession*.

But what does this give us? The idea that advertising is vulgar and commodities are crass? Or that there is a primitive magic at work, even in the commodity? Does it mean that perhaps the students are not to be admired for their political courage? After all, they were using one of the great 'capitalist' promotional symbols. Perhaps they were really capitalist exploiters and imperialists at heart. At any rate, if we cannot exactly oppose Western capitalism and its TV in this instance, we are invited to be ambivalent and wary. The noted critic W. J. T. Mitchell argues that it is an open question 'how to negotiate the border between struggle and dialogue, between the argument of force and the force of argument'.[16] He sounds the right note; but his elision of the word 'struggle' and the ambiguous phrase 'argument of force' makes it unclear whether Mitchell simply wants to disguise a conventional plea for free speech in revolutionary-sounding rhetoric, or whether he is furtively justifying organized violence against electoral democracies and their citizens. Rey Chow seems to go even further. She implies that anything is justified in the 'face' of Western imperialism and practically applauds the crushing of the students, because it shows the Western capitalists how foolish they are to think that they can bully China with 'visualism'. According to Chow, the corpses of the Chinese students were 'the casualties of unequally competing discourse networks none of which cared about their survival'.[17] In other words, they were killed by the media, and the selfish visualism of the Western public, whose stronger discourse network pushed the discourse of the police state into an awkward corner, where it had no choice but 'to put its best foot forward' and massacre its own citizens in defiance against 'yet another instance of Western imperialism dominating a "third world" culture'.[18]

What is almost entirely lost in all this political hairsplitting is any sense that the Chinese students themselves were trying to construct an idealized visual theatre for the media: that they *wanted* the media there in order to dramatize the tyranny of the fascist Chinese bureaucracy. According to this interpretation, the students were using the global media as a way of gambling their own lives, calculating that the risk to themselves would ultimately give them back their lives and political victory to boot. They did not necessarily want to be martyrs, but they were desperate enough to raise the ante, in the form of a provocative symbol, and they lost. From this point of view, it would be absurd to argue, with self-righteous contempt for the 'West', that the massacre was 'overdetermined by the presence of a massive publicity apparatus'.[19] If as Westerners we have no right to blame the Chinese authorities themselves, then surely at least we can allow that the students had a hand in their own deaths?

Analyses which pretend that nobody is responsible and that everybody is a victim of objects, systems and impersonal processes, are scarcely satisfactory. But then how should we characterize the views of Baudrillard, the great champion of such analyses? Would he delight in the moral lesson taught to the West by the brutal crushing of the student protest, just as he seemed to enjoy the irony of the West's inability to embrace Salman Rushdie as one of its own?

The answer is that, of course, many of Baudrillard's writings have a disappointing or ridiculous relationship with the world, and they usually lead nowhere. But this negative judgement is not true of Baudrillard in quite the way that it is generally true of so much work in social science and cultural theory. The difference in Baudrillard's approach is that he rarely if ever seriously attempts to persuade us of anything. He never pretends to achieve a balance of evidence, perspective or morality, never strives for objectivity, proportion or justice. Now, such defiance of the conventional norms of reasonableness and credibility usually suggests merely a different approach to the same problem of persuasion: not to be rational, but to exhort, by means of direct or indirect threats and attacks, usually of a guilt-inducing nature, to adopt a certain point of view or cause. Baudrillard will have nothing to do with causes. His hypotheses are not only incredible from the start, they are intrinsically unappealing to anyone looking for a cause to believe in. He advocates nothing. And though in a way he develops a rigorous point of view, he attaches little significance to it beyond its aesthetic and rhetorical unity, which persuades us less than it serves as the consistent frame for an abreaction of sociological *angst*, on the part of confused citizens of the 'new world order'.

And so there, at least, is one way of reading Baudrillard: to come to a realization that the discourses, including his own, which inform the object processes and events of modernity – the 'double hermeneutic' of which Anthony Giddens writes so eloquently in *The Consequences of Modernity* – are largely unreadable and thus indigestible. The social rate of metabolism is simply too ponderous to convert all the products of critical mediation into cultural nourishment ready for recycling. For lack of time and place, most of what is produced must be redistributed immediately; it cannot really be absorbed, and so it rarely even has the value of fertilizer when it is spread around.

As with the majority of the propositions of cultural metaphysics, there is little constructive to be done with insights like these. In a hyperBaudrillardian world, there is no time to think about anything seriously, nowhere to put anything, and little time to get to know anything intimately enough to internalize it, to miss it when it passes, to mourn its loss. 'It's just a mode of propagation by contiguity, like contagion, only faster – the ancient principle of metamorphosis, going from one form to another without passing through a system of meaning' (*FF* 78). If the register of the 'symbolic' is moribund in every form except death itself, as Baudrillard argues, this is nowhere more true than in the intellectual world. The academic universe has become so sophisticated and self-conscious that it no longer has much sense of a teachable culture, except in the rationalized form of a critical discourse on media and mediation. Nothing is worth passing on, except as a test of the student's naivété. Even world-historical confrontations such as Tienanmen, directly affecting the fate of nearly a third of the world's population, quickly resolve into a calculus of political 'positioning'.

These comments may seem out of sorts. But from a perspective sympathetic to cultural metaphysics as a sustained reflection on the disquieting strangeness of human civilization, they are unavoidable. Empty generalizations are the basic stuff of good cultural metaphysics. They take nothing away from the enormous promise which the world still holds for all who enter it. They only intend to strip the pretensions of our great modern theories to know in advance what the world will bring, and to lead us to its truth. On this view, social science is the contemporary version of all the foolish mummery which characterized the old world religions. And the abject absurdities of Baudrillardian texts are an attempt to bring social science down to Baudrillard's own level of inconsequential *nuisibilité* and *niaiserie*, to seduce us out of the imaginary space of the critical ego, where we might have been pretending that we were not actually participating in the global flux of raw sewage.

24

Cultural metaphysics and politics

A democratic society is not just a society that accommodates different groups and beliefs. . . . It is one in which members of society tolerate an *internal* discrepancy between different registers of society. A democratic society does not add up. It is a society of the discontinuous. This is why intellectuals, with their regressed preference for consistency, are frequently a threat to the necessarily strange and inconsistent nature of democracy . . . . There is only one price to pay – the recognition of the place of difference . . . . The 'freedom' or 'tyranny' of a society is in part to be measured by the capacity to tolerate or crush the difference between domains.[1]

Like many of the philosophical prophets of the modern era, particularly Nietzsche and Heidegger, Baudrillard confronts the contemporary intellectual with a kind of 'all or nothing' choice. Baudrillardian perspectives do not lend themselves to faith in organized political movements, to ideas for social programmes, to policies designed to reform human nature, or to plans for making the world a better place. They can be interpreted in essentially two ways, both of which are quite relevant to the end of the second millennium: either as inviting a total refusal of modern civilization, a call to terrorist arms; or as inviting a liberating abreaction of frustration over what cannot easily be changed. If we respond to Baudrillard at all on his own terms, it has to be either by becoming a fundamentalist, one who eagerly awaits (or brings about) the end of the world as we know it; or else by becoming a liberal (perhaps a closet liberal disguised as an aristocratic postmodern aesthete), one who accepts the world's imperfections, and stops trying to control its content, but looks nevertheless for new forms, frames, strategies, conventions within which interesting but unpredictable new possibilities might emerge, so that the human scenario can play itself out as freely and fully as possible.

In the 'all' strategy, politics usually becomes the final battleground of good and evil, in which individuals don't count. The only things that matter are truth and pornography, right and wrong. Are you a part of the solution, or a part of the problem? There has to be a final showdown, an irreversible conclusion.

In the 'nothing' strategy, politics is a cultivated area of societal life where everything is permitted, so long as it is expressed in a form which is not irreversibly destructive of another individual. In a liberal polity, there is (ideally) no such thing as an eye for an eye. Almost anything is reversible.[2] People do things – sometimes awful things – and they try to discuss them afterwards. They try to fathom the meaning and to decide what to do. They try to find better ways to discuss and decide. As for the question of good and evil, in the nothing strategy, this would gradually devolve onto the individual, and become largely a matter of public indifference. Evil would be considered a private affair, something to be worked out with one's conscience, spouse, friends, children – perhaps one's analyst. Or in a treatise on cultural metaphysics.

POSTSTRUCTURALISM AS RADICAL LIBERALISM: THE SURVIVAL OF ARISTOCRATIC LITERARY CULTURE IN THE POSTMODERN WORLD

When Marshall McLuhan published *Understanding Media* in the mid-1960s he precipitated a minor academic crisis in which serious scholars publicly disputed the importance of his work and dismissed his propositions as wild, irresponsible, inconsistent and false. The idea seemed preposterous at the time that attention might legitimately be paid to (and inferences drawn from) the aesthetic dynamics of communicative forms. Now, nearly everybody interested in media, mass culture and modernity draws (often unawares, and usually without footnotes) on the revised historical and social perspective which McLuhan established. It is not unlikely that Baudrillard's work, itself deeply informed by McLuhan's emphasis on social forms, will suffer a similar fate, as one trampled by the throng rushing through the door he left ajar.

In retrospect, we can see now that McLuhan helped to bring about a reformation in the relations between the 'two cultures'. What McLuhan achieved, effectively, was a literary colonization of the disputed borders of scientific culture. Once this ideological breach had been opened, structuralism and poststructuralism followed in short order. Undeterred by its failure to make social discourse scientific by reducing the literary to the textual, the structuralist revolution went on to play an important role in the consolidation of the literary ethos at the heart of our social scientific and technological culture. Its contribution has been to argue, apparently more successfully than hermeneutics and phenomenology, the widening scope of literary application which McLuhan promoted: to re-establish the pertinence of the literary sensibility in sociological, anthropological, epistemological and political discourses. In short, with the help of Freud, poststructuralism has succeeded in carrying forward the romantic concept of imagination – Coleridge's esemplastic power – into a contemporary frame of reference.

Once this has been recognized, the idea that poststructuralism poses a serious challenge to the 'Western episteme' will seem a little naive. Nearly all the ontological and epistemological claims of radical poststructuralist philosophy have been withdrawn, or are in the process of being redrawn in a more rational and liberal perspective. Militant poststructuralism now survives primarily as a means of brightening up the look of defunct systems of revolutionary thought. In practice, it has destroyed the Marxist historical significance machine, thus reopening the study of Western culture to the speculative imagination. Apart from a few theoreticians adhesively identified with collectivist utopian political programmes, poststructuralism has largely abandoned the grandiose theory of the 'epistemological break', and functions almost entirely within the boundaries of ongoing rational debate. Typical poststructuralist balloons, such as the once popular notions of society and gender as forms of discursive plasticine, have burst. The usable leftovers have settled down as regular features of the intellectual environment, scholarly routines whose value varies inversely with overuse. Applying deconstruction to itself, we realize that even poststructuralist metaphors grow more questionable the further they are extended.

What the era of poststructuralism has accomplished, in fact, is not an indictment of the West, but a salutary rediscovery of its essential values of freedom, of openness for openness's sake: of *play*. These poststructuralist insights into the metaphysical and social functions of play can be related to themes of collectivism, social integration and moral truth only in the most awkward and philosophically strained way. They lend themselves much more fluidly to discussions of diversity and difference, individuality and particularity. Oriented from the beginning in this distinctly liberal and un-Gallic style, the logical direction for poststructuralism was surely always towards a horizon of expanded communication: what Foucault might have called a 'heterotopia' of experimentation, expression and contestation.

It is now clear that the poststructuralist critique of 'foundationalism' in epistemology (a metaphysically hyped up version of Anglo-

American empiricism and pragmatism) has evolved satisfactorily into a much more useful critique of *fundamentalism* in social thought. In effect, it has doubled back to the conventional or non-essentialist foundations of an original liberal impulse at the heart of modern individualism. It was from this vantage point that certain poststructuralist philosophers began to elaborate a cultural metaphysics, as the present study of Baudrillard has tried to show. In this regard, the poststructuralist concept of difference has played a crucial role, by securing, at last, for the Nietzschean critique of equality and equivalence, a comfortable home in our scientific culture: as the idea of a Dionysian public sphere in a liberal democracy. And this has occurred just in time to save the 'public sphere' from the moral purposes of the egalitarians. Like Nietzsche, the liberal poststructuralists have understood that equality, like signification, is only a conventional form, a construction. It can never be realized as the stable content of social life, except as maximum entropy, or heat death.

From this neo-Nietzschean point of view, the still unfulfilled promise of democracy certainly does not lie in equality or fraternity, but in an expanded notion of liberty. For liberal postmoderns, the meaning of liberty resides not only in democracy's claim to guarantee an open and unfettered debate (threatened as ever today by political, religious and moral fundamentalism); but also in the enigmatic form which Donald Winnicott conceived as 'potential space'.[3] The latter view of freedom is of course much more controversial than habeas corpus or 'first amendment' rights, partly because it does not spring from modern convention, but rather from the mysterious depths of archaic symbolic ritual, as recuperated by psychoanalysis and cultural metaphysics. Elaborated in psychosocial terms, the idea of realizing liberty as potential space implies a radical conception of modernist culture as a realm of licensed amorality, where the intellectual distinctions between the me and the not me, the produced and the consumed, the created and the destroyed, the responsible and the irresponsible, can be held in suspense, if only so that the tedium of moralizing discourse can be ignored long enough to permit discoveries to be made and creativity to flourish.

If proposals for a Dionysian public sphere are to gain a political hearing, however, there will have to ensue a difficult debate about whether they imply merely a negative freedom, to be protected under constitutional law, or whether they suggest a kind of 'positive freedom' requiring the active promotion of the State. (A simple example of the dilemma in question is the emerging debate in the

United States over whether or not there should be meaningful public funding for the arts, that is, provision of tax revenues to be *administered by the arts community itself*, and not by the public or its representatives, who are too easily given over to feelings of being offended or abused.)

The idea that the promise of modernity lies in the institution of an irresponsible heterotopia is arguably the essential contribution of the poststructuralist movement, and no one has more effectively conveyed its central argument than Baudrillard. Indeed, the whole point of the theory of simulation is that life has always been overdetermined by the accidents of meaning. The regimes of biology and sociology must ultimately give way to the indeterminacy of a semantic body endowed with more and more intelligence, and more and more technology. Who can deny the intuition that in one privileged moment, delirium and hallucination might have the power to alter the course of a life?

Baudrillard's historical hypothesis, for what it is worth, is summed up in the triptychs 'ritual–law–code' (RLC) and 'metamorphoses, metaphors, metastases' (*Ecstasy* 45–56). One way of grasping his interpretation of the evolution of our experience is to consider how the art of persuasion – *rhetoric* in the traditional sense – has so far resulted, through successive technological refinements, from the syllogism to the computer, in a type of societal system which is transparently rhetorical, essentially persuasive from top to bottom, beginning to end. It is this unchartable new condition of social being which Baudrillard dramatizes through his blatant abdication of rhetorical credibility, his absurdist staging of Rationality as a metaphysical vanishing act. But what historical meaning could such a comedy of errors convey? If the tragic failure of rationality is degenerating into farce, then perhaps the dramatistic logic of the history of reason is to prepare the audience for the happy denouement. The irony and satire distilled from the tragedy of modernity are transformed into the moods of comedy, as Northrop Frye would say, 'stages in the life of a redeemed society'.

> At this point . . . comedy enters . . . the phase of the collapse and disintegration of the comic society. In this phase, the social units of comedy become small and esoteric, or even confined to a single individual. Secret and sheltered places, forests in moonlight, secluded valleys, and happy islands become more prominent, as does the *penseroso* mood of romance, the love of the occult and the marvellous, the sense of individual detachment from routine existence.[4]

This is the triumph of the liberal imagination and the apotheosis of cultural metaphysics. Within every individual, and through every local constellation of affective existence, there resides yet another incommensurable primitive society of symbolic exchange and seduction. Democracy rises as a sphere of radical deregulation. Responsibility is transformed into something which can only be claimed, and never imposed on others. The tragic-satiric age of metastasis and the code brings us full circle back to the fabulous ritual realm of comic metamorphoses. Interpreted in this light, Baudrillard's fictional sociology seems to unfold comfortably within the mainstream Western pragmatist project of forgetting Being and postponing the moment of Truth.

It comes down to the following question, for Baudrillard, as for Rabelais, Shakespeare, Nietzsche, Segalen, de Sade: how can the aristocratic privileges and vampire values[5] of moral independence,[6] cultivated difference, wasteful expenditure, cultural elitism and infantile acting out be translated into the modalities of a democratic society, without losing their symbolic intensity, but also without reverting to the brutal hierarchical and patriarchal symbolic social orders of the premodern era?

We moderns (or postmoderns) refer to the principle of freedom of expression as a 'right', but in fact we all recognize that rights are fictions, that they only exist as conventions, more or less rational or irrational. Modern 'democracy' is such a fiction, based on a rational bourgeois convention: namely, the habit of distinguishing the act of speech, more and more broadly defined, from all other actions. As this convention has taken hold through publicly programmed education, the emotional and symbolic significance of action in general has in the process been steadily attenuated. What remains is now more and more carefully specified for governmentalized remedy, or codified in terms of a generalized system of law. The law is thankfully still slanted in favour of respect for the moral independence of the individual. But the rationalization and universalization of law has a corrosive effect on collective forms of life. It is basically hostile to culture in the traditional sense, with its exotic tapestry of discriminatory lies, idealized hierarchies, and paranoid prejudices. When we specify actions, under rational democratic convention, we attempt to understand them on their own terms, rather than respond to them in terms of a moral absolute. When we codify actions, we strip them of meaning and submit them to a relatively impersonal system of justice where feelings are ruled out of court and judgments are given a practical rather than a symbolic explanation. In this bourgeois system, we are normally considered beyond the ultimate sanctions which traditional culture might prescribe; and even when we find ourselves in dire circumstances, accused of the worst transgressions, the modern convention is still to grant us at least a minimum of protection ('until proven guilty') from the revenge of the symbolic (for example, the death penalty). Devised as a check on divine power, the convention of civil rights and protections for the juridico-political individual rapidly generated a novel form of social privilege open in principle to any educated white male.

Now everybody wants to share this democratic privilege, and rightly so. But they resist the requirement that they construct the false, prosthetic, juridico-political self required for entry into the public sphere. Such is the strange, rationalizing power of modernity as a form: it absorbs, refracts and recombines all cultural contents, steadily stripping away their emotional form, their aura of symbolic power. The benefits in equality of opportunity are tangible and desirable, but the danger is cultural flatness. Moreover, concern over this prospect would appear to be more than just a battle of conventions, of ancients and moderns, as it was sometimes perceived in the eighteenth century. For though the modern convention which limits the political power to prescribe behaviour, and permits the reign of dunces in the Age of Lead, is based on a philosophically indefensible 'bourgeois' distinction between thought and action, private and public, symbol and reality, it is probably now historically irreversible (short of death, as Baudrillard claims). It has grounded itself in a massive, consumer-driven information, research and entertainment infrastructure which will be difficult to displace, and which may be inherently uncentralizable, if it survives the fundamentalist and evangelical attempts to hijack, destroy or regulate it.

The best poststructuralist case is that a procedural (rather than Platonic) understanding of science and society, invigorated and enlightened by a robust and speculative literary sensibility, will naturally want to secure terms for a liberal heterotopia within the 'technological dynamo' of global modernization. According to this scenario, the cultural dislocations wrought by modernity have shifted the traditional balance between common sense and primitive affect. Science has pushed morality almost entirely out of the practical sphere, leaving moral sentiment homeless, in search of shelter. Just as the science of the real world of phenomenal effects needed to be liberated from the primitive symbolic unconscious in order to bloom, now the symbolic itself needs to be protected from the wandering excess of disenfranchised morality, if culture is to flourish after the destruction of its traditional, integrated, biosocial forms. The violent, discriminatory, hierarchical quality of the symbolic must somehow be preserved (in spite of our commitment to equality of opportunity), or else culture will become a matter of complete indifference, censored into oblivion by moralizing defences against the dangers of associative living.

Arguably the most dangerous thing in the world is morality. This is particularly the case with remembered morality: the imagined loss of a golden age of harmony and chastity. In a globalizing age when there is no longer any possibility of escape from the cynicism of cosmopolitan culture, fictional utopias of social integration have broadcast appeal. Coupled with technology hallucinations of purity may have the power to destroy liberal culture entirely, if not the human race itself. In retrospect, however, we know that morality has always been questionable in any form, socially integrated or externally imposed. Cruelty and injustice have always been done in the name of the primitive superego, the seat of morality. Guilt is still thought of as a civilized emotion, arising through education and maturation of the personality. In fact, it is a destructive, narcissistic, unethical emotion which arises not through socialization and internalization, as is commonly supposed, but as a natural internal response to, or unconscious consequence of, our rage against helplessness and inevitable dependence. Given the treacherousness of these initial psychic conditions, it takes a long time for most of us to grow up, to develop a rational conscience (not the same as guilt or shame); and many of us never succeed. In the West, we have begun to recognize this problem. We are now much more understanding of the position in which small children find themselves. We are inclined to protect them from the sadism of institutionalized morality which has been traditionally designed into every culture as a programme of systematic intimidation (socialization or collectivization). Yet, as already noted, the danger of morality is as great as it ever was, perhaps worse. Ways to amplify the destructive effects of guilt are everywhere ready at hand, and the scope of amplification is practically unlimited. There is no longer a reliable series of intervals between the onset of moral outrage and panic and the societal levelling or complete destruction of the world. We are now, as individuals and societies, in full possession of the means of production of moral vision, that is, the elimination of all differences. It is a truly frightening prospect.

Science and society are now inextricably intertwined, and increasingly given over to more sophisticated mechanisms of self-regulation and unsupervised change. This automation includes the political process, the (re)production of public opinion and the evolution of social policy, as Baudrillard outlined in *Symbolic*

Exchange and Death. Here, short of complete destruction of modernity and repeal of the Enlightenment, the explicit claims of morality are all but exhausted. The public sphere still exists, but public morality does not. The latter survives mainly as an intellectual scrapheap for ministers of justice and attorneys general in search of materials with which to construct simulation models of decisive political action. In the real contemporary world, where action – especially economic action – is paralyzed by digitized administrative sludge, laws against violence in the media, the disintegration of family values, drugs, and sex are the only hope of seeming politically effectual. Either one passes oppressive new laws, or one generates a tide of fascist sentiment, in order to be swept along at its head. Governments have few other options under the conditions of societal overload which Baudrillard calls political 'hysteresis' (TE 11).

But if true morality is thankfully all but dead in the bourgeois public sphere, what remains of the human primitive in the social and symbolic dimensions is still hopelessly entangled in morality's webs, even and perhaps especially in the West. It is vital that science and the societal not be the only spheres of influence to be liberated from its arachnid grip. Morality today may be retreating back into the primitive symbolic unconscious whence it arose, but it still needs to be absorbed and neutralized if the spontaneity of human culture in the broadest sense is to survive and prosper. Remember that, unlike ethics, social morality is not a limit on the primitive unconscious, it is an expression of it. And unlike the ethical, the moral has no respect for individuality and freedom. The taming of the monster morality will require the cultural and constitutional elaboration of a clear ethical division between science and the symbolic, between the societal and the social, between the institutional and the individual. As is already evident among the higher primates, cultural learning only occurs if there is some freedom to play.[7] Freedom requires at least a relative degree of insulation from the behavioural constraints and vegetative necessities imposed by predators, hunger and climate, as well as from the authoritarian, instrumental social organizations they foster. In the scientific-societal world, we protect the sphere of play from both logic and morality in order to promote the exploration of practical effects, whether in the carefully bounded experimental set-up, or in the conventions of parliamentary and public debate. In the symbolic-social world, we try to establish a frame in which it is possible to explore without fear of sanction or loss of trust the emotional world of meaning, as in a marriage, a psychoanalysis, a work of art, or a treatise in cultural metaphysics. Both the scientific and the symbolic are equally distorted and corrupted by the constraints of morality; and so if we want cultural diversity and evolution to continue, we must try as hard as we can to get rid of morality in every sphere of human endeavour. We must find ways to do without this brutal instinctual legacy, before technology is used to reinforce it to a point beyond escape.

Perhaps one way to achieve this would be to create a specialized milieu in which it would be possible for thought to become genuinely 'rhizomatic'. In this potential space, the body would begin to experience what it means fully to enter the domain of imagination, and individuals in attempted association would experiment with regressions from the societal to the social, the fantastic emotional world of symbolic exchange and loss of prosthetic identity. The blueprint for such a liberation would require the creation, among the intelligentsia at least, of a broad consensus, and much sharing of wisdom, around a hypothetical project which today may still seem eccentric and irrational: the programmatic dissociation of social thought from any recognizable context of action, policy or politics. And that is exactly what Baudrillard has set out to do. Only when the symbolic social dimension has been released from the snares of governmentality can it become scientific in its own right: that is, free of morality and genuinely experimental. Only then will the Enlightenment have delivered its promise.

Notes

CHAPTER 1

1. Quoted in James Riordan and Jerry Prochnicky, *Break on Through: The life and death of Jim Morrison* (New York: William Morrow, 1991), p. 211.
2. Julian Barnes, *A History of the World in 10½ Chapters* (New York: Vintage, 1989).
3. Nicholas Mosley, *Hopeful Monsters* (London: Minerva, 1990).
4. Quoted from Alfred de Musset, *Confession d'un enfant du siècle* (1836) in Eugen Weber, *France, fin de siècle* (Cambridge, MA: Belknap, 1986), p. 15.
5. See e.g. Raymond Williams, *Culture* (Glasgow: Fontana, 1981), p. 10.
6. As so wonderfully described by Jane Goodall in *Through a Window: My thirty years with the chimpanzees of Gombe* (Boston: Houghton Mifflin, 1990).
7. Jean-Luc Nancy, *The Inoperative Community* ed. Peter Connor, trans. Peter Connor, Lisa Garbus, Michael Holland and Simona Sawhney (Minneapolis: University of Minnesota Press, 1991), p. 10.
8. Brian Massumi, 'Everywhere you want to be: introduction to fear', in Brian Massumi, ed. *The Politics of Everyday Fear* (Minneapolis: University of Minnesota Press, 1993), p. 91.
9. See Gianni Vattimo, *The End of Modernity: Nihilism and hermeneutics in postmodern culture* (Baltimore: Johns Hopkins University Press, 1988), especially 'An Apology for Nihilism'.

CHAPTER 2

1. Rosemary Jackson, *Fantasy: The literature of subversion* (London: Methuen, 1981), p. 65.
2. Pier Paolo Pasolini, *Heretical Empiricism*, trans. Ben Lawton and Louise K. Barnett (Indianapolis: Indiana University Press, 1988), p. 172.
3. Jonathan Culler, *On Deconstruction: Theory and criticism after structuralism* (Ithaca: Cornell University Press, 1982), p. 8.
4. Allan Megill, *Prophets of Extremity: Nietzsche, Heidegger, Foucault, Derrida* (Berkeley: University of California Press, 1985).
5. Jonathan Dollimore, *Sexual Dissidence: Augustine to Wilde, Freud to Foucault* (Oxford: Clarendon, 1991), p. 323.

6. Richard Rorty, *Consequences of Pragmatism* (Minneapolis: University of Minnesota Press, 1982), p. 66.
7. Jean Baudrillard, *Cool Memories* (London: Verso, 1990), p. 215.
8. Georg Lukács, *The Theory of the Novel*, trans. Anna Bostock (Cambridge, MA: MIT, 1971).
9. D. M. Thomas, *The White Hotel* (Toronto: Clarke, Irwin, 1981).
10. Wim Wenders, *The Logic of Images: Essays and conversations*, trans. Michael Hofmann (London: Faber & Faber, 1991), p. 64.
11. On the implications of these events, see Cornelius Castoriadis, 'The Hungarian Source', and Claude Lefort, 'The Age of Novelty', in *Telos* 29 (Fall, 1976), pp. 4–38.
12. His tormenter was Michel Foucault, who was director of philosophy at the time.
13. Very active during the 1960s, the Situationists were a tightly organized group of revolutionary anticapitalist theoreticians influenced by Georg Lukács, Henri Lefebvre, surrealism, Dadaism, and so on. Among those situationist works which influenced Baudrillard directly must be included Guy Debord, *La société du spectacle* (Paris: Buchet/Chastel, 1967).
14. Gerard Bonnot, 'Le terroriste de Nanterre', *Le Nouvel Observateur* (16 July, 1979), p. 44.

CHAPTER 3

1. See, for example, Jacques Derrida, *Positions*, trans. Alan Bass (Chicago: University of Chicago Press, 1981), pp. 68–71.
2. See Richard Rorty, ed. *The Linguistic Turn: Recent essays in philosophical method* (Chicago: University of Chicago Press, 1967).
3. W. R. Bion, 'Attacks on linking', *Second Thoughts: Selected papers on psycho-analysis* (New York: Jason Aronson, 1967), pp. 93–109.
4. Otto Rossler, quoted in James Gleick, *Chaos: Making a new science* (Harmondsworth: Penguin, 1987), p. 142.

CHAPTER 4

1. Theodor Adorno, *Negative Dialectics*, trans. E. B. Ashton (New York: Seabury, 1973), p. 181.
2. As we shall see later, it is primarily through this insight that Baudrillard attempts to differentiate himself from the element of subjective idealism in radical constructivist thought and poststructuralism generally.
3. Georges Bataille, *Theory of Religion*, trans. Robert Hurley (New York: Zone, 1989), p. 31.
4. *Ibid.*, p. 38.
5. There is already a very large literature on Heidegger's relation to postmodern thought. From the point of view of *cultural metaphysics*, see, for example, Theresa Brennan's *History after Lacan* (London: Routledge, 1993), which (without especially mentioning Baudrillard) is pitched on a Baudrillardian

level of abstraction. The book offers a passionate articulation of the basic Heideggerian themes in a broad synthesis – from Marx to Derrida – which brings them into line with feminist theory in an interesting way.

6. Karl Marx, *The Economic and Philosophic Manuscripts of 1844*, trans. Martin Milligan, ed. Dirk J. Struik (New York: International Publishers, 1964), p. 113.

CHAPTER 5

1. Ferdinand de Saussure in Jean Starobinski, *Words upon Words: The anagrams of Ferdinand de Saussure*, trans. Olivia Emmet (New Haven: Yale University Press, 1979), p. 8.
2. See Brian Spooner, 'Weavers and dealers: the authenticity of an oriental carpet', in *The Social Life of Things: Commodities in cultural perspective*, ed. Arjun Appadurai (Cambridge: Cambridge University Press, 1986), pp. 195–235.
3. For more elaboration of the notion of society as an extended anthropomorphic metaphor, see Mary Douglas, *Purity and Danger: An analysis of the concepts of pollution and taboo* (London: Routledge & Kegan Paul, 1966), and *Natural Symbols* (Harmondsworth: Penguin, 1970). See also John O'Neill, *Five Bodies: The human shape of modern society* (Ithaca: Cornell University Press, 1985).

CHAPTER 7

1. Mihaly Cziksentmihalyi and Eugene Rochberg-Halton, *The Meaning of Things: Domestic symbols and the self* (Cambridge: Cambridge University Press, 1981), p. 40.
2. Elias Canetti, *Crowds and Power* (Harmondsworth: Penguin, 1962).
3. Gilles Deleuze and Felix Guattari, *Anti-Oedipus: Capitalism and schizophrenia*, trans. Robert Hurley, Mark Seem and Helen R. Lane (New York: Viking, 1977).
4. Sigmund Freud, *Beyond the Pleasure Principle. Standard Edition of the Complete Psychological Works of Sigmund Freud*, XVIII, trans. James Strachey (London: Hogarth, 1955), p. 56.
5. Deleuze, *The Logic of Sense*, trans. Mark Lester, ed. Constantin V. Boundas (New York: Columbia University Press, 1990), pp. 253–66.

CHAPTER 8

1. James Carey, 'Time, space, and the telegraph', in David Crowley and Paul Heyer, eds, *Communication in History: Technology, culture, society*, 2nd edn (New York: Longman, 1995), p. 155.
2. Anthony Giddens, *The Consequences of Modernity* (Stanford: Stanford University Press, 1990), pp. 18–19; emphasis in original.
3. See Marshall Sahlins, *Stone Age Economics* (Chicago: Aldine, 1972).

CHAPTER 9

1. Karl Marx, *Capital*, 1, trans. Samuel Moore and Richard Aveling, ed. Friedrich Engels (New York: International Publishers, 1967), p. 47.
2. *Ibid.*, p. 35.
3. *Ibid.*, p. 47.
4. *Ibid.*, p. 74.
5. *Ibid.*, p. 51.
6. *Ibid.*, p. 37.
7. *Ibid.*, p. 39.
8. *Ibid.*, p. 47.
9. *Ibid.*, p. 71.
10. Georg Lukács, *History and Class Consciousness: Studies in Marxist dialectics*, trans. Rodney Livingston (Cambridge, MA: MIT, 1971).
11. Marx, *Capital*, pp. 52 (emphasis added), 57, 71, 76.
12. *Ibid.*, p. 35.
13. *Ibid.*, p. 72.
14. *Ibid.*, p. 75.
15. *Ibid.*, p. 72.
16. *Ibid.*, p. 85.
17. *Ibid.*, p. 74 (emphasis added).
18. *Ibid.*, p. 80.
19. Still, it is worth remembering that Marx would probably not have used the phrase 'mystical veil' if he had not believed that these social relations were but the *superstructure* of the productive system. Reification would disappear with the mode of production which gave rise to it.
20. Lukács, *History and Class Consciousness*, p. 85.
21. *Ibid.*, p. 83.
22. *Ibid.*, p. 171.
23. Max Horkheimer, 'Traditional and critical theory', in *Critical Theory: Selected essays*, trans. Matthew J. O'Connell (New York: The Seabury Press, 1972), pp. 188–243. The article first appeared in 1937.
24. Marcuse's concept of 'one-dimensionality' extends Lukács's theory of reification to account for developments in American capitalism since the New Deal. Baudrillard develops Marcuse's concept of 'repressive desublimation' in *La société de consommation*. See Herbert Marcuse, *One-Dimensional Man: Studies in the ideology of advanced industrial society* (Boston: Beacon Press, 1964).
25. Maurice Merleau-Ponty, *Adventures of the Dialectic*, trans. Joseph Bien (Evanston: Northwestern University Press, 1973).
26. A translation by Kostas Axelos appeared in 1960.
27. Louis Althusser, *For Marx*, trans. Ben Brewster (New York: Vintage, 1969), p. 222.
28. Louis Althusser, 'Avertissement aux lecteurs du *Livre I* du *Capital*', in Karl Marx, *Le Capital*: Livre I, trans. J. Roy (Paris: Garnier-Flammarion, 1969), p. 22.
29. Mike Gane, *Jean Baudrillard: Critical and fatal theory* (London: Routledge, 1991), p. 79.

30. Goldmann never failed to draw appreciative attention to Lukács's work in all his numerous publications. See his *Introduction à la philosophie de Kant* (Paris: Gallimard, 1967), which was originally published in 1948.
31. Walter Benjamin, 'The work of art in the age of mechanical reproduction', in *Illuminations*, trans. Harry Zohn and introd. Hannah Arendt (New York: Schocken Books, 1969), pp. 217–54.
32. In an early review of *Understanding Media*, Baudrillard characterized Marshall McLuhan's popular slogan, 'the medium is the message', as 'the very formula of alienation in a technical society'. According to Baudrillard, McLuhan's hypotheses about social communication are 'worth re-examining' because of the way they seem to reflect and confirm the 'abstraction' of social life through the 'imposition of models' (*FCPES*, p. 175).
33. Benjamin, p. 232. In his analysis of the upheaval in perception engendered by the advent of moving pictures (the 'sense of the universal equality of things', p. 223), he concentrated on the possibilities of the new medium for segmentation, rearrangement, analysis and 'permeation of reality' (p. 234). Apparently, the 'crisis' of the stage brought on by the advent of film appeared to him as a crisis of capitalist culture itself. In the increased division of labour which film imposed on theatrical performance (the fragmentation not only of the actor's performance, but also of the conceptualization of his role), Benjamin saw paradoxically a liberation of the actor: 'For the first time – and this is the effect of the cinema – man has to operate with his whole living person, yet forgoing his aura' (p. 229). Similarly, in the massive, functional extension of the reading public associated with the explosion of popular presses, Benjamin believed that 'the distinction between author and public is about to lose its character', and that publication is now a theoretical possibility for 'any gainfully employed European' (p. 232).
34. Walter Benjamin, *Charles Baudelaire: A lyric poet in the era of high capitalism*, trans. Harry Zohn (London: NLB, 1973), p. 148.
35. *Ibid.*, p. 151.
36. Jack Goody and Ian Watt, 'The consequences of literacy', in Crowley and Heyer, eds, *Communication in History*, p. 49.

CHAPTER 10

1. John Ardagh, *The New France: A society in transition, 1945–1977* (Harmondsworth: Pelican Books, 1977), p. 630.
2. Marie Leroy, *Le phénomène Beaubourg* (Paris: Syros, 1977), pp. 58, 8.
3. The first of these was entitled *Critique de la vie quotidienne 1: Introduction* (Paris: Grasset, 1947) reprinted (Paris: L'Arche, 1958). A second volume appeared in 1962 under the subtitled *Fondaments d'une sociologie de la quotidiennété*. In 1968, Lefebvre published *La vie quotidienne dans le monde moderne* (Paris: Gallimard, 1968).
4. Most of these essays can be found in Lefebvre, *Au delà du structuralisme* (Paris: Anthropos, 1971).
5. Sartre explained his plan to use this method in *Search for a Method*, trans. and introd. Hazel Barnes (New York: Vintage, 1968), p. 51. The original French version of this work was published together with the *Critique* in 1960.

6. On *Socialisme ou Barbarie*, see Mark Poster, *Existential Marxism in Postwar France: From Sartre to Althusser* (Princeton: Princeton University Press, 1975), pp. 201–9. See also, Richard Gombin, *The Origins of Modern Leftism*, trans. Michael K. Perl (Harmondsworth: Penguin, 1975), as an introduction to the radical Marxist background of Baudrillard's work.
7. Guy Debord, *La société du spectacle* (Paris: Buchet/Castel, 1967); Raoul Vaneigem, *Traité du savoir-vivre à l'usage des jeunes générations* (Paris: Gallimard, 1967). For a full account of the situationism, with reference to Baudrillard, see Sadie Plant, *The Most Radical Gesture: The situationist international in a postmodern age* (London: Routledge, 1992).
8. See André Breton, *Position politique du surréalisme* (Paris: Denoel/Gonthier, 1962).
9. See, for example, Epistémon (pseudonym), *Ces idées qui ont ebranlé la France* (Paris: Fayard, 1968), pp. 26ff.
10. Lefebvre, *Everyday Life in the Modern World*, trans. Sacha Rabinovitch (New York: Harper, 1971), pp. 110–27.
11. *Ibid.*, pp. 124–5.
12. *Ibid.*, p. 62.
13. Quoted in Dick Hebdige, *Subculture: The meaning of style* (London: Methuen, 1979), p. 117.
14. Edmund Husserl, *The Crisis of European Sciences and Transcendental Phenomenology*, trans. David Carr (Evanston: Northwestern University Press, 1970). Among other things, Husserl was concerned about the 'superficialization of meaning' attendant on the 'mathematization of nature' in which 'one operates with letters and with signs for connections and relations . . . [such that] the original thinking which genuinely gives meaning . . . is excluded' (pp. 44, 23, 46).
15. For a similar argument, which can be compared with Baudrillard's analysis of the art auction in *FCPES*, see Clifford Geertz, 'Deep play: notes on the Balinese cockfight', in *The Interpretation of Cultures: Selected essays* (New York: Basic Books, 1973), pp. 412–53.
16. Marcel Mauss, *The Gift: Forms and functions of exchange in archaic societies*, trans. Ian Cunnison and introd. E. E. Evans-Pritchard (London: Routledge and Kegan Paul, 1969).
17. Georges Bataille, *La part maudite, précédé de la notion dépense* (Paris: Editions de Minuit, 1967), p. 31.
18. See Jacques Derrida, 'From restricted to general economy: a Hegelianism without reserve', in *Writing and Difference*, trans. and introd. Alan Bass (Chicago: University of Chicago Press, 1978), pp. 251–77.
19. Michel Foucault's 1963 essay on Bataille, 'A preface to transgression', comes nearest to Baudrillard's reading of Bataille in many respects. In particular, the following passage invites close comparison to Baudrillard's conclusions about the failure of Marx's critique of political economy to 'transgress' the problems of the 'society of consumption':

    In a form of thought that considers man as worker and producer – that of European culture since the end of the eighteenth century – consumption was based entirely on need, and need based itself exclusively on the model of hunger. When this element was introduced into an investigation of profit (the appetite of those who have satisfied their hunger), it inserted man into a dialectic of production which had a simple anthropological meaning: if man was alienated from his real nature and immediate needs through his labor and the production of objects with his hands, it was nevertheless through its agency that he recaptured his essence and achieved the indefinite gratification of his needs. But it would undoubtedly be misguided to conceive of hunger as that irreducible anthropological factor in the definition of work, production, and profit; and similarly, need has an altogether different status, or it responds at the very least to a code whose laws cannot be confined to a dialectic of production. (Michel Foucault, *Language, Counter-Memory, Practice: Selected essays and interviews*, ed. and introd. Donald Bouchard, trans. Donald Bouchard and Sherry Simon (Ithaca: Cornell University Press, 1977), pp. 49–50.)

20. John Ashbery, 'On Raymond Roussel', in Raymond Roussel, *How I Wrote Certain of My Books*, trans. Trevor Winkfield (New York: SUN, 1977), p. 52.
21. Lucien Goldmann, *Towards a Sociology of the Novel*, trans. Alan Sheridan (London: Tavistock, 1975), p. 7.
22. *Ibid.*, p. 139.
23. Roland Barthes, *Critical Essays*, trans. Richard Howard (Evanston: Northwestern University Press, 1972), p. 199.
24. *Ibid.*, p. 203.
25. Georges Perec, *Les Choses* (Paris: Editions 'J'ai Lu', 1965).
26. The novel is briefly discussed in *Le système des objets*, pp. 235–8.

CHAPTER 11

1. Theodor Adorno, 'Cultural criticism and society', in Paul Connerton, ed., *Critical Sociology* (Harmondsworth: Penguin, 1976), p. 271.
2. Emile Durkheim and Marcel Mauss, *Primitive Classification*, trans. and introd. Rodney Needham (London: Cohen and West, 1963), pp. 82–3.
3. Claude Lévi-Strauss, *Totemism*, trans. Rodney Needham (Boston: Beacon Press, 1963); *The Savage Mind* (London: Weidenfeld and Nicolson, 1966).
4. Georges Charbonnier, *Conversations with Lévi-Strauss*, trans. John and Doreen Weightman (London: Jonathan Cape, 1969), p. 125.
5. Claude Lévi-Strauss, 'Introduction à l'oeuvre de Marcel Mauss', in Marcel Mauss, *Sociologie et anthropologie* (Paris: Presses Universitaires de France, 1950), p. xlix.
6. *Ibid.*, p. xlvii.
7. Claude Lévi-Strauss, *The Scope of Anthropology*, trans. S. O. Paul and R. A. Paul (London: Jonathan Cape, 1967), p. 18.
8. *Ibid.*, p. 18.
9. *Ibid.*, p. 19.
10. Ferdinand de Saussure, *Course in General Linguistics*, trans. Wade Baskin (New York: Philosophical Library, 1959), p. 16; emphasis in original.
11. Umberto Eco, *A Theory of Semiotics* (Bloomington: Indiana University Press, 1976), p. 73; emphasis in original.
12. Jonathan Culler, *Structuralist Poetics: Structuralism, linguistics and the study of literature* (London: Routledge and Kegan Paul, 1975), p. 18: 'Precisely because the individual signs are unmotivated, the linguist must attempt to reconstruct the system, which alone provides motivation.'

13. *Ibid.*, p. 14: 'Whatever the rights of the linguistic case, for the semiologist or structuralist concerned with the social use of material phenomena the *reduction of the continuous to the discrete* is a methodological step of the first importance' (emphasis added).
14. Roland Barthes, *Critical Essays*, trans. Richard Howard (Evanston: Northwestern University Press, 1972), pp. 214–15.
15. Giddens, *The Consequences of Modernity* (Stanford: Stanford University Press, 1990), pp. 15–16.
16. Marshall McLuhan, *The Medium is the Massage* (Harmondsworth: Penguin, 1967), pp. 74–5.

CHAPTER 12

1. See Julian Pefanis, *Heterology and the Postmodern: Bataille, Baudrillard, and Lyotard* (London: Duke University Press, 1991), pp. 59f., for a discussion of the relationship between Baudrillard's theory of simulacra and Plato's epistemology as articulated in the *Republic.* Pefanis's book also contains a superb discussion of Bataille's influence on postmodern theory and on Baudrillard's work in particular.
2. Alice Jardine, *Gynesis: Configurations of woman and modernity* (Ithaca: Cornell University Press, 1985), pp. 179, 25.
3. Judith Butler, *Gender Trouble: Feminism and the subversion of identity* (New York: Routledge, 1990), p. 142.
4. Donna J. Haraway, *Simians, Cyborgs, and Women: The reinvention of nature* (New York: Routledge, 1991), pp. 189, 190.
5. The privilege Derrida affords *writing* over speech can be seen as an attempt to give 'meaning' (as opposed to signification) to the concept of system, though in a very different way from Baudrillard's symbolic exchange.
6. Marcel Mauss, *The Gift*, trans. Ian Cunnison (London: Routledge, 1966), p. 1.
7. Georg Simmel, 'The metropolis and mental life', *The Sociology of Georg Simmel*, trans. Kurt H. Wolff (New York: Free Press, 1950), p. 413.
8. Paul Radin, *Primitive Philosophers* (1957), has argued persuasively that individualism and even 'personalism' run riot in 'primitive' societies, but that it is limited by a conception of society as an independent, objective reality, separate from the being of the individual. He surmises that it is this divergent ontology of the individual and the social which promotes the impression of conformity, not a cognitive failure to distinguish the self from the 'group mind', as Levy-Bruhl had hypothesized. It may be that a similar explanation would throw light on the 'postmodern', as I have tried to suggest elsewhere: 'Entre la chair et l'esprit: le corps social du nouveauné,' *Sociologie et Sociétés* 24: 1 (Spring, 1992), pp. 67–79.
9. See Allon White, 'Hysteria and the end of carnival: festivity and bourgeois neurosis', *Semiotica* 54: 1–2 (1985), pp. 97–111.
10. [Lévi-Strauss's anthropology]

    is a Cartesian anthropology that strips cognition of meaning and affect, denies the integral relations of theory and praxis, and thus represents men as the eternal victims of their brains, ceaselessly driving to assemble and disassemble mental elements, forced forever to enact these *ad hoc* schemes in an imitation of life. These are images of our own alienation. . . . (Eric R. Wolf, 'Foreword', in Stanley Diamond, *In Search of the Primitive* (New Brunswick: Transaction Books, 1974), p. xii.)

11. Peter Winch, 'Understanding a primitive society', in *Understanding and Social Inquiry*, ed. Fred R. Dallmayr and Thomas McCarthy (Notre Dame: University of Notre Dame Press, 1977), pp. 182–3.
12. Georges Bataille, *L'expérience intérieure* (Paris: Gallimard, 1943), pp. 15, 178: States of ecstasy, rapture, at least of meditated emotion. . . . Laughing through tears. – The killing/unveiling of God.
13. Freud used this expression to describe the superego in *The Ego and the Id*. Sigmund Freud, *The Ego and the Id. The Standard Edition of the Complete Psychological Works of Sigmund Freud*, XIX (London: Hogarth Press, 1953–74), p. 53.
14. Albert O. Hirschman notes many ironies in the ideological history of capitalism, including the fact that among those who have lamented the 'disenchanting' effects of bourgeois political economy, 'there was little recognition that, to an earlier age, the world of "the full human personality", replete with diverse passions, appeared as a menace that needed to be exorcized to the greatest possible extent' (*The Passions and the Interests: Political arguments for capitalism before its triumph* (Princeton: Princeton University Press, 1977), p. 133).
15. Michel Foucault, *The Order of Things* (New York: Vintage, 1970).
16. *Ibid.*, p. 387.

CHAPTER 13

1. Raoul Mortley, *French Philosophers in Conversation* (London: Routledge, 1991), p. 106.
2. Arthur C. Danto, *The Philosophical Disenfranchisement of Art* (New York: Columbia, 1986), p. 210.
3. Georges Bataille, *Theory of Religion*, trans. Robert Hurley (New York: Zone Books, 1989), p. 19.
4. A. Kojève, *Introduction to the Reading of Hegel*, ed. Allan Bloom, trans. James Nichols (Ithaca: Cornell University Press, 1969), p. 4.
5. Gilles Deleuze and Felix Guattari, *Anti-Oedipus: Capitalism and schizophrenia*, trans. Robert Hurley (New York: Viking, 1977).
6. Max Horkheimer and Theodor Adorno, *Dialectic of Enlightenment*, trans. John Cumming (New York: Seabury Press, 1972), p. 54.
7. Kojève, *Introduction to the Reading of Hegel*, p. 7.
8. Marx ('On the Jewish question') and Simmel ('The stranger') both recognized that in Europe this fantasmatic relationship (to Capital, the city and the market) was projected onto the Jew. The tragic drama of the 'stranger' climaxed philosophically in the bathos of Heidegger's embrace of the Nazi ideology.
9. Bataille, *Theory of Religion*, pp. 43–5.
10. *Ibid.*, p. 47.
11. Karl Marx, *Grundrisse*, trans. Martin Nicolaus (Harmondsworth: Penguin, 1973), pp. 750, 700.

12. Elias Canetti, *Crowds and Power*, trans. Carol Stewart (Harmondsworth: Penguin, 1962), pp. 226–34.
13. Donna Haraway, *Simians, Cyborgs, and Women: The reinvention of nature* (New York: Routledge, 1991).

CHAPTER 14

1. Lacan called this 'das Ding' and Kristeva called it 'abjection', but there is also the possibility of wonderment, beauty (Donald Meltzer), and rhythmic sensorimotor attunement with the mother/caretaker (Daniel Stern). These more benign, profoundly personal, and deeply social elements of prelinguistic experience are generally discounted in our civilization. As we have seen, Baudrillard alluded to them through the connotations of primitive innocence in his original concept of symbolic exchange, and the symbolics of the face; but he later discarded them in favour of a more brutal, 'tragic' vision of social being. In French social philosophy, Merleau-Ponty and Emmanuel Levinas offer the most fundamental explorations of this concept of a prerational, prelinguistic social form, as presupposed, but never systematically articulated, by Baudrillard. For a general account of the implications of infant research for social theory, see my 'An essay on the symbolic process', doctoral dissertation, Concordia University (Montreal, 1989).
2. William S. Burroughs, *The Four Horsemen of the Apocalypse* (Bonn: Expanded Media Editions, 1988), pp. 23–4.
3. I am thinking, in particular, of Scott Bukatman's fine study of postmodern science fiction, *Terminal Identity* (Durham: Duke University, 1993).
4. Mike Gane, 'Introduction', in *Death*, p. viii.
5. For discussion of these symbolic social forms, the locus classicus in the anthropological literature is Marcel Mauss, *The Gift*, trans. Ian Cunnison (Cambridge: Cambridge University Press, 1954).
6. Bruce Chatwin, *The Songlines* (New York: Penguin, 1987), p. 57. See also Mauss, *The Gift: Forms and functions of exchange in archaic societies*, trans. Ian Cunnison and introd. E. E. Evans-Pritchard (London: Routledge and Kegan Paul, 1969), pp. 8–10; and Malinowski's classic study of the Kula system of gift exchange in *Argonauts of the Western Pacific* (New York: Dutton, 1961).
7. Gianni Vattimo, *The End of Modernity*, trans. J. R. Snyder (Baltimore: Johns Hopkins University Press, 1988), pp. 24, 23.

CHAPTER 15

1. Karl Marx, *Economic and Philosophic Manuscripts of 1844*, trans. Martin Milligan, ed. Dirk J. Struik (New York: International Publishers, 1964), p. 114; emphasis in original.
2. See Max Horkheimer and Theodor Adorno, *Dialectic of Enlightenment*, trans. John Cumming (New York: Seabury Press, 1972). See also, William Leiss, *The Domination of Nature* (Boston: Beacon Press, 1974).

3. Freud himself was a formidable collector of objects. See Edmund Engelman's collection of photographs, *Bergasse 19: 1938* (Chicago: University of Chicago, 1976). Marianna Torgovnick's discussion of Freud's study (in *Gone Primitive: Savage intellects, modern lives* (Chicago: University of Chicago Press, 1990)) is often referred to, but should be consulted only as an example of Freud-bashing: she calls Freud's bas relief of *Gradiva* 'Gravida' and mistakes a photo of von Flieschl, his fellow student who died of cocaine addiction, with 'one of Freud's teachers, bearded and fatherly'. The burden of her interpretation is founded in these errors.
4. I shall leave it to the reader to interpret the unfolding of this predicament in the novel.
5. As often as not, what is meant by desire when advertisers or Lacanians or Deleuzians talk about it is *envy*, in Melanie Klein's sense of the term.
6. Freud singled out the self-absorbed confidence of some beautiful women, but it is easier for us to see now that his remarks apply just as well to the narcissistic male.
7. The French *charnier*, like the English charnel, connotes a mortuary, a charnel-house, or mortuary chapel, an ossuary, a deathly carnality.
8. See Jacques Lacan, 'The signification of the phallus', *Ecrits: A selection*, trans. Alan Sheridan (New York: Norton, 1977), pp. 287, 285.
9. Linda Williams, *Hard Core: Power, pleasure, and the 'Frenzy of the visible'* (Berkeley: University of California Press, 1989), pp. 189–95.
10. See Leo Bersani, 'Is the rectum a grave?', in Douglas Crimp ed., *AIDS: Cultural analysis/cultural activism* (Cambridge, MA: MIT, 1989), pp. 197–222, esp. pp. 215ff.
11. Compare Foucault, *History of Sexuality: Volume 1: An introduction*, trans. Robert Hurley (New York: Pantheon, 1978), p. 145.
12. The following passage from Bataille conveys a sense of the symbolic which Baudrillard feels is abstracted and neutralized in the semiological labour of suntanning:

The sacred is that prodigious effervescence of life that, for the sake of duration, the order of things holds in check . . . [In the sacred] this holding changes into a breaking loose, that is, into violence. It constantly threatens to break the dikes, to confront productive activity with the precipitate and contagious movement of a purely glorious consumption. The sacred is exactly comparable to the flame that destroys the wood by consuming it. It is that opposite of a thing which an unlimited fire is; it spreads, it radiates heat and light, it suddenly inflames and blinds in turn. Sacrifice burns like the sun that slowly dies of the prodigious radiation whose brilliance our eyes cannot bear, but it is never isolated and, in a world of individuals, it calls forth the general negation of individuals as such. (*Theory of Religion*, trans. Robert Hurley (New York: Zone, 1989), pp. 52–3.)

13. The relation between the face and the 'figure of alterity' – the problem of otherness – is an important subtheme in Baudrillard's writings. It was explored in great depth by Emmanuel Levinas, *Totality and Infinity*, trans. Alphonso Lingis (Pittsburgh: Duquesne University Press, 1969).
14. Bataille, *Theory of Religion*, p. 43.
15. *Ibid.*, pp. 50, 29.
16. *Ibid.*, p. 52.

17. Compare Roland Barthes's discussion of French striptease in *Mythologies*, trans. Annette Lavers (London: Paladin, 1972), pp. 84–7.
18. Lacan, *Ecrits: A selection*, trans. Alan Sheridan (New York: Norton, 1977), p. 288.

CHAPTER 16

1. Arthur Kroker, 'Baudrillard's Marx', in *Theory, Culture and Society*, Vol. 2, No. 3 (1985), 69–83.
2. Teresa de Lauretis, *Technologies of Gender: Essays on theory, film, and fiction* (Bloomington: Indiana University Press, 1987), p. 82.
3. Marguerite Duras, in *New French Feminisms: An anthology*, ed. and introd. Elaine Marks and Isabelle de Courtivron (Amherst: University of Massachusetts Press, 1980), pp. 174–5.
4. The French *sexe* (m) does double duty for sex and gender, but has not been rendered as 'gender' anywhere in the English translations of Baudrillard.
5. It should be remembered that Baudrillard's arguments were made in a context where feminist discourse on sex and gender was dominated by Lacanians, ex-Lacanians and deconstructionists, all of whom were utterly immersed in the binary Lacanian terms of reference they were disputing. For some comments on the effects of Lacan-inspired textualism on feminist theory, see my 'Lacanian psychoanalysis and feminist metatheory', in *The Hysterical Male: New feminist theory*, ed. Arthur and Marilouise Kroker (London: Macmillan, 1991), pp. 235–52.
6. Judith Butler, *Gender Trouble: Feminism and the subversion of identity* (New York: Routledge, 1990), p. viii.
7. Rose, in Juliet Mitchell and Jacqueline Rose, eds, *Feminine Sexuality: Jacques Lacan and the Ecole Freudienne* (New York: Norton, 1982), p. 43.
8. G. W. F. Hegel, *Phenomenology of Mind*, trans. J. B. Baillie (New York: Harper, 1967), p. 496.
9. For a brief discussion of the repercussions, see David Macey, *The Lives of Michel Foucault* (London: Vintage, 1993), pp. 358–60. According to some widely circulated rumours, Baudrillard's decision to publish the piece on Foucault spoiled some interesting plans for collaboration with Foucault, Deleuze and others. See Douglas Kellner's study of Baudrillard, *Jean Baudrillard: From Marxism to postmodernism and beyond* (Stanford, CA: Stanford University Press, 1989), pp. 132, 231. Baudrillard himself stated: 'I was put into a sort of quarantine, and I am still suffering the consequences' (quoted in Macey, p. 359). It should be pointed out, however, that contrary to the available English translation of *Oublier Foucault*, Baudrillard's propositions are in the infinitive – not in the imperative mood.
10. Alice Jardine, *Gynesis: Configurations of woman and modernity* (Ithaca: Cornell University Press, 1985), p. 66; emphasis in original. Jardine rightly identifies Baudrillard's nostalgia for the symbolic and mythic forms of sexuality, but incorrectly accuses him of blaming women and feminism for the disenchantment of modernity and the loss of the symbolic dimension.
11. Sara Kofman, *The Enigma of Woman: Woman in Freud's writings*, trans. Catherine Porter (Ithaca: Cornell University Press, 1985), p. 207; emphasis in original.

12. Often ignored in these discussions, however, is the likelihood that 'core gender identity' is established very early. John Money considers it difficult to reverse after eighteen months, *regardless of anatomy*. We are talking about a very 'primitive' and also very *profound* impersonation indeed. See John Money, 'Hermaphroditism', in Albert Ellis and Albert Abarbanel, eds, *Sex and Today's Society* (New York: Ace, 1967), pp. 24–47, 34. For an interesting discussion of the issues, see Robert J. Stoller, *Sexual Excitement: Dynamics of erotic life* (New York: Simon and Schuster, 1979).
13. See Jessica Benjamin, *The Bonds of Love: Psychoanalysis, feminism and the problem of domination* (New York: Pantheon, 1988); Camille Paglia, *Sexual Personae: Art and decadence from Nefertiti to Emily Dickinson* (New York: Vintage, 1990).
14. In this regard, Baudrillard's seduction might be seen as the inverse of Althusser's 'interpellation', or 'hailing' of the subject.
15. See Arthur Kroker, 'Baudrillard's Marx'.
16. Lacan defined the signifier as 'that which represents the subject to another signifier'. (*Ecrits: A selection*, trans. Alan Sheridan (New York: Norton, 1977), p. 316.)
17. Foucault, *History of Sexuality: Volume 1: An introduction*, trans. Robert Hurley (New York: Pantheon, 1978), p. 159.
18. Perhaps Baudrillard felt that the publication of Foucault's *History of Sexuality* in the same year as *Symbolic Exchange and Death* had diluted the impact of his own work. There are striking parallels between the two authors' views on the theme of sexuality as a normalizing production.

CHAPTER 17

1. Victor Segalen, *René Leys*, trans. J. A. Underwood (Woodstock, New York: The Overlook Press, 1988). Page references will be provided in the text.
2. Edward Said, *Orientalism* (New York: Pantheon, 1978), p. 3.
3. This is W. Clifford M. Scott's version of Freud's original instruction to his patients (personal communication).
4. Pierre Bourdieu, *Outline of a Theory of Practice*, trans. Richard Nice (Cambridge: Cambridge University Press, 1977), pp. 177ff. '[P]ractice never ceases to conform to economic calculation even when it gives every appearance of disinterestedness by departing from the logic of interested calculation (in the narrow sense) and playing for stakes that are non-material and not easily quantified.' From a Baudrillardian point of view, statements like this are either true in the trivial sense (everything is connected to everything else, everything is discontinuous with everything else, everything is like everything else, everything is different from everything else); or it is a case of functionalist self-deception, of trying to have it both ways: the fantasy of a non-reductionist reductionism.
5. Hugh Trevor-Roper (London: Eland, 1976), p. 156.
6. *Ibid.*, p. 279.

7. Quoted in Trevor-Roper, p. 156. During his truly remarkable career, Backhouse managed to deceive several large British and American multinationals, and during the First World War, the entire British government, with one grandiose scheme after another, involving millions of dollars in forged contracts for battleships, machine guns and banknotes. His greatest achievement, however, was the complete fabrication, from scratch, of a Manchu courtier's diary, which remained for more than two decades a cornerstone of Western scholarship on the Empress Dowager's regime.
8. Trevor-Roper, *Hermit of Peking*, pp. 359–62.
9. Quoted in Robert Laliberté, *L'imaginaire politique de Victor Segalen* (Montreal: Institut Québécois de recherche sur la culture, 1989), p. 25. 'Entropy is a more terrible monster than Nothingness. Nothingness is icy and cold. Entropy is tepid. Nothingness is perhaps hard like a diamond. Entropy is bland, a lukewarm paste.'
10. *Ibid.*, p. 25.
11. *Ibid.*, p. 25.
12. Gilles Deleuze, *Cinema 1: The movement-image*, trans. Hugh Tomlinson and Barbara Habberjam (London: Athlone Press, 1986), p. 73.
13. Pier Paolo Pasolini, *Heretical Empiricism*, trans. Ben Lawton and Louise K. Barnett (Bloomington: Indiana University Press, 1988), p. 172.
14. Otto Rank, *The Double*, trans. Harry Tucker (New York: Meridian, 1971).
15. C. F. Keppler, *The Literature of the Second Self* (Tucson: University of Arizona Press, 1972), p. 33.
16. Guy de Maupassant, *Le Horla* (Paris: Livre de Poche, 1984), p. 27.
17. *Ibid.*, p. 50.

CHAPTER 18

1. Especially in the original stage version, he is the stereotypical product of a sexist education, pornography and all. This heavy-handedness has been removed from Cronenberg's film version, the screenplay for which is credited to the playwright.
2. David Hwang, *M. Butterfly* (New York: Plume, 1988), p. 95.
3. See especially Jane Gallop, *The Daughter's Seduction: Feminism and psychoanalysis* (Ithaca, NY: Cornell University Press, 1982); and *Reading Lacan* (Ithaca, NY: Cornell University Press, 1985).
4. See in particular George Butterworth ed., *Infancy and Epistemology: An evaluation of Piaget's theory* (New York: St. Martin's Press, 1982).
5. Julia Kristeva, *Powers of Horror: An essay on abjection*, trans. Leon S. Roudiez (New York: Columbia University Press, 1982).
6. See Charles Levin, 'Thinking through the hungry baby: toward a new pleasure principle', *Psychoanalytic Study of the Child*, vol. 47 (1992), pp. 119–37.
7. Barthes, *The Pleasure of the Text*, trans. Richard Miller (New York: Hill and Wang, 1975), p. 47.
8. Bersani, 'Is the rectum a grave?' in Douglas Crimp ed., *AIDS: Cultural analysis/cultural activism* (Cambridge, MA: MIT, 1989), p. 221.

CHAPTER 19

1. Julia Kristeva, *Powers of Horror: An essay on abjection*, trans. Leon S. Roudiez (New York: Columbia University Press, 1982).
2. Jean-Paul Sartre, *Being and Nothingness*, trans. Hazel E. Barnes (New York: Washington Square Press, 1966), p. 784.
3. Derrida, 'Freud and the scene of writing', in *Writing and Difference*, trans. Alan Bass (Chicago: University of Chicago Press, 1978), pp. 196–231.
4. Michel Foucault, interview in *La quinzaine littéraire*, 15 April 1966. Quoted in Didier Eribon, *Michel Foucault*, trans. Betsy Wing (Cambridge, MA: Harvard University Press, 1991), p. 161.
5. Jacques Monod, *Chance and Necessity: An essay on the natural philosophy of modern biology*, trans. A. Wainhouse (New York: Vintage, 1971), p. 112.
6. *Ibid.*, p. 116.
7. *Ibid.*, p. 116.
8. Jacques Derrida, 'Spéculer – sur "Freud"', in *La carte postale: de Socrate à Freud et au-delà* (Paris: Aubier-Flammarion, 1980), p. 305.
9. See my 'Thinking through the hungry baby: toward a new pleasure principle', *The Psychoanalytic Study of the Child* 47 (1992), pp. 119–37.
10. Gilles Deleuze, *Sacher-Masoch: An interpretation*, trans. Jean McNeil (London: Faber and Faber, 1971), p. 100.
11. Karl Marx, *Grundrisse*, trans. Martin Nicolaus (Harmondsworth: Penguin), p. 600.
12. Karl Marx, *The Economic and Philosophic Manuscripts of 1844*, trans. Martin Milligan, ed. Dirk J. Struik (New York: International Publishers, 1964), p. 102.
13. Marx, *Grundrisse*, p. 706. Of course, with the same premises, Marx argues the opposite of Baudrillard – that the predominance of capital creates 'the material conditions to blow this foundation sky high' – i.e. to liberate the subject from the object.
14. Jean-François Lyotard has developed a similar analysis of 'techno-scientific "monad"'. See for example, 'Time today', in *The Inhuman: Reflections on time*, trans. Geoffrey Bennington and Rachel Bowlby (Stanford: Stanford University Press, 1991), pp. 58–77.
15. Gilbert Simondon, *Du mode d'existence des objets techniques* (Paris: Aubier-Montaigne, 1969).
16. *Ibid.*, pp. 25–6.
17. *Ibid.*, p. 25.
18. *Ibid.*, p. 26.
19. Gilles Deleuze and Felix Guattari, *Anti-Oedipus: Capitalism and schizophrenia*, trans. Robert Hurley *et al.* (New York: Viking, 1977), p. 221.
20. Arthur Kroker, personal communication.
21. Michael Heim, *The Metaphysics of Virtual Reality* (Oxford: Oxford University Press, 1993).
22. Norbert Wiener, *God & Golem, Inc.: A comment on certain points where cybernetics impinges on religion* (Cambridge, MA: MIT, 1964), p. 46.
23. James R. Beniger, *The Control Revolution: Technological and economic origins of the information society* (Cambridge, MA: Harvard University Press, 1986), p. 9.

24. Gilles Deleuze and Felix Guattari, *A Thousand Plateaus: Capitalism and schizophrenia*, trans. Brian Massumi (Minneapolis: University of Minnesota Press, 1987), pp. 406ff.
25. Miguel de Landa, *War in the Age of Intelligent Machines* (New York: Zone, 1991), p. 107.
26. Nicholas Mosely, *Hopeful Monsters* (London: Minerva, 1990), p. 445.
27. Of course, deconstructionists and grammatologists would immediately deconstruct this opposition.
28. Michael Benedikt, *Cyberspace: First steps* (Cambridge, MA: MIT, 1992), pp. 1, 3.
29. Howard Rheingold, *The Virtual Community: Homesteading on the electronic frontier* (Reading, MA: Addison-Wesley, 1993), p. 80.
30. Benedikt, *Cyberspace*, p. 2.
31. Rheingold, *The Virtual Community*, p. 67.
32. See *ibid., passim.*
33. Julian Dibble, 'A rape in cyberspace: how an evil clown, a Haitan trickster spirit, two wizards and a cast of dozens turned a database into a society', in *The Village Voice*, 21 December, 1993, pp. 36–42.
34. Harley Hahn and Rick Stout, *The Internet Complete Reference* (Berkeley: McGraw-Hill, 1994), pp. xix–xx.
35. Mark Poster, *The Mode of Information: Poststructuralism and social context* (Chicago: University of Chicago Press, 1990), p. 111.
36. *Ibid.*, p. 119.
37. *Ibid.*, p. 121.
38. *Ibid.* This quotation is taken slightly out of context, but still invites the analysis suggested here.
39. Jacques Derrida, *Aporias*, trans. Thomas Dutoit (Stanford: Stanford University Press, 1993), p. 43.

CHAPTER 20

1. Jay David Bolter, *Writing Space: Computers, hypertext, and the history of writing* (New Jersey: Lawrence Erlbaum, 1991), pp. 233, 235.
2. Derrick de Kerckhove, 'The new psychotechnologies', in *Communication in History*, eds. David Crowley and Paul Heyer, pp. 333–4.
3. Marshall McLuhan, letter to Margaret Atwood (1972), *The Letters of Marshall McLuhan*, ed. M. Molinaro, G. McLuhan and William Toye (Toronto: Oxford University Press, 1987), p. 457.
4. Bolter, p. 230. Bolter uses the term 'symbolic' in a sense related to signification, rather than symbolic exchange.
5. Niklas Luhmann, 'Autopoiesis: what is communication?', *Communication Theory*, 2: 3 (1992), p. 254.
6. *Ibid.*, p. 253.
7. There is no doubt that simulation is inevitable, which is perhaps why Baudrillard is so drawn to traditional cultures, like the Japanese, who appear to have refined simulation into a cultural art form.
8. Denise Schmandt-Besserat, 'The earliest precursor of writing', in *Communication in History: Technology, culture, society* (2nd edn), ed. David

Crowley and Paul Heyer (White Plains, New York: Longman, 1995), pp. 21–9.

9. Thus George Landow's interesting *Hypertext: The convergence of contemporary critical theory and technology* (Baltimore: Johns Hopkins University Press, 1992), pp. 19–22 involves a common misreading of Baudrillard.
10. Speculations about such transcorporeal dimensions of social being have been explored with most enthusiasm by poststructuralist feminists, such as Theresa Brennan, *History after Lacan* (London: Routledge, 1993).
11. Julia Kristeva, *Revolution in Poetic Language*, trans. Margaret Waller (New York: Columbia University Press, 1984).
12. Michel Serres, *Hermes 1: La communication* (Paris: Minuit, 1968), p. 41.
13. *Ibid.*, pp. 32–3.
14. Claude Lévi-Strauss, *Totemism*, trans. Rodney Needham (Boston: Beacon Press, 1963), p. 16.
15. See John Fekete, *Moral Panic: Biopolitics rising* (Montreal: Robert Davies Publishing, 1994) and Christina Hoff Sommers, *Who Stole Feminism? How Women have Betrayed Women* (New York: Simon and Schuster, 1994).
16. Albert Borgmann, *Crossing the Postmodern Divide* (Chicago: University of Chicago Press, 1992), pp. 136, 137.
17. William Gibson, *Neuromancer* (New York: Ace, 1984).
18. Primo Levi, *The Drowned and the Saved*, trans. Raymond Rosenthal (New York: Vintage, 1988), pp. 38–9.
19. Clifford Geertz, *Local Knowledge: Further essays in interpretive anthropology* (New York: Harper, 1983), p. 62.
20. Baudelaire apparently adapted the phrase from George Sand's *Un hiver à Majorque*, according to Donna Dickenson, *George Sand: A brave man – the most womanly woman* (Oxford: Berg, 1988), pp. 1, 80, 99, 149.

CHAPTER 21

1. Richard A. Shweder, *Thinking Through Cultures: Expeditions in cultural psychology* (Cambridge, MA: Harvard University Press, 1991), p. 249.
2. Anthony Giddens, *Modernity and Self-Identity: Self and society in the late modern age* (Stanford: Stanford University Press, 1991).
3. Sigmund Freud, 'Instincts and their vicissitudes', *Standard Edition* XIV, p. 139.
4. Anthony Giddens, *Modernity and Self-Identity: Self and society in the late modern age* (Stanford: Stanford University Press, 1991), p. 121.
5. Giddens, *The Transformation of Intimacy*, p. 182.
6. The idea of GARAP is taken up again briefly in Baudrillard's *La Guerre du Golfe n'a pas eu lieu* (Paris: Galilee, 1991), p. 19.
7. Marshall Sahlins, *Culture and Practical Reason* (Chicago: University of Chicago Press, 1980), pp. 112–13.
8. *Ibid.*, p. 116.
9. *Ibid.*, p. 117.
10. Louis Althusser, *Lenin and Philosophy*, trans. Ben Brewster (New York: Monthly Review Press, 1971), p. 165.

11. Michel Foucault, *The Archeology of Knowledge* (New York: Harper, 1972), p. 200.
12. See Norman Denzin, '*Paris, Texas* and Baudrillard on America', *Theory, Culture and Society* 8 (1991), pp. 121–33.
13. Mike Gane, 'From the Beaubourg to the Bonaventure Hotel', in *Baudrillard's Bestiary: Baudrillard and culture* (London: Routledge, 1991).
14. Isabel Allende, *The House of the Spirits* (New York: Bantam, 1985), p. 432.
15. Paul Piccone, 'The crisis of one-dimensionality', *Telos* 35 (Spring, 1978), p. 47.
16. The fact that many died as a result does not in itself invalidate Baudrillard's point – that the war was a sham.
17. Gane, 'From the Beaubourg to the Bonaventure Hotel', p. 156.

CHAPTER 22

1. Daniel Boorstin, *The Image: A guide to pseudo-events in America* (New York: Atheneum, 1961).
2. For a more sober treatment of these issues, see John Fekete, *Moral Panic: Biopolitics rising* (Montreal: Robert Davies, 1995).

CHAPTER 23

1. Gilles Deleuze, *The Logic of Sense*, trans. Mark Lester (New York: Columbia University Press, 1990), p. 257.
2. Anne Rice, *The Vampire Lestat* (New York: Ballantine, 1985), p. 10.
3. Quoted in Naomi Greene, *Pier Paolo Pasolini: Cinema as heresy* (Princeton: Princeton University Press, 1990), p. 133.
4. *Ibid.*, p. 138.
5. *Ibid.*, p. 145.
6. Lisa Appignanesi and Sara Maitland, eds, *The Rushdie File* (London: ICA Documents, 1989), pp. 140–1.
7. R. J. Hollingdale, from *Guardian* 17 February 1989, reprinted in Appignanesi and Maitland (eds), *The Rushdie File*, pp. 118–20.
8. Lata Mani, 'Cultural theory, colonial texts: reading eyewitness accounts of widow burning', in *Cultural Studies*, ed. L. Grossberg *et al.* (New York: Routledge, 1992), p. 400.
9. Rey Chow, *Writing Diaspora: Tactics of intervention in contemporary cultural studies* (Bloomington: Indiana University Press, 1993), pp. 166–7.
10. Michel Foucault, *Discipline and Punish: The birth of the prison*, trans. Alan Sheridan (New York: Pantheon, 1977), p. 3.
11. Robert Darnton, *Berlin Journal: 1989–1990* (New York: Norton, 1991), p. 12.
12. Paul Virilio, *The Vision Machine* (London: British Film Institute, 1994), p. 60.
13. Andrew Wernick, 'Global promo: the cultural triumph of exchange', *Theory, Culture and Society* 8 (1991), p. 89.
14. *Ibid.*, pp. 106–7.

15. *Ibid.*, p. 108.
16. W. J. T. Mitchell, 'The violence of public art: *Do the Right Thing*' in *Art and the Public Sphere*, ed. W. J. T. Mitchell (Chicago: University of Chicago Press, 1992), p. 47.
17. Chow, *Writing Diaspora*, p. 167.
18. *Ibid.*, p. 165.
19. Mitchell, 'The violence of public art', p. 30, n. 2.

CHAPTER 24

1. Mark Cousins and Parveen Adams, 'The truth on assault', *October* 71 (Winter 1995), pp. 93–102.
2. Like Baudrillard, Hannah Arendt stressed that it is our capacity to construct a world where it is possible, symbolically, to undo or reverse the consequences of our actions (she emphasized forgiveness), which saves us from complete immersion in productivist instrumentalism. See Hannah Arendt, *The Human Condition* (Chicago: University of Chicago Press, 1958), e.g. pp. 237–8.
3. D. W. Winnicott, *Playing and Reality* (Harmondsworth: Pelican, 1971). Hannah Arendt also used the phrase 'potential space' to describe the creative arena which springs from the 'condition of plurality' (differences): *The Human Condition*, p. 200. See my 'Baudrillard, critical theory, and psychoanalysis', *Canadian Journal of Political and Social Theory*, Vol. 8, Nos 1–2 (Winter–Spring), pp. 35–52, for an outline of the links between Baudrillard's concept of the symbolic and Winnicott's 'potential space' and 'transitional object'.
4. Northrop Frye, *Anatomy of Criticism: Four essays* (Princeton: Princeton University Press, 1957), p. 185.
5. For the original discussion of vampire value, in a related but different register, see John Fekete, 'Vampire value, infinitive art, and literary theory: a topographic meditation', in John Fekete, ed., *Life After Postmodernism: Essays on value and culture* (St. Martin's: New York, 1987), pp. 64–85.
6. For technical discussion of the concept of moral independence, see Ronald Dworkin, *A Matter of Principle* (Cambridge, MA: Harvard University Press, 1985), pp. 353–70.
7. Jerome Bruner, 'Nature and uses of immaturity', in *Play: Its role in development and evolution*, eds J. S. Bruner, A. Jolly and K. Sylva (Harmondsworth: Penguin, 1967), pp. 28–64.

Glossary of key terms

Note: While it is not always possible to provide transparent definitions of the following terms, it is hoped nevertheless that the entries, in combination with the discussion in the text, will help the reader to piece together the layers of Baudrillard's thinking, and their connection with the central themes of poststructural philosophy.

Accursed share (La Part Maudite; the Devil's share): Georges Bataille thought that the essential characteristic of a 'general' economy, viewed as a natural totality, such as the terrestrial environment feeding off the solar system, is to dissipate excess energy, or in human terms, to squander wealth through useless expenditure. It is possible to defer this moment of prodigal waste through accumulation and growth, which 'channels a disorderly effervescence into the regularity of productive operations' (p. 45). However, because growth requires restraint (through rational planning: saving, investing, working), Bataille called this second type of economy 'restricted'. 'Nothing is more different from man enslaved to the operations of growth than the relatively free man of stable societies. The character of human life changes the moment it ceases to be guided by fantasy' (p. 45).

Once utility becomes the conscious guiding principle of life, as in the modern Western economies, a clearer knowledge of certain things results, but this 'cannot become full self-knowledge' (p. 46), according to Bataille, because the latter depends upon acceptance of the exuberant and irrational waste of life's energy: 'the fact that the ground we live on is little other than a field of multiple destructions' (p. 23). To deny the necessity of destructiveness, the 'glorious' destiny of 'useless consumption', is to deprive ourselves 'of the choice of an exudation that might suit us . . . . For if we do not have the force to destroy the surplus energy ourselves, it cannot be used, and, like an unbroken animal that cannot be trained, it is this energy that destroys us; it is we who pay the price of the inevitable explosion' (p. 24).

The devil's share is this excess which must be destroyed, the part which, if held in 'reserve', becomes a curse on its holder. In effect, Bataille is saying that passion is a 'hot potato' – if you don't discharge it, it will consume you. One must be willing to let go, give up and, above all, *lose*. Loss is the 'name of the game', as Baudrillard frequently asserts (see especially *FCPES* 204–12). Melanie Klein understood loss in terms of the need for mourning and reparation – the 'depressive position'. Bataille gives the same theme a 'manic' twist, emphasizing the importance of turning oneself over in the heat of passion, rather than holding oneself prudently in reserve. The extreme ambiguity of the experience of loss (exaltation and abnegation) suggests the secret and seductive link between radical waste and conservation in the manic social functions of ritual: the emotional intensity of the gift, of *rites de passages* and religious sacrifice (in which the sacred is forged through destruction of the profane); the creation of useless objects, which have no logic or meaning; the stretching of experience to the point of stupefaction. There is a thematic continuity between the devil's share and the festival, the carnival, the grotesque, spirit possession, ceremonial or compulsive intoxication, and the intense, agonistic intimacy of symbolic exchange and seduction. In all cases, the reversal of social order and the transgression of emotional limits (what V. W. Turner calls 'liminality') is symbolically fused with the affirmation of limits and structures. As Baudrillard points out, another name for this ambiguity is 'reversibility' – the traditional symbolic view, upon which the fatal strategy is based, that nothing ultimately escapes the cycle of creation and destruction. (Apparently it is only in modern growth societies that the idea of a radical break, or total rupture with the past, becomes part of the social imaginary.)

Bataille thought that societies sum themselves up in the way they dispose of their excess energy. This is another way of saying that one gains a deeper understanding of a social organization when one understands how it deals with its aggression. In societies of gift exchange, the sense of obligation to the giver is often personified in a 'spirit' which will destroy the receiver of the gift if he does not eventually reciprocate. For the Maori, this was the *hau*, for Malinowski's Trobriand Islanders, it was the *tauvau*. Whatever one's theory about the moral basis of social and economic exchange, the primordial gift form is not just an expression of altruism, mutuality, reciprocity, or an archaic mode of distribution, trade, marketing: it is also an act of hostility. (In other words, it channels the ambivalence which Baudrillard mentions in his discussions of symbolic exchange.) In Bataille's favourite examples of the West Coast *potlatch* ritual and the Aztec human sacrifice, it is easy enough to identify the hatred which accompanies the gift. But the same principle is discernibly at work in Christ's loving offer of salvation to mankind through his own self-sacrifice. Not only is His personal gain in status enormous (the potlatch principle) – but He succeeds in cursing all humanity in the process, reducing his followers to an abject state of eternal obligation, guilt, humiliation and ineffectuality – for who can ever repay His totalitarian gift?

The page references are to Georges Bataille, *The Accursed Share. An Essay on General Economy. Volume 1: Consumption*, translated Robert Hurley (New York: Zone Books, 1988). See also Mikhail Bakhtin, *Rabelais and his World*, trans. Hélène Iswolsky (Cambridge, MA: MIT Press, 1968); V. W. Turner, *The Ritual Process: Structure and Anti-Structure* (Ithaca: Cornell University Press, 1969); Gananath Obeyesekere, *Medusa's hair: An Essay on Personal Symbols and Religious Experience* (Chicago: University of Chicago Press, 1981).

Alterity: *See* Other, Evil.

Anagram: Before he worked on the posthumously published *Course in General Linguistics*, which became a canonical text in the French *sciences humaines*, Saussure had already begun to fill several boxes with notes on a theory of anagrams. Some of these notes have been published in a small volume by Jean Starobinski, *Words upon Words: The Anagrams of Ferdinand de Saussure* trans. Olivia Emmet (New Haven: Yale, 1979). Saussure's idea was apparently that anagrams and 'hypograms', etc. had served as an organizing principle in classical poetry. Detailed phonetic analyses of Homer, Virgil, Lucretius, Horace and Ovid, among others, are provided in the notebooks. Saussure thought that the letters or sounds in a word or name, representing a formal theme or motif in the poem, would appear at the beginning of each verse, or scrambled in the metred line, or dispersed throughout a stanza, in complicated ways which cannot be summarized here. Whether or not Saussure's hypotheses have the general application he hoped, they do touch on an essential element of the poetic impulse: the utterly arbitrary, ritual, frivolous, 'meaningless', manipulation of language as sheer ludic material, without communicative purpose or semantic function, such as we find in the complex conventions of metre and rhyme which dominated poetic practice until the rise of modern poetry, or in the highly idiosyncratic writerly systems of modernists like Mallarmé, Joyce and Georges Perec.

Baudrillard's discussion of the anagrams (*Death*) seems to represent his final working through of ambivalence about the formal structuralist theory of language which dominated French thought. According to Baudrillard, the anagrams are to Saussurian structural linguistics what the death instinct was to Freudian psychodynamics or the gift to Mauss's sociology – the point of entry into an alternate universe where the orderly, functional, accumulative aims of social science collapse in the self-cancelling form of play. 'Play' in this context means an activity in relation to rules which have no point or ulterior motive other than the construction of a ludic situation. The concepts of ritual and ceremony can easily be read into this, as well as Baudrillard's subsequent preoccupation with seduction as an anti-utilitarian principle of meaning.

What is of interest here is the illustration of Baudrillard's view that radical thought fails because it only reinforces and balances the system it opposes. Functionalism is opposed with fantasies of improved functioning, utilitarianism with claims for greater utility, rationalism with the pretence of superior rationality, oppressive cultural systems of signification with more, rather than less, control of meaning. We speak of modern verse as 'free', and celebrate its 'liberation' from traditional conventions of composition. But perhaps this use of the word free relies on a typical modern misunderstanding, if not delusion. Would not a poetry without idiosyncratic constraints just be prose – free of useless forms, perhaps, but imprisoned in the compulsion to communicate?

In a recent collection of essays (*IF* 169–70), Baudrillard asks playfully: 'Couldn't we transpose the games of language on to social and historical phenomena: anagrams, acrostics, spoonerisms, rhyme, strophe, catastrophe? Not just the dominant figures of metaphor and metonymy, but those spontaneous, childish, formalistic games, the irregular and deviant tropes which delight the vulgar imagination'?

Chaos theory (*See also* Fractal; Strange Attractor): The term chaos theory refers to a still somewhat controversial branch of physics addressing problems of indeterminacy in dynamic systems. Like quantum theory before it, chaos theory encapsulates a number of intriguing ideas about causality which would not have been conceivable within the framework of classical mechanics. The basic idea is that the behaviour of systems becomes unpredictable when they reach a critical point of disequilibrium. This unpredictability turns out to be a window into nondeterministic forms of order. Temporal processes become reversible. The uniformity of an entropic field becomes improbably asymmetrical, and therefore uniquely structured. Universally valid laws of system functioning are suspended in favour of singularities and peculiarities. Trivial features are randomly amplified into fluctuations which become new organizing principles (strange attractors). Systems become self-organizing in statistically unusual ways.

From this sophisticated mathematical perspective, which can model regular irregularities and patterned incoherence, Chaos is just a different form of Order, and vice versa. The claim to study the formal properties and deep structures of randomness and turbulence implies dissolution of the mythic duality which opposes primordial Chaos to a human, natural or divine Order. Thus chaos theory tolls another in the endless series of death knells for creationism and essentialism in human culture.

Baudrillard's fondness for natural science metaphors derives primarily from the way they suggest the precariousness of the human scale of experience. According to Baudrillard, social life is increasingly governed by the abstract extremes – everything that is either too small or too large to perceive (let alone comprehend). The micromolecular combinatorial world of DNA coding is at one extreme, and the global flux of international currency markets is at the other. Both are equally remote from the local, sensory-cognitive order of everyday life, where experience seems to have the most semantic density. In short, for Baudrillard, the proximal realm of human intercourse is steadily attenuating between the biomedical and globalizing pressures of abstract societal systems.

Baudrillard's use of words like 'fractal' and 'strange attractor' is imprecise and ambivalent. On one hand, they represent a kind of entropic degradation of (social) Being, the engulfing of the particular in the general and the dilution of the individual in the universal. The 'fractal stage' of culture refers to a state in which values become infinitely divisible, completely random and mobile. This is the fourth, or 'viral' order of simulation, characterized by 'metastasis', 'the rule of propagation through mere contiguity, of cancerous proliferation' (TE 7).

On the other hand, the fractal pattern of culture conjures for Baudrillard the exquisite possibility of metaphysical revenge against the 'artificial paradises' of 'present-day systems', against the 'consensus' of societies which 'sometimes succeed only too well and get lost in the delusion of their own functioning' (TE 107). The 'contrary energy' of the accursed share and of the mythic, symbolic principle of evil appears 'in the malfunctioning of things, in viral attacks, in the acceleration of processes and in their wildly chaotic effects, in the overriding of causes, in excess and paradox, in radical foreignness, in strange attractors, in linkless chains of events' (TE 106–7). To capture such strange events, according to Baudrillard, critical theory itself must become (as in the fatal strategy) a strange attractor, 'in the hope that reality will be naive enough to fall into it' (TE 110).

The metaphor of a 'theory' of chaos thus suggests the final triumph of systematicity – an ultimate reduction of meaning and control of experience through a kind of epistemic institutionalization of randomness, chance, particularity, texture – the codification of alterity itself. For Baudrillard this means the disappearance of 'destiny'. In contrast to 'chance' and chaos, destiny refers to the spiritually impassioned, agonistic, ritual fatefulness of the symbolic world of illusions. It is not the environment of random and incalculable differences, but a theatre of 'enigmatic duality', where there is a secret but contradictory will. The end awaits, but everything one does to avoid it brings one closer to the 'fateful resolution'. Yet there is presentiment of 'total reversal' (*IF* 158–9).

In the chaotic universe of 'exponential stability and instability' (*IF* 155–60), the illusions of poetic justice have been replaced by a disillusioning system of 'indefinite fractal scissiparity' and of statistical chance (*IF* 159). But at the same time, 'the poetic form is not so remote from the chaotic form' (*IF* 168): the advent of chaos in history portends for Baudrillard the trivialization of all functional logic, a kind of anagrammatic reversal, a subversion of 'consensus', a liberating 'parody of sociality', as envisaged in the Borges tale of the Babylonian Lottery (*Seduction* 150).

See James Gleick, *Chaos: Making a New Science* (New York: Penguin, 1987); and Ilya Prigogine and Isabelle Stengers, *Order out of Chaos: Man's New Dialogue with Nature* (New York: Bantam, 1984).

Chora: This term was drawn from Plato's *Timaeus* by Julia Kristeva in *La révolution du langage poétique* (1974) to denote 'a nonexpressive totality formed by the drives and their stases . . . an essentially mobile and extremely provisional articulation' (p. 25). According to Kristeva, this nonexpressive, provisional articulation is 'anterior to sign and syntax' (p. 29). Since it pre-dates the acquisition of language in the ontogeny of the subject, the *chora* is pre-Symbolic, and therefore also 'pre-Oedipal'. It is closely related to Freud's concept of *primary process*, which functions as if beyond time, in the absence of negation and the law of contradiction. To distinguish it from the *Symbolic* (i.e. the signifying modality of language), Kristeva links the Chora to the *Semiotic*, which she defines as the 'psychosomatic modality of the signifying process' (28). This is the sensorimotor dimension of the body as signifying *material*: rhythm, beat, texture, pitch, timbre, shape, volume, gesture, etc., and their primitive relations to the erogenous zones, to the flows, breaks, densities, intervals, fragmentations and condensations of proto-articulate experience. The semiotic dimension is 'indifferent to language, enigmatic and feminine . . . rhythmic, unfettered, irreducible to its intelligible verbal translation' (p. 29). According to Kristeva, 'the mother's body is . . . the ordering principle of the semiotic *chora*, which is on the path of destruction, aggressivity, and death' (pp. 27–8). As an irreducible dimension of the body, the *chora* serves as both the precondition and the disruptive negation, or dissolution, of linguistically and socially constituted identities, notably the imaginary ego-identity of the subject in the 'mirror phase', and the phallocentric organization of the Oedipal subject. In this respect, the *chora* is reminiscent of Baudrillard's concept of *symbolic exchange*, which anticipated some of Kristeva's ideas (*FCPES* 1972), but was also elaborated in response to them (*Death* 1974). See Julia Kristeva, *Revolution in Poetic Language* trans. Margaret Waller (New York: Columbia University Press, 1984).

Code: Like much of Baudrillard's technical vocabulary, the term code is drawn metaphorically from linguistics and semiotics, where its meaning had already been stretched to breaking point by ambitious panlinguists. Baudrillard uses it very skilfully to suggest that there exists a kind of supraordinate combinatorial 'logic' (or code) which restricts the range of meanings possible to express, or experiences possible to share, in a given social or cultural 'system'. Although Baudrillard never specifies in detail what such a code might look like for a contemporary society, he does outline a fairly comprehensive abstract theory of the codes governing social forms in modern industrial and postindustrial societies (*FCPES, Mirror, Death*), including the three orders of simulation (*Death*). In these studies from the early and mid-1970s, he makes it quite clear that he is referring to a historical process of progressive formalization, in which functional and utilitarian principles – particularly the principle of equivalence – come increasingly to control the organization of social forms from within.

Dedifferentiation: Dedifferentiation (for example, dedifferentiation of subject and object, figure and ground) refers to an active form of perception, in which differences are noticed but still transgressed. Dedifferentiation is particularly important as a phase of the creative (or deconstructive) process, and should be distinguished from the imaginary state of undifferentiation, which nobody can actually report having experienced, since it refers to an inferred lack of perception, or an original state prior to cognition. See Anton Ehrenzweig, *The Hidden Order of Art* (Berkeley: University of California Press, 1967).

Différance: A philosophical neologism which Jacques Derrida coined by adding a gerundial *a* to the noun 'difference' so as to combine the active and passive connotations of the verbs to differ (non-identity), and to defer (delay). Like Baudrillard, with his distaste for the utopian 'realization' of what would otherwise have remained an inspiration, Derrida abhors a plenitude. Following Lacan in certain respects, Derrida emphasizes the facilitating features of 'castration', the gaps, holes, absences and destructions (erasures) in 'Being'. Like the margins and the spacing of words in a text, these make the semantic effect possible. Différance is not an 'existent' thing (one of Heidegger's mere phenomenal beings (*seiendes*) which 'conceal' true 'Being' (*Sein*)). But it is not Being either, because différance is reputedly too diaphoric, too much of a movement across, always inconclusive, hesitating at the eleventh hour. It is not supposed to serve as an ontological substratum. Nor is it supposed to be a sort of God-like absence, the non-being of negative theology. Différance is not a concept, not a sign, not a signified, not even a signifier; not the will to power, not a force, not a drive, not libido, not even Freud's death instinct, though perhaps closer to that. A vulgar description of différance might be: the play of spacing and tracing which somehow occurs as silence passes into utterance and back. That is an interesting (non)concept for a theory of culture. It has a certain affinity with Kristeva's *chora*, and aspects of Baudrillard's symbolic exchange, seduction, and fatal strategy.

Evil (Principle of Evil; Evil demon; Noise): There is an interesting connection between Baudrillard's principle of evil and Descartes' 'evil demon', who tries to fool us into thinking that our dreams are real perceptions, thus threatening to undermine any possibility of certain knowledge. Our fear of the evil demon is proportional to the angry violence which can be so easily mobilized against anything marked as the enemy of our convictions. As Baudrillard points out, following Freud, 'evil' is whatever disturbs our sense of security and comfort. Descartes' demon may be taken as the equivalent of 'noise' in modern communication theory – we try to eliminate it at all costs.

When a society is on its way to becoming completely operational and euphemistic, or 'hyperreal', as Baudrillard believes about ours, the primordial Symbolic duality of Good and Evil undergoes a fundamental mutation. Good becomes a utilitarian value judgement ('the greatest good for the greatest number'), a functional quality ('smooth and easy to handle'), or an operational feature ('the "push-button" convenience of remote control'). People are no longer good or evil, but they may be happy, or they may be unhappy because they come from a dysfunctional family.

Evil drops out of the picture almost entirely. According to Baudrillard, it takes on an anamorphic quality, so that it can only be recognized from a specific angle, like the skull representing mortality in Holbein's *The Ambassador*. From every other point of view, 'evil' is just an incomprehensible blur.

> In a society which seeks – by prophylactic measures, by annihilating its own natural referents, by whitewashing violence, by exterminating all germs and all of the accursed share, by performing cosmetic surgery on the negative – to concern itself solely with quantified management and with the discourse of the Good, in a society where it is no longer possible to speak Evil, Evil has metamorphosed into all the viral and terroristic forms that obsess us. (TE 81)

In a fundamental sense, Baudrillard's concept of Evil is a variation on the theme of endangered otherness. Evil is radical alterity – an otherness in the world which is irreconcilable, and which resists our good intentions to 'recognize' it as 'different', and to welcome it into our midst. Baudrillard sees in our attempt to 'redeem' the accursed share the arrogance of the humanist subject of the 'good' who does not merely demonize the other, as Christ did the Pharisees; but worse, who greets the other wholeheartedly as a candidate for tolerance and rehabilitation ('forgive them for they know not what they do').

Baudrillard's insistence on a formulation based on such archaic metaphysical principles as Evil has met with much moral displeasure, particularly among promoters of radical cultural politics. This is because it appears to allow only three points of resistance to the functional administration of life: suffering and death by act of God (plagues, conflagrations and catastrophes); fundamentalist terrorism; and finally, the practice of writing cultural metaphysics. The discourse on evil makes Baudrillard sound not only irrational and 'reactionary', but also quite insensitive to actual misery in the world. He has a tendency to welcome anything which disrupts the smooth functioning of the 'system' as a portent of the re-enchantment of the universe, or at least as a satisfying revenge on behalf of the Symbolic.

'Fortunately', he states 'the evil genie has taken up residence in *things*: this is the *objective* energy of evil' (TE 108). The point here is not nominally a moral one, but a conscious refusal to speak or write willingly in a way which supports the 'consensus' that the world in which we live is 'real'. Baudrillard distinguishes his attitude from Descartes' radical doubt by saying that he is a sort of Manichean who admits of 'no possibility existing at all of reconciling the "illusion" of the world with the "reality" of the world' (*Evil* 40–3). In this Gnostic sense, then, the principle of evil does not imply a moral choice, but an ontological choice between belief in a rational material world which is consistent with itself and can be taken at face value (even if supported by a belief in a creating God) and an irrational ludic world of illusion, play and seduction (which could only have been 'seduced' into existence by an 'evil demon' or 'Trickster').

Fatal strategy: The book *Fatal Strategies*, like *Symbolic Exchange and Death* and *Seduction*, is a major classic of contemporary cultural metaphysics. As an exercise in pure speculation (in the sense of irrational and excessive gambling) it is also an extraordinary *tour de force*. One might say that the fatal strategy is to *become* a pure object, which is to say, to be seduced out of oneself, to 'not give a damn about one's own being' (*FS* 139) – at which point, one is delivered over to the 'play of the world', its appearances, illusions and secrets. The 'irony' passes into things and events, which have been pushed to the extreme beyond which they no longer make sense in their own terms. The fatal strategy lies also in this – the hidden extremes, or 'ecstatic' forms, which contain the secret of the real:

> The real does not efface itself in favor of the imaginary . . . [but] the more real than real: the hyperreal. The truer than true: this is simulation.
>
> Presence does not efface itself before emptiness, but before a redoubling of presence which effaces the opposition between presence and absence. (*FS* 11)

Many would disagree, but Baudrillard insists that the fatal strategy is not a political strategy in the sense of a subject 'position' in relation to an object or goal, which would involve an exercise of instrumental will. The fatal strategy is in a way neither active nor passive, but a kind of magical identification with the actions of things. It is somehow to merge with this 'objective irony' of things – 'an irony which belongs to the system, [which] arises from the system because the system is constantly functioning against itself' (*Evil* 48). Thus one's 'opposition' comes out of the system itself, requiring at most the effort of nudging phenomena to the point of revealing their intrinsic absurdity.

> The world is not dialectical – it is sworn to extremes, not to equilibrium, sworn to radical antagonism, not to reconciliation or synthesis. This is also the principle of Evil, as expressed in the 'evil genie' of the object, in the ecstatic form of the pure object and in its strategy, victorious over that of the subject. (*FS* 7)

Baudrillard's statements do seem to read at cross purposes with themselves in a most interesting way, which perhaps represents the 'objective irony' of 'Baudrillard', as a 'thing' in the world of social scientific discourse: for what emerges is a subject making a highly personal statement – not about the world, but of his feelings about social theory, which he identifies with the 'real':

> This is the key to the whole position: the idea is that of a most fundamental and radical antagonism, of no possibility . . . of reconciling the 'illusion' of the world with the 'reality' of the world . . . . It is, to say it one more time, the issuing of a challenge to the 'real' – the attempt to put the real quite simply, on the spot. (*Evil* 42–3)

Fractal (*See* Chaos theory; Strange attractor): The term 'fractal' was coined by the French mathematician Mandelbrot, whose reaction to the formalist Bourbaki school of mathematics parallels the post-structuralist revolt against the structuralism of Piaget and Lévi-Strauss. A fractal is a fractional and fractured dimension, for example, a dimension which is more than one, but less than two. Thinking in fractals involves a kind of realism which goes beyond perceptual norms. A straight line is just an abstract idea which we never really see. Viewed microscopically, any example of a line reveals a jagged and broken thread, endlessly deviating from the straight and narrow. A fractal geometry of the line therefore involves more than one, but less than two dimensions. A Koch curve is another example. It is formed by adding to each side of an equilateral triangle three more triangles one-third its size, and then adding to their exposed sides triangles one-third their size, and so on, *ad infinitum*. The resulting circumference never becomes a circle, but it gets longer and longer – unendingly so. The infinite self-embedding of a fractal structure is comparable to the semantic abysses described in deconstructionist philosophy and literary criticism. Like the imploding symmetry of the Quaker Oats box, with its logo of the quaker presenting a Quaker Oats box with the same image of the quaker presenting the same box, any search for the 'transcendental signified' results in a recursive *mise en abyme*: the ultimate reference of the signifier is never finally fixed.

Gestell [German: frame]: Loosely translated, this was Heidegger's term for 'technological system', as he described in *The Question Concerning Technology*. Baudrillard does not actually use the word *Gestell*, or refer directly to Heidegger; but the influence of Heidegger's reading of 'Western metaphysics' is everywhere in his work. In brief: Heidegger saw 'metaphysics' as the tendency in European thought since Plato to assume that 'reality' is transparent and rational – in other words, structured according to the forms of reason and the principles of logic. Before Plato, Pythagoras had already been speculating in a mystical way that 'natural' harmonies and numbers provide the key to the essence of Being (hence the distinction between 'rational' and 'irrational' numbers). The credibility of this intuition has been amply reinforced by modern science, particularly through the awesome conceptual power of mathematical physics. Heidegger could see that the abstract rationalism of the ancients was rapidly achieving more and more concrete embodiment through the material social shaping power of technology. The problem is that the *Gestell* of metaphysics and technology is not just a framework, but a filter which screens out anything resistant to codification in rational form. In consequence, Heidegger believed, upper case 'Being' was devolving into lower case 'beings' – mere phenomena. Since Heidegger's death, it has become clearer that physical engineering technologies and abstract knowledge technologies have been converging, especially through the computer, into an ever more consequential consolidation of the *Gestell*. Baudrillard was one of the first to elaborate Heidegger's theory of technology in this way, particularly in his 'critique of the political economy of the sign' (*FCPES*), his analysis of the digitalism of the 'third order' of simulation, and the 'structural revolution of value' (*Death*).

Heteronomy (143): Poststructuralists liked to use this term to mark their dislike for Kantian ideas about the 'autonomy' of the subject. The structuralist and poststructuralist subject is not autonomous because he or she is a slave to pre-existing structures and systems ('subjection'). However, poststructuralist theorists later came to argue that individuals should be granted moral autonomy in the legal sense (political rights and freedoms) in order to balance heteronomy with heterogeneity. Michel Foucault was the most important of the philosophers to make this liberal turn, so uncharacteristic of the French intelligentsia, explicit. The move can be justified on the grounds that Enlightenment and individualistic values by no means commit one to a naive form of naturalistic or foundational thinking, since they may be defended quite adequately as historical and cultural 'constructions'. Indeed, such individualistic constructions can be seen to form the ethical cornerstone of antinaturalist and antifoundationalist thought. There are three good biographies of Foucault, but see in particular James Miller, *The Passion of Michel Foucault* (New York: Doubleday, 1993). See also James Bernauer and David Rasmussen, eds, *The Final Foucault* (Cambridge, MA: MIT Press, 1988), esp. p. 19, where Foucault defends 'the ethical research which allows individual liberty to be founded'.

Hyperreality: Hyperreality corresponds to the third order of simulacra; in effect it is both the aesthetic and epistemological form of simulation (*Death* 70–6). There is a thematic connection between the hyperreality of simulation and Heidegger's *Gestell* (the framing of our experience of Being through technology) which can be articulated most effectively through consideration of the enhanced deconstructive, reproductive and reconstructive capacities of digital technologies. But hyperreality is not a separate category from reality (nor is simulation). Rather, it is a way of presenting and receiving reality – in brief, it is reality conceived without otherness. In a sense, it abolishes the space within which the 'scene' of reality can be represented. This is why Baudrillard, playing off a non-existent etymological connection, sometimes says that hyperreality is '*ob*-scene'. 'Obscenity begins where there is no more spectacle, no more stage, no more theatre, no more illusion, when everything becomes immediately transparent, visible, exposed in the raw and inexorable light of information and communication' (*Ecstasy* 21–2). In the same vein, he says that hyperreality is the 'ecstatic' form of reality, which means that hyperreality is reality *as if* overexposed, pushed to an extreme, in manic flight from itself. The distance across which one might perceive something as real, or imagine something different in its place, has been abolished. In its place an overwhelming excess of reality has been poured. The gaps which might have allowed perception to have a certain character are filled up; and the veils which situate perception within a particular history are torn aside. There are no longer any secrets, or illusions of interiority.

Yet at the same time, the hyperreality of simulation has the eerie quality of the uncanny, of the *déjà vu* – 'a hallucinatory resemblance of the real to itself' (*Death* 72). The real reduplicates itself indefinitely, fractally, *en abyme*, and we feel trapped inside it: 'we have passed alive into the models' (*FS* 9). Baudrillard draws the analogy of the dreamer who is aware he or she is dreaming: a kind of symbolic distance is established which allows the dream process to continue undisturbed (*Death* 74). By theorizing hyperrealism in this way, as a cultural evolution occurring within an ongoing 'crisis of representation', which has already struggled through realism and surrealism, Baudrillard effectively reopens the gap into which presentiments of otherness can be invited; and redraws the veil through which they can be expressed.

Hysteresis: In physics, hysteresis is a phenomenon in which a physical effect on a body lags behind its cause. Baudrillard carries the term over into his pataphysical accounts of globalized media politics and history (see *IF passim*; esp. 161–71). By 'hysteresis of the political' Baudrillard seems to be saying that he thinks social and geopolitical events have become stuck in a kind of fractal loop, in which they reiterate themselves indefinitely, without issue. This is an extension of Baudrillard's metaphor of the 'precession of simulacra', regarding the extreme contemporary forms of social simulation, in which the cultural model seems to circulate in advance of any of its performances, almost as if society had slipped into Plato's Realm of Forms, where everything would be experienced in its most perfect and completely realized form (Utopia) before it actually occurred in the partial and imperfect realm of sensory experience.

Imaginary (*See also* Mirror): The Imaginary is the most interesting of Lacan's three psychic registers: the Real, the Imaginary and the Symbolic. The Real refers roughly to what is beyond subjective knowing and symbolization, the frightening intimation of which may dominate in psychotic states of mind. The Symbolic refers to the dimension of social otherness and uncertainty – metaphorically equated with the alien, paternal structure of language – whose acceptance signifies the subject's successful working through of 'castration', or separation from the Imaginary world of identification with the virtual image of the ideal self reflected in the fusional relationship with mother (Mirror phase).

In the 1970s, synthesizing Lacan's formulations with Althusser's 'scientific' theory of ideology, cultural studies theorists forged a link between the psychological illusions of subjectivity, as described by Lacan, and the social illusions of capitalist ideology, as described by Marx and Engels. The resulting style of sociological and cultural analysis persists to this day, though nearly everyone practising it has repudiated the simple equation upon which it is based. Baudrillard has always avoided this psychologically reductive style of cultural theorizing. See in particular Louis Althusser, *Lenin and Philosophy and Other Essays* trans. Ben Brewster (New York: Monthly Review Press, 1971), pp. 127–219. For an introductory guide to the original sources in Lacan, see Madan Sarup, *Jacques Lacan* (Hemel Hempstead: Harvester Wheatsheaf, 1992).

Interpellate: Louis Althusser introduced this term to refer to the manner in which ideology 'hails' the subject. There is a sense in which, when the policeman tells us to 'stop', he acts as the connecting point through which we, as the subjects of his address, are 'positioned' by the social system: thus, in a rudimentary way, we are already interpellated. *See also* Imaginary.

Mirror (Lacan's mirror phase): Baudrillard's frequent use of the mirror metaphor is not reducible to Lacan's concept of the 'mirror stage', but it is immensely richer for it. Lacan's idea was that the *corps morcélé*, or fragmented infantile body, converges in the *virtual* image of the integrated body as an *imaginary* ego identity – an illusion of homogeneous uniformity, or intentional consistency. The identification with this virtual image need not occur literally in a mirror reflection. In fact, it is more likely to be established in the narcissistic relationship, whether liberating or confining, mediated by the mother's informing presence, and the quality of her gaze. According to Lacan, 'the sight alone of the whole form of the human body gives the subject an imaginary mastery over his body, one which is premature in relation to a real mastery'. He continues: 'This is the original adventure through which man . . . has the experience of seeing himself, of reflecting upon himself and conceiving of himself as other than he is – an essential dimension of the human, which entirely structures his fantasy life' (*The Seminar of Jacques Lacan. Book 1: Freud's Papers on Technique 1953–1954* trans. John Forrester (New York: Norton, 1991), p. 79).

In *The Mirror of Production*, Baudrillard used the mirror trope to elaborate Heidegger's insight that Western 'metaphysics' is organized around the idea of production (*pro-ducere*), or making visible, measurable, manageable, useful. He described with devastating precision the imaginary self-certainty of the Marxist analytic ego contemplating its own virtual image in the 'mirror' of modern utilitarianism, or political economy.

Nihilism: In *fin de siècle* fiction, nihilism referred to the sort of anarchist terrorism described by Dostoevsky in *The Devils* (also translated as *The Possessed*) and by Joseph Conrad in *Under Western Eyes* (prophetic titles all). The philosophical meaning of the term comes primarily from Nietzsche. It refers to the tendency of 'Western Metaphysics', variously interpreted since, to degrade and destroy absolute moral and epistemological values.

Other, Otherness (*See also* Evil): The other is supposedly what one is not, or at least something different from oneself. But is this difference absolute or relative? Is it a matter of a fundamentally different order of being – an *essential* difference – or just a diacritical differentiation, like the formal distinction between linguistic phonemes? It is difficult not to experience the other as an extension of oneself, or to define the other in terms of an understanding of oneself and one's own experience. On the other hand, the history of one's own experience is probably dominated by the influence of the other, which means that the real problem is not to discover the difference of the other, but to establish one's own difference from the other, whose sameness to ourselves reveals our own failure to be different. Fine. But then the problem of identifying the other returns, since it becomes crucial to understand what it is that we have failed to differentiate ourselves from. Freud talked about this problem in terms of transference. It seems like a frivolous game, but the history of ideas would be shallow without it.

Part maudite, la (*See* Accursed share)

Pataphysics (sometimes spelled 'pataphysics): The celebrated 'Professor of pataphysics', created by Alfred Jarry (1873–1907), appeared in two guises, the raucous bully Père Ubu (*Ubu Roi* (1896)) and the absurdist visionary, Dr Faustroll (*Exploits and Opinions of Doctor Faustroll, Pataphysician* (1911)). Ubu was a sort of grand guignol clown whom Jarry depicted, in a famous woodcut, wearing a pointed hood and gown (like a potentate of the Ku-Klux-Klan) over his 'Gidouille', or prominent belly decorated with a galactic swirl. Dr Faustroll, who is perhaps a troll-like version of Faust, represents the less destructive side of Jarry's contempt for the 'traditional universe'. According to Jarry, Faustroll's pataphysics 'is the science of that which is superinduced upon metaphysics'. It deals with 'epiphenomena', often 'accidental', which means that 'pataphysics will be, above all, the science of the particular'. Since the classical physical laws of the traditional universe 'possess no longer even the virtue of originality', 'pataphysics will examine the laws governing exceptions, and will explain the universe supplementary to this one'. It is 'the science of imaginary solutions, which symbolically attributes the properties of objects, described by their virtuality, to their lineaments'. For example: 'Instead of formulating the law of the fall of a body toward a center, how far more apposite would be the law of the ascension of a vacuum toward a periphery' (Roger Shattuck and Simon Watson Taylor, eds, *Selected Works of Alfred Jarry* (New York: Grove Press, 1965), pp. 193–4).

Jarry's pataphysics may be taken as one of Baudrillard's fundamental theoretical inspirations, starting with *Symbolic Exchange and Death* (*ESM* 1976), but particularly since *Fatal Strategies* (1983). In 'The ascension of the void towards the periphery' (*IF* 29–37), he argues, tongue-in-cheek with Jarry, against the inductive illusion that historical events follow one another because they are related: 'Simulation is just like this irresistible unfolding, this sequencing of things as though they had a meaning, when their only principle of organization is artificial montage and nonsense' (*IF* 30). Jarry's *fin de siècle* buffoonery is a fitting metaphorical vehicle for Baudrillard's expressions of ironic disillusionment with mass-mediated politics. It is as if the vacuum created by the perfections of simulated culture had sucked history up towards the periphery, the edge or end of history, which keeps reiterating itself fractally, infinitely, like the turbulence around a strange attractor, without ever being able to resolve itself.

The richness of Jarry's pataphysical parodies is indicated in his interesting anticipations of post-relativity physics, notably his reference to Lucretius's concept of the 'clinamen', or accidental 'swerve' in matter, which anticipates both Heisenberg's uncertainty principle, and the concept of 'exponential instability' in chaos theory (i.e. the spontaneous self-reorganization of a system arising from a slight fluctuation which eventually gives rise to a 'singularity', or emergent property, not deterministically related to the initial condition of its emergence).

Potlatch: Cultural practices reminiscent of the potlatch ceremonies have been found in many parts of the world, but the most famous examples are the aboriginal ceremonies recorded by nineteenth-century anthropologists on the West and Northwest Coast of Canada and Alaska, among the Kwaikutl, Haida, Tlingit, and other tribes. These were reputedly sometimes wild, orgiastic and destructive affairs, a form of compulsive feasting which sometimes dragged on for months in unsanitary, winter conditions. The Canadian government made the potlatch illegal in 1884. What bothered the officials was the impression of economic waste. The Indian Reserve Commissioner Sproat reported that 'it is not possible that Indians can acquire property, or become industrious with any good result, while under the influence of this mania' (quoted in Douglas Cole and Ira Chaikin, ' "A worse than useless custom": The potlatch law and Indian resistance', *Western Legal History*: 5, 2 (Summer/Fall 1992), 188).

Marcel Mauss wrote that potlatch was 'really nothing other than gift-exchange'. But he added: 'The only differences are in the violence, rivalry and antagonism aroused' (*The Gift* trans. Ian Cunnison (London: Routledge & Kegan Paul, 1954), p. 33). *See also* Accursed share.

Seduction:

> What makes you exist is not the force of your desire (wholly a nineteenth-century imaginary of energy and economy), but the play of the world and seduction; it is the passion of playing and being played, it is the passion of illusion and appearance, it is that which comes from elsewhere, from others, from their face, their language, their gestures – and that which bothers you, lures you, summons you into existence; it is the encounter, the surprise of what exists before you, outside of you, *without you* – the marvellous exteriority of the pure object, the pure event . . . [B]eing doesn't give a damn about its own being; it is nothing, and exists only when it is lifted out of itself, into the play of the world and the vertigo of seduction. (*FS* 139)

Simulacra, simulation: Samuel Beckett (*Molloy* 26) once remarked wittily that 'the shadow in the end is no better than the substance', which captures the atmosphere of Baudrillard's theorizing about simulation in society and culture as well as any single phrase is able.

In the early 1970s Baudrillard frequently referred to the simulation effect of organized signs systems. At first this referred to the way that the sign heightens and intensifies the capacity of political economy to 'project' utilitarian values as natural 'finalities' or irreducible values. Thus, for Marx and the political economists, 'need' and 'use value' appeared to be the biological and anthropological ground of the commodity system. All that was required, according to Marx, was to 'liberate' these natural ontological values from the artificial shackles of 'exchange value' (money and the market system). Baudrillard questioned the claim that something natural could be recovered from the commodity economy. He showed how the commodity (use value/exchange value) had combined with the 'sign-form' (signified/signifier) to form the discourse of 'sign-objects' in a powerfully closed system (the 'object system') which generates a simulacrum – the collective hallucination that there is something solid outside the system, i.e. the natural values (need, use value, functionality) and the 'grand referents' (Man, Health, Happiness, Freedom, Fulfilment, Satisfaction, Equality, Justice) which establish the fundamental validity of the system and serve as alibis for its existence (*SO, SC, FCPES, Mirror*).

In *Symbolic Exchange and Death*, Baudrillard elaborated this into a tripartite scheme of historical periodization calibrated roughly to Marx's schema of feudalism/capitalism and Foucault's schema of epistemes, in *The Order of Things*: the Renaissance world of magical or divine correspondences; the Classical Rationalist world of orderly identities and taxonomies; the historical world of Man, political economy, and evolution; and the emerging contemporary world of language and communication systems. Baudrillard describes the 'three order of simulacra, running parallel to the successive mutations of the law of value since the Renaissance' thus:

- The *counterfeit* is the dominant schema in the 'classical' period, from the Renaissance to the Industrial Revolution.
- *Production* is the dominant schema in the industrial era.
- *Simulation* is the dominant schema in the current code-governed phase.

> The first order simulacrum operates on the natural law of value, the second-order simulacrum on the market law of value, and the third-order simulacrum on the structural law of value. (*Death* 50)

Prior to the three modern orders of simulacra, Baudrillard posits the cruel and archaic world of primitive and feudal societies, where signs are clearly bound to a rigid social order of caste, rank or role. But this is also the emotionally fluid world of symbolic exchange and seduction, where life is frankly accepted as an illusion, and there is no predominant problematic of 'reality', no pretence to know or discover the natural scientific relationship between signs and what lies beyond the extraordinary effects they create.

To this schema, Baudrillard soon added a fourth 'viral' or 'exponential' or 'metastatic' order of simulacrum. Its principle of value is 'fractal', and follows the 'natural', 'commodity' and 'structural' stages of value.

The general idea of simulation is tied basically to the intellectual revolution of cybernetics and communications, structural linguistics, poststructuralist 'textualism', and systems theory, all of which dissolve substances into relations and entities into patterns of organization. The schematic ordering of simulacra demonstrates the basic historical trend of modernization: increasing formalization, step-by-step invalidation of ordinary sense experience, trivialization of emotional certainties. It is the geometric expansion in the real power of digital technology which gives the schema its greatest plausibility as a contribution to cultural studies and social history. But the links with observed social phenomena are indirect at best. Not that there is any shortage of detailed analyses of the complex processes of social simulation, of which the most brilliant recent example is Ian Hacking, *Rewriting the Soul: Multiple Personality and the Sciences of Memory* (Princeton: Princeton University Press, 1995). Baudrillard's most effective referent is always at the epistemic level – not social reality as such, whatever that is, but the successive *theories* of social reality, and their ambiguous interpenetrating loops with social and societal life.

In the following commentary, delivered in an interview, Baudrillard alludes to the subtlety of the conceptual distinctions involved in his own work, and the specificity of cultural metaphysics as a level of analysis:

> The problematic of the disappearance of the referent was not an issue according to the first logic of illusion; rather, there was simply no referent. So in a sense, we are going back towards an anterior state – but nevertheless with a difference.
>
> Is this revolution an *historical* one? I do not think it is. It is, rather, a *metaphysical* one: the universe of the media which we are currently immersed in is not the magical universe or the cruel universe which we had at an anterior stage, where the sign was operational purely on the basis of its own functioning as sign. With the advent of the media, it seems to me that we have lost that prior state of total illusion, of the sign as magic. We are, in other words, in that state of 'hyperreality' as I have called it. Now we are dealing with a sign that posits the principle of non-reality, the principle of the absolute absence of reality. We went beyond the reality principle a long time ago, and now the game which is being played is no longer being played in the world of pure illusion. It is as if we are now in a shameful and sinful state, a post-illusion state. (*Evil* 46–7, emphasis added)

Strange attractor: An attractor might be described as the point of maximum equilibrium around which the dynamics of a system are organized, like the central point in space where the pendulum comes to rest. A strange attractor is essentially the coherent but eccentric organizing pattern of a 'chaotic' system with many variables. It has a fractal structure which allows the dynamic process to undergo an infinity of variations within a finite space, such as a three-dimensional figure of eight, without ever intersecting itself, or repeating itself in periodic fashion. Baudrillard states: 'The strangeness of the strange attractor is only metaphorical. Radical strangeness belongs to the enigmatic duality of a world, and of the inexorable contradiction (of our will and its loss), which maintains the indestructible illusion [of destiny, and of a spiritually impassioned world]' (*IF* 159).

Uncanny: In his extraordinary study of the psychodynamics of the aesthetic dimension, Freud said of the 'uncanny' that, among other things

> it is marked by the fact that the subject identifies himself with someone else, so that he is in doubt as to which his self is, or substitutes the extraneous self for his own. In other words, there is a doubling, dividing and interchanging of the self. And finally there is the constant recurrence of the same thing – the repetition of the same features or character-traits or vicissitudes, of the same crimes, or even the same names through several consecutive generations.

Freud's English editor Strachey comments that this passage echoes Nietzsche's 'eternal recurrence'. Freud also discussed the idea that 'a particularly favourable condition for awakening uncanny feelings is created when there is intellectual uncertainty whether an object is alive or not, and when an inanimate object becomes too much like an animate one'. Sigmund Freud, 'The "uncanny" ', *The Standard Edition of the Psychological Works of Sigmund Freud*, XVII (London: Hogarth, 1953–74), pp. 234, 233.

Index

Film and television references